The Three-, Four-, and Five-Year-Old in a School Setting

The Three-, Four-, and Five-Year-Old in a School Setting

Grace K. Pratt-Butler
Long Island University

Charles E. Merrill Publishing Company
A Bell & Howell Company
Columbus, Ohio

Published by
Charles E. Merrill Publishing Company
A Bell & Howell Company
Columbus, Ohio 43216

This book was set in Janson.

The Production Editor was Lynn Walcoff.

The cover was designed by Will Chenoweth.

Cover photos courtesy of the University of Maryland and Richard E. Farkas.

Library of Congress Catalog Card Number: 74-26189

International Standard Book Number: 0-675-08724-4

1 2 3 4 5 6—80 79 78 77 76 75

Printed in the United States of America.

To   Alan J. Butler

great Professor
    and
wonderful Human Being
    and
my dearly beloved Husband

Illustrations: Credits

Preface

This book was written for the student and beginning teacher. It may serve, also, to alert the parent, aide, and the experienced teacher to possibilities not hitherto considered.

The book is an introduction to preschool education and is designed to present three-, four-, and five-year-olds as they are and as they learn in various types of preschool groups. Concrete suggestions and plans are given for implementing learning experiences conducive to maximum realization of these children. In order to do this, examples are presented, often at the beginning of a particular discussion, as a means of focussing the reader's attention on common activities. Then, apt learning experiences are developed from these. It is hoped that this procedure will keep theories and practices on a functional level. The writer hopes to have accomplished this unity of theory and practice, by keeping active children central in the text, by developing learning experiences from the activities of the children in the discussion, and by indicating the underlying reasons for what is done. This method of presentation should foster reflective thinking in the reader and encourage him/her to consider relevant problems of his/her own. It should aid discussion in college classes, too.

After making necessary contextual adjustments, the preschool educator can take the book and use it. Problematic situations should be provocative to the teacher who, justifiably, may meet them differently than is implied here. Although underlying educational philosophies differ, and the writer has her own, it is hoped that the presentation is clear enough to be accepted in general with individual situational differentiations. In a sense, then, this book should serve as a catalyst—a stepping-off place from which each reader moves forward in terms of his/her theoretical and practical context.

From many years of working with the children as well as from teaching and administering undergraduate and graduate students, the writer is convinced of the importance of seeing children for what they are: generally, alike in certain expectable behavior and reaction; specifically, different in every possible nuance of feeling and expression of their changing developing selves. As they experience each day and undergo the consequences of what they do, it is hoped that their teachers will have guided each child into rich paths of interaction with the people and things which surround him. As the child's purposes are reached, convictions of longer range begin to develop. No child should be deprived of attention, affection, and regard for what he is as well as expectations for what he may become. However, this book is about what can be done with three-, four-, and five-year-old children now, which in turn fosters these expectations for what they will be.

Special appreciation is due to my husband, Alan J. Butler and to my mother, Grace Clark Pratt, for the numerous inconveniences suffered when some sections of this manuscript had to be completed; to Celeste Muschel, of the Ethical Culture Schools, who is also one of my former "parents," for her time and for making possible the inclusion of many pictures; to Lois Overbeck, Director of the Brooklyn-Parma Coop Preschool, Cleveland, Ohio, for the many pictures which she made available to me; to Dick Swartz of the Department of Health, Education and Welfare for the pictures sent in response to my request. Thanks are extended, too, to the following for their assistance in supplying appropriate illustrations: The Society for Crippled Children of Cleveland and especially to Jane Safford; Mary Jane Townsend of Cleveland Heights, Ohio; Richard E. Farkas and the University of Maryland. Especial thanks is expressed to Chris Economakis of New York, who made possible the inclusion of many of these pictures due to his careful work in making copies from the originals which were in color and black and white and of all sizes and shapes, and to Lynn Walcoff my patient and cooperative editor at the Charles E. Merrill Publishing Company. My gratitude goes out, too, to Louise Antz and Theodore Brameld, Professors of Educational Philosophy, and Algernon D. Black, Leader of the New York Society for Ethical Culture for fostering my continuous scholarly pursuits in educational philosophy and in ethics which are continually interwoven with what is here; to Victoria Wagner, former Educational Director of the Ethical Culture Schools, and Emily Henry, former Principal of the Midtown Ethical Culture School, who for many years shared interest in what the children and I were trying to do together; to former colleagues Ruth Berkman and Antoinette Wiggins for their support and encouragement. Appreciation is expressed, also, to the children, most of whom were in the writer's classes—many in the Ethical Culture School and in various other schools, centers, and neighborhood houses—who are in these pages, sometimes with their parents; to the university students, whose experiences and questions formed a constant learning arena, especially during the many years at the Brooklyn Center of Long Island University and for two years at Cleveland State University, for the sharpening of ideas, thoughts, and projections which resulted from my own experiences and problem-solving attempts; to the numerous others, who contributed a thought in the past, an idea in the present, or whose very presence caused projection into future possibilities.

Grace K. Pratt-Butler
November 17, 1974

Contents

CHAPTER 1

Three-, Four-, and Five-Year-Olds

INTRODUCTION

Young children are neither dolls nor babies, although they may look like the former and sometimes behave like the latter. Three-, four-, and five-year-olds are boys and girls, who have lived thirty-six, forty-eight, or sixty months. They have grown and developed physically, mentally, socially, and emotionally. They have evidenced needs and interests, acquiesced to certain social-cultural demands, and each one, to a greater or lesser extent, has manifested some unique behaviors and characteristics. Just what does this mean? To what extent can characteristics and behaviors be guided? Can actions be changed? Should they be directed or left alone? Will children develop anyway or must their lives be channeled carefully toward preconceived goals? Are their interactions, as living organisms in an environment of people and things, to be left unstructured? Are there extremes? Is there some middle way which accounts for evaluating new findings and yet encourages individual experience?

It is our purpose to examine these questions and to provide the kind of answers which will be of service to those who work with children of these ages. First, let us look at the children themselves.

WHO ARE THEY?

Emily sat silently at the book table, but she was not looking at the books. The little five-year-old girl was pale. She began to twist her braid slowly into a coil. Mrs. Sanger came over and sat down beside Emily. Emily looked at her, turned

1

her eyes away, and then she turned them back as she said slowly, "My Mommy only has a dollar in her pocketbook. When it's gone, she don't know what we can have to eat."

Lee ran out onto the roof of the playground, grabbing a building board as he went. He sped to the jungle gym and climbed to the top keeping the board tightly under his arm. "Bang, you're dead," he shouted, as he waved the board from his perch on top of the horizontal ladder. "Billy, come on, David's dead. Bang." The agility of the four-and-a-half-year-old enabled him to maneuver himself and his board into the place best suited to see everything.

Mandy entered the three-year-old group's room very slowly. Both arms were wrapped tightly around a bulky cotton laundry bag. When she walked into the room, Mandy stopped and looked about until she saw the teacher. She smiled and walked slowly over to her. "Why Mandy, here you are, good morning," was the cheerful greeting. Smiling more broadly, Mandy adjusted the laundry bag slightly and then swayed from one side to the other. "Shall we take off your coat, Mandy?" asked her teacher. Still smiling, Mandy shook her head "No." "You hold your bag Mandy and I'll take off your coat." Mandy smiled broadly, stopped swaying, and vigorously nodded "Yes." After the coat was off, Mandy clutched the laundry bag more tightly to her stomach and continued to stand there seeming oblivious to the activity all around her. "Mandy, let's hang up your coat" seemed unheard as Mandy continued to stand there silent and alone.

Janet, age four years and one month, walked into the prekindergarten room and up to her teacher. "Good morning," she said. "I took off my coat, it's in my locker." She smiled as her teacher greeted her, turned, and calling "Johnny, Johnny," ran off to join him in the housekeeping corner. John was engaged in putting doll dishes on the doll table. "Shall I cook dinner?" asked Johnny, taking a doll pan from the cupboard and moving toward the stove. "I'm hungry," he announced. "Can I be the sister, if you're the mother, Janet?" asked Gayle as she walked into the corner. "I'll put the baby to bed," she added, picking up the doll from the rocking chair.

Tony, age five years and four months, marched directly into the kindergarten, "Here I am, Miss Schwartz," he shouted. "I have brought my harmonica, and I want to play it. Do you want to hear me now?" As Miss Schwartz greeted him, Tony added, "My mother says I make an awful noise, but then you'll *like* my harmonica when I play!"

How does an educated teacher work with these children? How is their particular behavior to be interpreted? What should the teacher do in each case?

UNDERSTANDING BEHAVIOR

Understanding behavior requires knowledge of children, skill in analyzing action, and the ability to interpret individual behavior in relation to general underlying theory. This is an on-going process in which the teacher learns, evaluates, and reconstructs her role constantly.

Emily's teacher knew that the family was on welfare. She also knew that Emily was an intelligent, capable child. This was evidenced constantly as Emily settled difficulties with equipment and made suggestions for group play. Emily frequently went to the store for her mother. Sometimes she watched her baby brother, who was just two. Responsibility sat well on five-year-old Emily's shoulders. In fact, it sat so well that Emily tended to take charge of the various routines in the daily program. She identified with authority, but lacked the ability to form give-and-take social relationships with her peers. Her suggestions, often stated in an authoritarian manner, were not always accepted. The other children liked and respected her, but rarely initiated dramatic play with her. Emily needed to be guided into situations where she would be a relaxed five-year-old playing with other five-year-olds. Emily needed assurance, too, that food would be forthcoming. Basic needs had to be met.

Emily's acceptance of responsibility had developed from the egocentric concerns of the three-year-old. Three-year-olds learn to care for themselves and their belongings. A few months earlier, Mandy, for instance, had had the average three-year-old's sense of achievement. She could take off her coat, put equipment away, wash and dry her hands, and put napkins around the table for lunch. However, Mandy's self-image had been severely damaged by her brother Joe. When Joe was able to walk by himself, he literally "got into everything." Mandy's possessions were seized, tossed about, removed, and broken. Nothing was ever where she left it when she returned home from school. Mandy solved her problem by taking a laundry bag and putting her most favorite possessions into it every morning. Then she would come to school, only if permitted to bring the laundry bag. In a practical way, Mandy had solved her problem of trying to preserve her possessions from Joe's destructive actions. However, the situation created great anxiety in Mandy, and her insecurity was evidenced in a number of ways. She insisted on staying near her teacher. Inasmuch as she would not relinquish her laundry bag, this meant that she frequently stood very close to the teacher, her bag in her arms, while everyone else was busily doing something. Other children would ask why Mandy didn't put her cup on the tray or get her coat. She definitely needed help. However, her mother needed to be led to see Mandy and to understand her problems. And although Joe made overt demands, Mandy also had her requirements which needed to be met.

On a four-year-old level, Janet displayed the kind of behavior which one might expect. Her self-sufficiency enabled her to hang up her coat, greet her teacher, and join her friends in dramatic play in the housekeeping corner. Janet had developed self-sufficiency at three. Her physical coordination enabled her to manage gross motor movements, she was outgoing, and she had achieved a positive self-image. Her development had been fostered by understanding parents. Unfortunately, Emily, in contrast, had been expected to do more than should be expected from a three-, four-, or five-year-old. By the time she was five, her anxiety was closely identified with that of her mother. In the school situation she transferred this to her teacher and sought constantly to ally herself with the security of the teacher's authority. Self-sufficiency, responsibility, or the ability to manage certain things for one's self is part of maturing. Of the three children mentioned, Janet had developed optimum independence, within a well-rounded personality, for her age level.

Janet had developed self-sufficiency at three. (Courtesy Department of Health, Education and Welfare and Dick Swartz.)

Leo's physical activities displayed the kind of coordination generally expected of a mature four-year-old. This was in direct contrast to David, toward whom Leo's hostility was directed. David, at four and one-half still walked up and down stairs baby fashion—putting both feet together on each step. His gross motor control was very underdeveloped in comparison with that of most others his age. Riding a tricycle at moderate speed was his sole physical activity on the playground until his teacher persuaded him to give someone else a turn. Although David could feed himself, his hand coordination as well as the control of his other small muscles was underdeveloped. This was obvious to an alert youngster like Leo. Whereas Leo needed to develop some interest in quiet pursuits in order to broaden his means of satisfaction, David needed to develop his

The ability to manage certain things for one's self is part of maturing. (Courtesy Department of Health, Education and Welfare and Dick Swartz.)

coordination. He needed to run freely and to climb. Once able to manage the motor skills necessary for active physical play, David would be able to keep up with the other children and their activities.

Mandy had solved a problem of her own by bringing her favorite possessions with her. They were protected from her brother Joe. However, Mandy's insecurity prevented her from full use of her physical, social, and mental abilities. Mandy's need to protect her possessions prevented her from voicing choices about what she wanted to do.

Although their attention spans are usually not very long, most three-year-olds can solve simple problems such as those connected with block building, riding a tricycle around an obstacle, hammering a pegboard and turning it over for further hammering, and following simple requests. By four, they can do as Janet did. She followed the simple routine of hanging up her coat, saying "Good morning," choosing an activity, and following it through. Janet would listen attentively to a story for fifteen minutes, and then she might be found later utilizing some of the dialogue and/or activity in her play. Tony's behavior was of the type Janet might well display by her kindergarten year. Five-year-olds are masters of what they do in a number of ways. They relate several items, connect simple

Four-year-olds listen attentively to a story. (Courtesy University of Maryland and Richard E. Farkas.)

cause and effect relationships, have a sustained span of interest, and are beginning to clarify temporal relationships. Experiences are related and become data for solving difficulties. There is a build-up, and understanding becomes considerably broader and deeper by the time a child is five.

Although developmental areas are interrelated and every child is a whole, it is helpful to consider each of the major areas, namely the physical, social, emotional, and mental, separately.

PHYSICAL DEVELOPMENT

Leo had been encouraged at three to try out what the nursery school had to offer. He was encouraged to climb the jungle gym, to run, to hammer, and to cut with blunt scissors. Block building was a favorite activity. He carried full watering cans to sprinkle flowers, he put together puzzles, and in general utilized all of the equipment available. At four his large muscular coordination was developed to the extent that he had excellent control over activities requiring his large muscles. His small muscles, were, as is to be expected, less developed. His

*Block building provides fine learning experiences,
and it's fun to build with fathers when they visit.
(Courtesy Ethical Culture Schools, New York City
and Celeste Muschel.)*

finger control enabled him to put the cube blocks into their container easily. In-
tercoordinations, such as those of his hand and eye, developed to the point where
he could hammer a large-headed nail into a soft pine block, saw off another
piece, and nail the two together. Thus, he was active and well-coordinated.
During his kindergarten year he probably would be able to build usable struc-
tures with large building blocks, cut out pictures, hammer nails well, and do
all of the things that five-year-olds need to do to work through the problems
they solve with materials, to develop the interests they have, and to meet the
needs that require physical responses. Physically, Leo was healthy looking, and
he ate and slept well. The childhood diseases ran their course rather quickly. He
was healthy, active, and physically capable according to all of his teachers.

According to Todd and Heffernan, "In one sense the entire nursery group
and kindergarten program is a program in physical education, planned in terms
of helping each child move himself safely and smoothly through space."[1] It is
too easy to think that physical development will take care of itself. All too often
this belief fosters small muscle development and skill, and gross motor skills
may be so poor that a child literally cannot "move himself smoothly and safely
through space."

The writer remembers Phil who was a handsome, socially adept four-year-old. Phillip's physical coordination was so poor that it retarded normal four-year-old physical activity. His social development had become a masterful means to keep his friends physically quiet so that he would not be left behind. After consultation with his mother, it was discovered that Phillip's nurse had kept him sitting quietly on a park bench each afternoon. This had been the

Phil needed a chance to develop control of his large muscles.

pattern for the two years preceding his entrance into the four-year-old group. Phil needed a chance, which his teacher gave him, to develop control of his large muscles. As he began to do this, his "movement through space" became smoother and more rapid. By the end of the year, he climbed, ran, and jumped off the ladder gym onto the mat. Physical activity became natural and gave him great satisfaction. It also made his social relationships smoother because he became less dominating.

   Physical activity is basic. Children need it in all areas. Sinclair offers a clear summary for more particularized consideration of the young child's basic movement patterns. Her discussion of the eight general characteristics of movement (opposition, dynamic balance, total body assembly, rhythmic two-part loco-motion, eye-hand efficiency, agility, postural adjustment, dominance) is apt here. It serves to remind us again of the necessity for a variety of materials and equipment in ample space for fostering active physical growth.[2] In urban areas, children may spend their lives in apartments, in riding tricycles on the sidewalk, and in walking. Such children need to climb and to carry large blocks and build with them. Suburban children frequently do have opportunities for large muscle development, but less attention is given to their small muscle control or intermuscular coordinations. Enough physical activity for balanced development does not come of itself. necessarily. A further discussion of physical activity appears later in the book.*

SOCIAL DEVELOPMENT

Although Mandy did not reject the other children, her emotional anxiety caused her to withdraw from social interaction. She could not relate to others either verbally or through materials. Relating through materials would mean relinquishing the laundry bag. Verbal communication was not forthcoming because she had become withdrawn. Her experiences at home with Joe were negative; others would destroy her things. As a result, Mandy would not permit anyone to see or to touch what was in her bag. The size of it precluded using other materials.

At three, children tend to develop give-and-take relationships with others. This is most often evidenced in relating to one other child at a time. The child,

At age three, children tend to develop give-and-take relationships. (Courtesy Ethical Culture Schools, New York City and Celeste Muschel.)

---

*See chapters on program and on equipment.

who has not been with other children, may poke with a finger experimentally to get a reaction. Speech has developed later than ability to move one's arms and hands, and when in a new situation, a child tends often to regress to earlier patterns of behavior.

Ted always approached new objects or toys by poking them first with his forefinger. If all seemed well, he then opened his hand and grasped the toy. Ted's experimental approach led to the purposeful use of materials. During the first day at nursery school, Ted poked Mike. When there was no response, he grabbed Mike's sweater and pulled it toward him. Screams from Mike surprised him and he withdrew. Later, when he poked Debra, with one exploratory finger, she hit him on the head. Ted moved back and stared with a bewildered look on his face. His habitual approach toward new materials did not work with other people. Ted's teacher was aware of his need to use his voice to attract the attention of others and of his need to have his behavior interpreted to Mike and to Debra. Ted required the kind of techniques necessary to relate to other children:

"This is Mike, Ted. Say Mike and he will answer you. This is Debra. Here is a pail and shovel. Sit here near Debra. Can you fill your pail?"

Ted's teacher was aware of several things: Ted's behavior needed to be explained to Mike and Debra; Ted needed to be told their names and be reminded to *speak* to them. Ted was placed in a parallel play situation near Debra which would permit him to be near her but which would not require any social adjustment. His teacher realized that in the normal course of filling their pails some interactive behavior might occur.

Thus Ted's teacher had given him a verbal technique. More importantly, she knew that parallel play—doing what another was doing near him—was a typical preliminary to give-and-take relationships. Ted and Debra would need careful supervision. One might reach too far and preempt what the other considered *his sand.* Accidentally touching the other with shovel or pail might be misinterpreted. *But,* chants, laughter, or talk could result.

Ted and Debra might well begin to chant. Debra chants while scooping sand, "Fill it, fill it, fill my pail," or "Shov-el, Shov-el . . .". Ted soon joins and both chant together. After three or four minutes, both laugh together. A "bridge" has been created. Five minutes later, Debra drops her pail and runs to the swings, Ted follows. Soon both are swinging. Ted's teacher, who is watching, notes this and remembers the successful parallel play situations. There was no real interaction, but each child developed an awareness of the other.

Most adults who work with very young children are aware of processional play patterns. Although these usually precede parallel play and are in evidence from fifteen or sixteen months on, by those whose coordination permits it, such play is observable in the nursery school from time to time, usually for short periods.

For instance, Donna seizes a unit outdoor block from where they are stacked. She runs across the room and sets it by the opposite wall. As she runs back to the stack, Rosa follows her. After Donna has seized another block and started for the opposite wall with it, Rosa grabs a block from the stack and runs after Donna. She places her block next to Donna's. This pattern is repeated eight times. The fourth time, shrieks and laughter are heard, first from Donna and then from Rosa. Each is well aware of the other, but no direct interaction has taken place as yet.

By age four, Ted and Mike are observed frequently to be in each other's company. They greet each other upon arrival and go off together. Block building together is a frequent activity. There is discussion and occasionally some disagreement. By now, Ted has developed the ability to defend himself verbally first. If things don't work out to his satisfaction, he may hit, but he has learned to speak first. By age four and one-half both boys are joined by two, three, or four other boys and girls. Mike tends to be the leader. For several days, "Come and ride on our bus. Come and ride on our bus," is shouted as dramatic play centers around a block bus complete with steering wheel.

Ted tends to support Mike. "This way to the bus. This way—tickets."

After flying to Miami and back, Ted takes the lead in airplane play. After watching a minute, Mike follows Ted's lead. "Flight No. 340. Ready for boarding. Non-stop to Miami."

By age five, Ted is able to work well with almost anyone in the kindergarten. He tends to make worthwhile suggestions for class activities. "Let's build a store." Occasionally, everyone follows his ideas, and the group carries them out together. At times Ted resents the leadership of Mike, or Tim, a new child. However, generally speaking, he has developed excellent give-and-take relationships.

His teachers had watched and recorded Ted's social development with interest. By the end of nursery school, he could play in an interactive relationship with one other child. Although he poked or hit occasionally, he had learned to speak first.

During his prekindergarten year he progressed from playing with Debra to watching on the fringes of the more organized activities of groups of three or four children. His early attempts to join dramatic play were centered around the props needed. For instance, he would get a needed block for a child. There was occasional intervention and guidance from his teacher.

For example: "Ted, Jonathan is the father. Why don't you take this (*handing him a basket*) and be the grocery man? You could deliver the order." Thus he was placed in an important supportive role which was no threat to those who were in the primary roles of mother, father, or baby. His "groceries" were cheerfully accepted.

By the end of the prekindergarten year, Ted occasionally led the dramatic play with five children. The others were usually rather placid children. When a follower, he accepted the suggestions of the other active children cheerfully.

He often invited one other child for lunch on Saturday and was an occasional guest. He began to consider himself as part of a social unit and would say "On Saturday Rand and me, we went on the big slide in the park." "We" became a concept of real importance to him. Thus he was ready socially for the more organized activities which were carried through in the five-year-old kindergarten.

Social development is allied so closely to emotional development that they are considered separately only for reasons of clarity. It is in order, therefore, to look more closely at the emotional aspect of development.

EMOTIONAL DEVELOPMENT

Mandy's behavior at three has been described. Her anxiety was understandable and her teacher led her mother to a more complete appreciation of the little girl and her difficulties. In several months Mandy began to regain her self-confidence and to participate as an active three-year-old.

Janet's behavior is, and had been, in definite contrast to that of Mandy. Janet entered the three-year-old nursery school alert to what it had to offer. Her parents had built up positive associations with school. She had had the usual visit the preceding June, had attended a summer playgroup in the morning for four weeks, and was looking forward to nursery school.

Janet's cheerful, outgoing personality stood in sharp contrast to that of Gina, who clung to her mother and cried. Janet could not understand this and said to Gina, "Come girl, play." Routines were accepted by Janet as part of "the way we do things." She rested moderately well from the beginning, ate a little of everything, took care of herself at the toilet, learned readily to put toys and materials away, and accepted suggestions.

By age four, Janet was a strong, stable child. She greeted visitors cheerfully. Her mother reported that she slept through the night with a tiny night light and that she could accept change. Both her teacher and her parents noted that she showed no pronounced fears, although she tended to show some anxiety when dogs were nearby. Janet did not regress in behavior.

By age five she was capable and responsible. Janet could find her way about the school building, was willing to have the first shot injected when the doctor came, and helped Dora overcome fear of climbing on the jungle gym. Janet cried when hurt, but she was comforted easily and always helped put on her own bandaid.

In contrast, Leo had been a withdrawn, apprehensive three-year-old. Dissension at home finally resulted in divorce, and Leo had difficulty adjusting to the woman who cared for him. At the same time, he missed his father and watched for him at the window for long periods of time. At three and one-half, he began to hit. He had tantrums occasionally, and always announced at such times, "I will go far away." His nursery school teacher succeeded in diverting some of his aggressive behavior into pegboard pounding and other physical activity. He began to climb and rode a tricycle at full speed. When he learned that the latter was not for bumping into people, he identified with the policeman and looked for "bad people." His hostility and the aggressive behavior he displayed was overt and could be handled.

At four he was more calm, but he tended to victimize a weaker child. David was a quiet apprehensive boy. Leo soon found out how to make David cry and did this repeatedly. However, his means were verbal and though pretending to injure through materials, he did not strike David. Through working out calming influences, planning for special times alone with each parent, and being sure that he was participating in activities, which gave him satisfaction, Leo was readied for kindergarten. During that year, he was a positive contributor to constructive activities. Inasmuch as his attention span was shorter than that of most of the others, he needed help in order to channel his energies into positive behavior. He tended to be impatient when others wouldn't stop when he wanted to do something. However, he began to overcome this partly through being led to see more possibilities in things and partly by finding his own way to wait until others were finished. He would sit at the book table and look through books rapidly. All went quite well until his mother remarried. Despite an understanding stepfather, Leo was slow to accept this new male figure in the home. By the end of the kindergarten year, however, he had made considerable headway.

Emotionally secure children are usually confident and happy. They express their likes and dislikes and can handle simple frustrations. In a calm environment, the wise teacher is aware of the emotional development of each child and tries to gauge how much he can manage for himself. Bullying by older or stronger children, for instance, should be stopped. However, attempts of his peers to take his things should be manageable. Taking turns, the ability to solve simple problems—which usually involve materials—and disappointments which are not too shattering should be managed by a preschool child. Temper tantrums are behavioral extremes which need special attention.* Overcoming hesitancies concerning touching finger paint, anxiety about hearing a cork popped out of the test tube by steam, or covering the ears when hearing the roll of thunder are common enough. As a child matures, he gains more control over his own explorations and gains the self-confidence displayed in a positive image of himself. He increases his own emotional development.

A positive self-image enables the confident child to utilize his potentialities, to develop new possibilities, and to further his mental development through worthwhile learning experiences. The expectations for mental development in the preschool when reached, continue to serve the child throughout his life. This area of development is considered next.

*See chapter 4, p. 55.

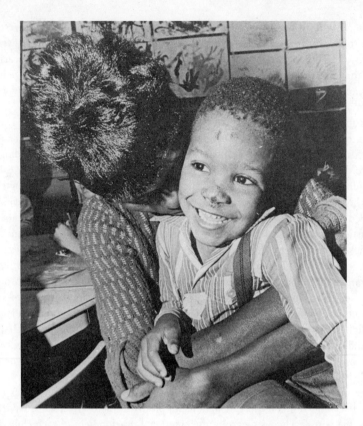

Emotionally secure children are confident and happy. (Courtesy of Department of Health, Education and Welfare and Dick Swartz.)

MENTAL DEVELOPMENT

Children like Janet do what is expected. At three Janet had adapted easily to school routines. She washed and dried her hands after using the toilet, put her cup on the tray after mid-morning snack, and placed her boots in front of her to distinguish which boot went on the left and which boot went on the right foot. Janet's teacher encouraged Janet to choose what she, herself, wanted to do. She had to establish her individual activity patterns. This was different from doing it because John was doing it or because she wanted to take it home to show her parents. Janet began to find that she could choose what she wished, could carry through the activity, and could achieve satisfaction from it. Her self-image was positive. Self-initiative was quite evident. Furthermore, Janet was encouraged to solve the problems that arose in the course of her work and play activities.[3]

For instance, when Janet at age three and one-half was building with the five-inch unit blocks, she wanted to make a simple bridge of three blocks in order to drive her car under it. She placed the two upright blocks too far apart and the third would not bridge the space across the top between the two uprights. Janet had alternatives: she could move the two upright blocks closer together, call for help, put a third upright between the other two, or give up. Janet decided to move the left upright closer to the right one with her left hand while she held the third block over the two uprights. Janet solved this simple problem for herself as well as a number of others. Thus Janet's teacher encouraged her to think with materials. Thinking with materials is problem solving at this level. It is basic and is a foundation for future problem solving. Her teacher refrained from solving Janet's problems but stood ready to prevent frustration. Too many failures would assure neither initiative nor problem-solving behavior. Unfortunately many adults too often have the tendency to solve children's problems for them as they work and play.

By prekindergarten, Janet's attention span was long enough to assure carrying activities through to satisfying conclusions. She tended to develop her own reasons for continuing what she was doing because her initiative had always been fostered. Young children should not be physically quiet for too long a period of time, but by age five may spend twenty minutes alone painting, for example. Janet had participated in a wide spectrum of experiences and was beginning to connect cause and effect.

> If we rattle the pellets in the container of the guinea pig just before he is fed, he will squeal. He knows he will be fed. If Miss Jones attaches that wire from a dry cell battery to the other battery, the bell will ring. If I plant a bean near the edge of a jar of vermiculite and give it water and set it in the sun, I can see the roots begin to grow. Something is done and something follows.

Janet began to relate verbally some of her experiences and the connections among them. Her vocabulary grew and she expressed herself with clarity.

By age five, Janet was a popular leader. Her ideas and plans were well expressed, and she was able to lead others into rich dramatic play activities.

Janet's teacher knew that a five-year-old who can choose and has an attention span of sufficient length to follow through, who can solve the simple problems that arise, who knows simple cause-and-effect relationships, and who can express her plans well enough to gain a following was developing very well.

Janet had had teachers whose conscious concern for fostering her mental development had been motivated by a similar underlying point of view. All her teachers had fostered initiative and self-direction in an environment which allowed and invited considerable free activity. Janet's teachers believed that through dealing with the problems which arose from the little girl's own experiences with the materials and equipment available and in the company of her peers, Janet would develop her means of solving difficulties. In her early years this would be largely with objects, as in the example with blocks.

They knew that Janet had to establish her own patterns and that, although she would be guided when necessary, her actions and her solutions to problems as well as her conceptual development were primarily connected with what she, herself, and in company with her peers, did.

In a sense, action solution is concept formation during the preschool years.[4] Janet's teachers, while believing that Janet should be competent in various specific ways as part of their general expectations about her, did not try to teach her a sequence of specific actions geared toward preplanned behavioral competencies. Instead constant interactions in an environment abundant in people and materials experienced under their guidance were deemed preferable. Some of the further ramifications of this arrangement will be discussed in later chapters. Both Dewey and Piaget seem in accord here because the sensorimotor adaptive actions of Piaget[5] appear to have some equivalency in Dewey's learning by doing.[6]

INTERRELATIONSHIPS

We have seen how in some of the cases cited above, there are interrelationships between physical prowess and social development, between emotional stability and problem solving, and between physical ability and emotional development. In other words, there is a constant interaction and interrelationship going between the physical, mental, social, and emotional growth and development aspects of the young child. Given a school situation which is aware of the importance of each, the young child should develop the kind of balance that is necessary.

It might be added that special concern should be given to problems of deprivation.* A child like Emily who had an emotionally insecure past due to real physical want based on the economic need of her family requires special attention. Deprivation can have a physical effect on children. The writer has seen children deprived of the right food suffering from rickets; she has noted skin diseases and various evidences of lack of proper diet. On the other hand, emotional deprivation may be reflected in lack of physical well-being. Eating too much is a familiar method of overcompensation.

Social deprivation frequently shows in lack of ability to get along with other children. More seriously it may show in actual emotional fear as the child tries to avoid seeing anyone else. The writer remembers a little girl who had had very bad experiences with women before coming to this country. Once here, she felt the fear and the strangeness of a new country to which she had come, and she also had to adjust to new surroundings in her immediate household. Her fear of women became intense, and she would retire behind her mother, the

*See chapter 2, p. 20.

only woman she would accept, or her father, whenever another woman approached her. This kind of deprivation of a normal, natural childhood shows up in various ways. Deprivations may be physical, social, emotional, and/or mental. The child who is never encouraged to ask a question and given an answer, who is never given a chance to find out for himself and to explore his environment, who is never given a chance to "tag along while someone else is busy doing something" has never had a chance to find fulfillment of his needs for growing intellectually. For example, simple problem solving, as mentioned earlier, needs to go on constantly if the child is to develop his own ability to find out the possibilities a new piece of equipment holds. To try and then to have the feelings of success accompanying the solution of a simple problem gives the child the kind of positive self-image he/she should have.

In this chapter, we have seen some examples of physical, mental, social, and emotional growth and development and have had some indication of how these aspects of growth and development are interrelated. The various behavioral and characteristic illustrations of three-, four-, and five-year-old children are not extraordinary but are examples of the kinds of concerns which are part of the preschool teacher's daily life. The skilled teacher knows that, although there are general expectations for each age level, each child develops individually. Even though a general air of self-sufficiency may pervade a five-year-old kindergarten, for example, some one or two individuals may be very dependent. One may not yet have reached this level of maturity, and the second may have regressed to an earlier stage of development. With understanding, the teacher guides the first to achieve greater independence while she tries to interpret the regressive behavior of the second in order to fulfill whatever need is lacking and to enable him to reach the developmental level of which he is capable. Careful clarification of the problems presented by each child and collection of all possible data relevant to these from her own general knowledge, from specifics observed, and from particulars given by the parents during interviews help the teacher to plan possible ways to meet the difficulty. Changes in the child's behavior to ways more akin to acceptable expectations for the age level are the test of how the teacher is succeeding in meeting the situation.

The reader has been introduced to preschool children. Today, a growing number of children go to nursery schools, day care centers, Head Start classes, prekindergartens, and kindergartens. However, such education is not new. In the next chapter some of the types of education available to preschool children at present and the contributions of some past educators will be considered briefly. Underlying philosophical theory will receive consideration in the third chapter, and theory and practice will be interwoven. Too frequently, excellent practices have been carried out in preschool education without the practitioners being aware of why they were doing what they were doing! The unity of theory and practice gives preschool education purpose and significance.

Notes

1. Vivian Todd and Helen Heffernan, *The Years Before School* (New York: The Macmillan Co., 1970), p. 240.

2. Caroline B. Sinclair, *Movement of the Young Child Ages Three to Six* (Columbus: Charles E. Merrill Publishing Company, 1973), Chapter 4, especially.

3. Grace K. Pratt, "Developing Concepts about Science in Young Children," in *Foundations of Early Childhood Education: Readings*, ed. Michael Auleta (New York: Random House, Inc., 1969), pp. 296-300, for a discussion of problem solving.

4. Ibid.

5. Ronald K. Parker, *The Preschool in Action* (Boston: Allyn and Bacon Co., 1973), p. 95.

6. John Dewey, *Democracy and Education* (New York: The Macmillan Co., 1916), p. 323.

CHAPTER 2

The Present Scene

THE CONTEMPORARY SITUATION

Figures indicate that approximately four million children attend preschool. Of these, 76.8 percent are age five; 22.8 percent are four; 8.3 percent are three. As a result of the Federal Education Act of 1965, there has been accelerated interest in this age group because of the increase in federal funds. About three of every four children, according to a recent survey, attend kindergarten.[1] Another source states that one of every four mothers of children under six is in the labor force.[2] Although funding suffers temporary setbacks, the increase in preschool enrollment is continuing. The number of working women is steadily increasing, and many women, who previously had little or no concern about early education, now find themselves part of parent groups because as "working" mothers their children are attending some preschool group.

The diversity of patterns for set-up and operation and for the funds to operate the various groups serving children ages three, four, and five is varied. Kiernan states it well, "Although it is an obvious over-simplification, education continues to be a local function, a state responsibility, and a federal concern." Concerning the latter, he says, "a dozen federal cooks have attempted to prepare each fiscal meal and distribute emergency government largess through separate and unrelated agencies, rather than channeling these efforts through Washington's only logical agency, the United States Office of Education. Too many blue plate specials have been offered. . . ."[3] The writer remembers earlier discourses on the "bugaboos" of federal control.[4] Controls have been there, but they have been related for the most part to each of Dr. Kiernan's "blue plate specials."

19

FUNDED CENTERS

The average citizen hears a great deal about Head Start and about day care. To some, these are vague terms. To others, they refer to a single structure. Just what each is is not always clear.

There are three types of day care centers described in the Federal Interagency Day Care Requirements of the United States Department of Health, Education and Welfare, Office of Economic Opportunity for federal funds. They are:

1. The daily day care home which serves from one to five young children in a home;
2. The group day care home which gives family-like care in a large residence for ten to twelve children;
3. The day care center for twelve or more children of mixed ages part of whose day is directed by a professional teacher.[5]

The last is the most common. Programs are varied; many tend to follow some, or all, of the educational precepts as developed in this book at the same time that they give children necessary shelter, food, and rest.

Baumrind tells us that one third of the centers with which the Department of Public Welfare contracts, offer only custodial and protective care. Many lack the healthy, stimulating environment that can contribute to positive child development.[6]

Head Start programs began in the summer of 1965 and enrolled over 550,000 in approximately 2,500 child development centers.[7] They were initiated as a result of the Economic Opportunity Act of 1964 and $150 million was allotted to them.[8] They became year-round centers later. The underlying theory behind the program was that the centers were an answer to the cultural deprivation of children whose parents could not "provide a foundation for success in the larger society."[9]

Cultural deprivation has received considerable attention in recent years. The accumulating deficit of such deprivation appears to mount as children mature. For instance, Biber holds that three different levels of deficit can be associated with family life patterns in negative conditions of poverty. She lists them as: immature language and thinking; lack of close relationships; physical and psychological uncertainties.[10] In a similar vein, Brittain says that the assumptions about the characteristics of "culturally deprived" children which underlie their inferior academic performance include "poor language facility, constriction in dealing with symbolic and abstract ideas, narrowness of outlook because of the narrowness of the familiar environment, passivity and lack of curiosity, low self-esteem, and lack of motivation for achievement."[11] The Head Start Centers were to function as nuclei for wider reform and to coordinate various forms of social services for the whole family.

The general idea of a child development center was to draw together family, community, and professional resources to focus on the child's total development.[12] Unfortunately, generalizations about the "deprived" were too pat. In many cases, the focus was placed on listening and on prereading—the paths to tomes of knowledge hitherto kept for the advantaged! But in many cases, there was neglect of underlying theories and practices to encourage physical, social, emotional, and mental growth and development. Years of careful research, observation, and experience with these young children in a variety of settings for various socioeconomic levels were ignored. Independent school groups for middle and upper classes, university demonstration classes, and the settlement houses, which had served the underprivileged for years, were almost entirely ignored. Indeed, in many cases, those struggling to establish new centers probably did not know that such education had existed. The sincere as well as the adventurers emerged quickly and grasped the opportunity to start groups for the preschool-aged child with the federal money available. The environment was hostile, in some cases, to those outside of the particular center and its program. For example, rival programs were set up in close proximity to each other.

In some other cases, the results of experience to expedite evidences of knowledge and prereading skills was accepted. Programs focussed on the first grade *to come* rather than on rich experiences *now* for a fuller present year. Immediate results were sought in order to prove the need for continued funding. The theory of the child developing as an individual was often disregarded. The stress on language and prereading led to formidable clashes over English versus "dialect" speech. New "hardware" flourished.

This type of controversy continues. Professional educators, in a number of instances, have withdrawn from this "bandwagon" in American education. Others have tried to penetrate a stone wall. A few have made some initial headway and have been able to continue to consolidate their gains and to make these centers, and their successors, genuinely educational.

There is nothing new about education for children under six. What have some predecessors in preschool education done? A brief summary of selected instances may lend perspective to the present situation.

SOME PREDECESSORS

The Federal Emergency Relief Administration authorized the establishment of Federal Emergency Nursery Schools in 1933. (Thus it was a predecessor to preschool funding in this country.) In 1940, there were 1,500 W.P.A. nursery schools with 50,000 children enrolled. In 1941, nursery schools were established on Farm Security Administration Projects. These employed staff furnished by the W.P.A. and N.Y.A. Migratory camps accounted for about forty-one such groups in 1940.[13]

However, there was education at earlier dates in America for preschool children.

Mrs. Carl Schurz, a pupil of Froebel,* established the first kindergarten in the United States in 1855. This was a private kindergarten for German speaking children in Watertown, Wisconsin.[14]

Elizabeth Peabody began the first English speaking kindergarten in Boston in 1860. She influenced Matilde Krieger and her daughter to begin a training school for teachers in 1868.[15]

Susan Blow taught in the first public kindergarten which opened as part of the St. Louis public school system in 1873. Graves states that twelve kindergartens were opened at first; others were opened as soon as competent directors could be obtained. Directors were trained in Miss Blow's training school. Within ten years, nearly eight thousand children attended over fifty public kindergartens in St. Louis. In 1880, San Francisco authorized that kindergartens be incorporated in public schools.[16]

In 1878, in New York City, handbills announcing a free kindergarten were distributed. Two children appeared on the first day of the Workingman's School which was the first free kindergarten east of the Mississippi. However, the school grew rapidly and some of the initial tenets held by Felix Adler, the

Scene in 1879 at the Workingman's School which is now the Midtown Ethical Culture School. It was the first free kindergarten east of the Mississippi. (Courtesy Ethical Culture Schools, New York City and Celeste Muschel.)

*See pp. 37-38 in chapter 3 for further information about the "Father of the Kindergarten."

founder, are still incorporated today in the programs of the Ethical Culture Schools. Of special importance were two emphases: (1) there should be as great a mixture of children of different backgrounds as possible; (2) about one-third of the children should be given scholarship assistance in order to assure maintenance of the variety.

In England, Rachel and Margaret McMillan began their preschool on the London dumps in 1909, primarily, to protect children from physical harm.[17] This protection extended beyond cognitive stimulation and work to medical and dental care as well. The nursery school was to make up for the poverty, apathy, and neglect which had been the lot of these children.[18] It is interesting to note that the term "Nurture School" was used because the McMillans believed that the nursery school, as a supplement to the home, was a nurturing force which would release the child from "the prison of the slums." To this end, intellectual, social, and moral behavior would provide the means.[19]

In Rome, Maria Montessori began her first preschool, *Casa di Bambini*, for slum children. She agreed with Froebel's emphasis on self-teaching, but she made her materials larger and easier for children to use than those of Froebel. She believed that children should have a spontaneous interest in learning and that a child should choose from a variety of materials and then "occupy himself" with what he has chosen. The materials are graded in difficulty, and the children progress constantly to finer differentiations. The Montessori method has stressed the theory that cognitive abilities develop from sensory discrimination.[20] Since the development of the first Montessori preschool, numerous schools using the Montessori method have come into being. Baumrind is a helpful authority here.[21] In 1971, there were said to be more than one thousand Montessori schools.[22]

SOME TYPES OF PRESCHOOLS

The kindergarten of the Workingman's School, which was known later as the Ethical Culture School, has been mentioned earlier. This was just one, among many preschool groups, in what are usually known as *Independent Schools*. In New York, for instance, such schools as the Harriet Johnson Nursery School, the City and Country School, the Walden School,* both old and new Lincoln School, and the Downtown Community School are a few which had, and still have, such preschool groups. These schools have followed Progressivism** in education in varying degrees. Children have learned actively and entered at three, four, or five years of age and then continued on through the higher grades in the school. Although these schools have charged tuition, most have had some scholarship plan to enable them to serve a wider student body. Parents have vis-

---

*The Walden School had two-year-olds for many years.
**To be discussed in chapter 3.

ited, conferred with teachers, attended meetings, and participated in the Parent Teachers Association. In many schools, this association has been a dynamic part of the school.

Other schools, especially those of Essentialist and Catholic persuasion* have added preschool groups until one could find examples of most educational philosophies in the preschool classes of *Independent Schools.* Programs vary, but most have a full day with a hot meal, rest on cots, and transportation. They look upon the preschool as the initial part of the school's educational program.

Another type of preschool began to develop in the late thirties and early forties. Today this type forms a large, though varied branch of preschool education. This is the school of the group which may be rather loosely designated as the *Cooperative Nursery School.* Two of the first and most noteworthy were (1) the one established by faculty wives at the University of Chicago in 1915, and (2) the Nursery School started at Smith College in 1926.[23]

Schools of the above type are usually started by a parent who may or may not have an education herself in Early Childhood Education. Some states have sought to regulate such groups, and although standards and requirements vary, the educational requirements now usually include provision for at least one teacher who meets acceptable educational standards. This person is in charge. The parents take turns as assistants on a regular basis, and in most instances, they help to govern the school.

Many of these groups began and still are housed in churches because the space is usually available at a low fee. Others are frequently housed in community centers, and sometimes in homes. These schools vary in setup, in length of day, and in the age levels served as well as in the manner in which the children are grouped. Many do an excellent job and have become community focal points for parent education and family activities.

Many universities have established preschool groups. Departments of Psychology wanted children for their students to observe and test. Departments of Home Economics needed children for their students. Departments of Education wanted *Campus Schools* for demonstration purposes, for observation, and for student teaching. Two of the earliest universities to have preschool classes were the University of Minnesota and the University of the State of New York at Buffalo. Landreth tells us that Elizabeth Merrill Palmer left a bequest to establish a school for teaching homemaking and the care of young children to girls in Detroit in 1922. As a result, a research and testing program was started,[24] and the Merrill Palmer School is still a leader in work with young children.

In the thirties and forties, especially, such campus schools were fully utilized for demonstration purposes. As Landreth says, "in the United States, nursery schools were organized around 1921 to furnish laboratories for the study of young children."[25] Although the trend at present is away from such campus-based demonstration schools and classes, due to limitations of space, money, and

---

*To be discussed in chapter 3.

varied clientele, some do exist and serve well. However, many administrators believe that the function they perform is served best elsewhere.

The concept of a school of practice right on campus is being replaced by field-based programs in schools which are already in operation and therefore not limited by space or finances. Their populations, too, may be more varied. However, there is a great deal in favor of a well-run campus-based demonstration school. These advantages exist despite the fact that their location frequently precludes attendance by a varied group of children. It does afford varied learning experiences for students from numerous college groups and classes; it is a checkpoint for various spot matters for the students; and it has a faculty which is part of the university, and therefore, accountable to it.

Within recent years, advocates of the women's liberation movement have been instrumental in getting preschool classes on college campuses. While the women want the advantages of preschool for their children, some get little more than child care by volunteers. Other such groups function as genuine educational centers and serve children and college students much as the demonstration groups mentioned above. Although housed on campus, the attitude, interest, and rapport of education departments to these classes vary. In some cases, the latter have been called in to "patch up" groups already underway, and in others, they have cooperated to establish and man them from the start.

SPECIAL EDUCATION AND LEARNING DISABILITIES

Numerous groups have been started to serve children of preschool age who have specific handicaps. For instance, the Society for Crippled Children in Cleveland has an excellent program for preschool children which includes all the usual activities in necessarily modified form. The children have a full program, take trips, and develop as fully as their handicap permits. Other groups serve other handicapped children.

In 1966, the Bureau of Education for Handicapped was established by congressional mandate. This bureau serves as (1) a coordinating center for federal efforts, (2) coordinator for state and local efforts, (3) administrator for federally funded programs, (4) facilitator of educational efforts for the handicapped. With this bureau in operation, duplication of services can be avoided and numerous advances in service may be anticipated.

Associations for children with learning disabilities are growing in various areas. These are often sponsored largely by parents who usually succeed in getting others interested and thus gain support for the necessary services. The child with a learning disability is one who needs help in a way or ways which may not be completely diagnosed at preschool age. By noting deviant behavior and responses at nursery school, teachers can perform a valuable service. Once these children have been noted, special attention can be given to the learning disability.

Gearheart tells us that the lines are not always clearly drawn. Children with a specific disability, who may benefit from a specific learning disabilities program, are often placed in a general program because there is nothing specifically available for them. He states that there are only three characteristics that all children with learning disabilities may be said to have in common. Summarized briefly, these are:

1. the child must have average or above average intelligence;
2. the child must have adequate sensory acuity;
3. the child must be achieving considerably less than would be predicted by a composite of I.Q., age, and educational opportunity.[26]

Children with a specific disability can participate in many activities. (Courtesy Society for Crippled Children, Cleveland, Ohio.)

In other words, there is a significant educational discrepancy. Gearheart says that these children often exhibit one or more other characteristics which he lists. These range from hyperactivity to lack of coordination. Their difficulties usually lead to difficulties with symbolic processes.

For these reasons, it seems to be especially important that these children receive attention early. In the preschool, the informal situation, the length of the day, and the intimacy of the teacher with the children should facilitate early recognition and intervention. Although Gearheart's third characteristic would be hardest to recognize at any early age, the teacher of three- and four-year-olds is an excellent situation to gain preliminary insight into a possible discrepancy between potential and achievement at an early age. The teacher's insights may indicate a basic problem.

In Special Education circles, the present trend is to keep children segregated as little as possible and, if special help is necessary, to give it. Then when the child is able, he joins regular groups. One school, for instance, has the Special Education in one wing of the building, so that when children are able, they go down the hall and around the corner in their wheelchairs and join a regular class at certain times during the day. Emotionally disturbed children often join other groups for certain parts of the day. Ramps and special equipment are necessary, but the price is small in terms of service to the children.

OPEN EDUCATION

Open Education as a term is new, but as a concept or set of concepts, it is a different and loosely inclusive term for a group of attitudes and beliefs which has numerous historical antecedents. Many teachers in large and small schools and other educational groups practiced education which was generally pragmatic and in many cases tinged with Reconstructionism* through the years. This meant that the child was considered:

1. as an individual different from other children;
2. as an active person capable of making simple choices;
3. as one able to solve simple problems;
4. as one able to benefit from undergoing an increasing variety of experiences;
5. as an individual able to relate to those around him regardless of race, nationality, or creed;
6. as one capable of developing and maintaining a strong self-image at the same time that he became increasingly aware of others and of the group of which he was a part.

It meant that the group was looked upon as:

1. a small social unit which encouraged a plurality of individuals at the same time that it gave a sense of security and a unity that was "ours";
2. capable of formulating and maintaining simple agreements for the benefit of the group as a social unit;

---

*See next chapter.

3. able to assimilate a new member within its rather free association without denying individuality and free expression so long as this was not deterrent to the actions of others;
4. developing interrelationships in an ever-widening sphere;
5. a unit for implementing and judging initial ethical actions, attitudes, and beliefs.

Programs based on this kind of theory emphasized physical, mental, social, and emotional growth and development toward maximum individual and group realization or potentiality and achievement. In some cases, this has been stated as furthering conscious concern for others in an ever-widening sphere of ethical concern.

Unfortunately, for present preschool education, the teachers in learning situations which functioned on the above premises neither wrote a great deal nor tried to sell themselves to the public. They did, and are doing, a fine job. They were and are concerned about practice related to theory rather than the latter as a written entity in itself. Certainly in most ways, many did have open rather than closed classrooms.

Silberman has stated that he uses the terms "informal education," "open education," and "the open classroom" . . . more or less interchangeably. He also says that he refers "to a change in atmosphere—toward more humaneness and understanding, toward more encouragement and trust." He refers also to "a change in learning style— . . . to the teacher as a facilitator of learning, . . . to more concern with individualized learning."[27] Does one need to go to England to find this? I think not.

The British purveyors of "open classrooms," however, do seem to the writer to have more space. Many American buildings are old and the walls solid. However, in many cases children did, and do, move back and forth and in and out. Halls have been used because the space was needed, but no one thought of calling it a "corridor" even though it did expand interrelationships. Larger groups, as in many of the English classes, have not been as favored here. This it seems to the writer has been for two reasons, primarily: (1) old buildings have smaller rooms and the spatial set-up is not always conducive to it (though when it is, it is often so utilized); (2) teachers believe that in the preschool, each child in making the transition from home to school should develop a close relationship to his teacher. Once he is secure and feels that he *belongs* and has *his* teacher and *his* place or room, he is ready to expand his exploration of the physical-spatial environment and to add breadth and variety to his social relationships.

The present book is based on the theories and practices of the writer. As the reader will find, the view is not restrictive but urges freedom for choosing, for experiencing, for creating, and for time and opportunity to understand what the outcome was. Activity, yes! Freedom and activity for purposes—and the actions of young children are purposeful—not just for random action which tends

Freedom for choosing, for experiencing, for creating. (Courtesy Ethical Culture Schools, New York City and Celeste Muschel.)

to lead nowhere. Purposeful activity initiates a three-part act with a motive, the action itself, and the consequence of so acting.*

Before considering in detail more theories and practices, it is necessary to consider briefly the current philosophies which underlie education. These are often discernible, too, in the demands and expectations of parents. The teacher must deal with these expectations and her/his own formulations. The following chapter presents the philosophies now dominant in education in summary form.

Notes

1. William P. McClure and Audra May Pence, *Early Childhood and Basic Elementary and Secondary Education Needs, Programs, Demands, Costs* (Urbana, Ill.: University of Illinois, College of Education, Bureau of Educational Research National Education Finance Project, Special Study #1, 1970), Chapter 2.

2. Robert Anderson and Harold Shane, eds., *As the Twig Is Bent* (Boston: Houghton Mifflin Company, 1971), p. 223.

*See chapter 12.

3. Owen Kiernan, *American Education,* ed. Weldon Beckner and Wayne Dumas (Scranton: International Textbook Company, 1970), p. 457.

4. Theodore Brameld, *Toward a Reconstructed Philosophy of Education* (New York: The Dryden Press, 1956), p. 296.

5. McClure, *Early Childhood and Basic Elementary and Secondary Education,* pp. 22-23.

6. Diana Baumrind, "Will a Day Care Center be a Child Development Center?" *Young Children* 28 (February 1973): 154.

7. Keith Osborn, in *Early Childhood Education Rediscovered,* ed. Joe Frost (New York: Holt, Rinehart and Winston, Inc., 1968), p. 281.

8. Anderson and Shane, *As the Twig Is Bent,* p. 281.

9. Ibid., pp. 29-30.

10. Barbara Biber, *Young Deprived Children and Their Educational Needs* (Washington, D.C.: Association for Childhood Education International, 1967), pp. 9-11.

11. Clay Brittain, in *Early Childhood Education Rediscovered,* ed. Joe Frost (New York: Holt, Rinehart and Winston, Inc., 1968) p. 287.

12. Osborn in *Early Childhood Education Rediscovered,* p. 282.

13. Catherine Landreth and Katherine Read, *Education of the Young Child* (New York: John Wiley, 1942), pp. 10-13.

14. Ryland W. Crary and Louise Petrone, *Foundations of Modern Education* (New York: Alfred A. Knopf, 1971), p. 73.

15. Edith M. Dowley, "Perspectives in Early Childhood Education" in *As the Twig Is Bent,* ed. Anderson and Shane (Boston: Houghton Mifflin Co., 1971), p. 14.

16. Frank P. Graves, *A History of Education in Modern Times* (New York: The Macmillan Co., 1914), p. 249.

17. Grace K. Pratt-Butler, "Ethical Imperatives for Head Start," *The Educational Forum* (January 1972): 215-16.

18. Dowley, in *As the Twig Is Bent,* p. 14..

19. Bettye M. Caldwell, "On Reformulating the Concept of Early Childhood Education—Some Why's Needing Wherefore's," in *As the Twig Is Bent,* ed. Anderson and Shane (Boston: Houghton Mifflin Co., 1971), p. 254.

20. Ibid., p. 78.

21. Baumrind, "Will a Day Care Center be a Child Development Center?" pp. 154-69.

22. Dwight Allen and Eli Seifman, *The Teacher's Handbook* (Glenview, Ill.: Scott-Foresman Co., 1971), pp. 497-98.

23. Landreth and Read, *Education of the Young Child,* pp. 8-9.

24. Ibid., p. 8.

25. Ibid., p. 7.

26. B.R. Gearheart, *Learning Disabilities: Educational Strategies* (St. Louis: C.V. Mosby Co., 1973), pp. 9-10.

27. Charles E. Silberman, ed., *The Open Classroom Reader* (New York: Vintage Books, 1973), pp. xvi, xviii.

CHAPTER 3

Contemporary Philosophies of Education

Below surface descriptions, there are underlying philosophies of education. Some of these were developed by educators who worked out their theories in practice with children. Others left it to their followers to give practical credence to their theories.

Today, the term philosophy is often misused. The man on the street says, "My philosophy is that kids should work." His friend says, "My philosophy is that TV hurts kids." In both cases, these are opinions. In simple terms, a genuine philosophy contains the following:

1. a theory of reality

    What is most real? Is it God? Is it what your senses tell you? Is it nature? Is it experience?

2. a theory of knowledge

    What is knowledge? Is it information? Is it facts in sequence? Is it primarily method, or "know how"?

3. a theory of value

    What is value? Is it an absolute truth which is always the same and which brooks neither difference nor alteration? Is it a set of beliefs which are relative to one's life and experience and which may change?

Although interrelated, a theory of reality (or ontology), of knowledge (or epistemology), and of value (or axiology) are the necessary ingredients for a philosophy in the full sense of the term.

Today, there are various educational philosophies. Some are pure, and others are eclectic. People often hold to one philosophy except for some special area. For instance, they may maintain that reality is some sort of Absolute Being, but that a methodology based largely on the individual's own testable experience is most valid. If they are very clear as to where they draw their lines, this philosophy may be maintained, but if not, they possess something other than a well thought-out philosophy. In the above case, this is necessary because the methodology carried out completely can refute the ontology or theory of reality. If, however, a person is clear about his boundary lines, he can consciously maintain an eclectic point of view. Many students new to the education field are eclectic. A brief exposition of each of the educational philosophies most current in present education follows.

The education of young children is not new. A philosophy of education is not new either. Plato discussed it in his *Republic*[1] and the ancient Hebrews prescribed how children should behave toward their teacher and what should be derived from early education.[2] Between then and now, earnest theorists and practitioners have attended to the education of young children.

Teachers study educational philosophy and to a greater or lesser degree it influences how they set up and conduct their classes, teach their children, and interpret the statements of their children's parents in terms of an educational philosophy.

The articulate parent, too, voices what he thinks should be done. In many cases, these convictions fall loosely into the categories of contemporary educational philosophies. In a few instances, they are voiced as carefully weighed philosophies, bolstered by psychological and sociological speculations.

Some typical instances follow.

THE CATHOLIC PERENNIALIST

Alicia is a good child. She seemed to know what was right as a toddler. My sister is a nun and she thinks that Alicia is turned to God already, even though she is only five years old.

As long as there are underlying truths, we have tried to show Gerard what these are. His partial knowledge is, after all, related to underlying principles and, of course, ultimately to the Infinite Good. Perhaps we have stressed this too much. He is a serious child.

Jose and Carmencita tell truth. No lie. Go to church every Sunday. Maybe be better than me. Good kids.

We choose Paul's books carefully and watch the approved lists for occasional movies suitable for him. Children's books and movies should be censored. Don't you think so? There is so much to lead them astray.

Beverly knows she's black. She knows, too, that she's a child of God.

The articulate Catholic parent often tends to emphasize certain principles which he defines as truths. Some of these are evident in the above statements made to their children's teacher. Underlying Catholic Perennialism, as Scholasticism or Thomism in education is sometimes termed, are principles defendable as truths received through faith and given by God as he works within the mind and heart of man. A few points of importance may be summarized briefly.

According to the Catholic Perennialist philosophy, man is made in the image of God. However, inasmuch as he is not pure soul or form as is God, he is imperfect. His matter, or material body, houses his true being or spirit. Thus man is composed of the material or matter or body and form or soul or spirit. As the person slowly actualizes his spiritual as well as his intellectual potential, he moves toward the ends set for him by God, or toward the greatest possible actualization obtainable by him. A child therefore is directed toward truth and away from falsehood, toward what is right and away from what is wrong, toward the spiritual good and away from more sensuous pleasure. He is "set" in the right direction and is turned away from "wandering fires," or the errors which come from following the senses to useless or completely material ends.

Permitting full exposure to all sorts of experience is to do an injustice because a child is unable, as yet, to choose for himself. Adults know more than children inasmuch as they have achieved greater actualization and thus they direct the child. The home, the school, and the church each are responsible for certain aspects of the child's education and guidance.

According to this philosophy, it is the teacher's responsibility to cause the child to relate the particular bits and pieces of partial knowledge to the more fundamental principle which underlies them. "He [the teacher] brings the material for knowing to the mind of the student, lays that material out in order, removes the impediment to knowing; and then hopes for the splendid result of knowledge."[3]

Basic to belief in God is faith. The Catholic Perennialist believes man can, and does, develop his reason to varying degrees. He is dependent, also, upon revelation. As Aquinas stated, "Through faith man comes to know God as God knows Himself. Human reason can never discover what God is in Himself . . . If man is to know the deeper mysteries of the life of God, then God must reveal them to man and man must accept these truths on faith."[4] The teacher seeks to actualize the child's reason insofar as he is able. Older students learn to think logically and are well trained in Aristotelian logic. The young child, however, starts his actions from the senses, and then should turn inward to utilize his actualizing reason, and then upward to the contemplation of God. The Absolute is unchanging. It is the particulars which change. Saint Augustine held that only God can teach us; we do not learn through signs or words.[5] Habits of the right kind can assist us. The child can be habituated in certain ways until his reason can take over the command of his senses. Aquinas tells us that human passions were made to operate under reason and that under reason, they "reach their greatest perfection."[6]

Religion is basic to the Catholic, and education cannot be considered apart from it. The major emphases of this educational philosophy are to stress goodness and spiritual being, to set certain controls for children through adult selection, and to give a child only carefully chosen experiences insofar as this is possible. It may be seen that right habits are stressed and that selection of materials is important. If a child is set in the way he should go, he will not deviate later. Thus the Catholic parent expresses certain needs which he considers of primary importance. Therefore, the Catholic child is surrounded by things Catholic because these are the best influences that his parents know.

THE LAY PERENNIALIST

As a professor of ancient Greek history, I am, of course, an intellectual. I do insist that Bruce be well educated. Does he seem intelligent to you?

Jim reasons with me now. Of course, we have always reasoned with him.

After all, it is our minds that distinguish us from lower animals. Gertrude must develop her mind. Then she will be genuinely free.

Do you think that this school fosters elitism? There are those who say that this is undemocratic. Is it democratic to hold back my child, if he is more intelligent than someone else?

Do you think kindergarteners too young for some of the old myths? They are a part of the cultural heritage.

The educational preferences of the above parents have been indicated. Although the view known in general philosophy as neo-Aristotelianism and to educational philosophers often as Lay, or nonreligious, Perennialism focusses on secondary and college education, the major emphases may be anticipated in terms of the preschool child.

Aristotle distinguished man from animals by his rational-intellectual faculties. The good man was the one in whom reasoning was functioning at the maximum, ". . . the good and happy man, therefore, is he who behaves in accordance with the dictates of reason."[7] Each has a potential intellect which should be actualized as fully as possible. Inasmuch as this actualization develops through actual functioning, reasoning is stressed. The child's physical-sensual self was to be developed through habit training until such time as the gradually developing intellect could assume responsibility for the whole person. The golden mean served as a standard for much of the former—the intellect functioning according to logical precept was the criterion for the latter.

Although the emphasis is on older children, the stress on education is important at all levels. According to this philosophy, children's time should not be wasted. The mind cannot be neglected. Young people should study the one hundred Great Books, but children, too, should have intellectual stimulation. As Hutchins has said, "The aim of liberal education is wisdom. Every man has the duty and every man must have the chance to become as wise as he can . . . to enable every human being, . . . to achieve his highest potentialities."[8]

The parents who tend to emphasize this philosophy are concerned about what is learned, rational explanation, and classical studies, and they bring a serious, thoughtful approach to their children's education. Inasmuch as intellectual interaction and reflection upon ideas is so important, the young child can be initiated into this liberating atmosphere.

THE IDEALIST ESSENTIALIST

Yes, but is this best for Charles? You see, that although we do not have a great deal of money, we want him to have every chance and advantage. His father keeps saying, "Charles will have everything as perfect as possible." We shall set the best example possible, and endeavor to bring out the best that is in him. Character is important, you know.

Well, said Mrs. Snowden, if Peter is to spend a whole year here in pre-kindergarten and another in kindergarten, he will be two years late in setting up his law practice. "Setting up his law practice?" Why, yes, his father and I want him to become a perfect lawyer. If he wastes two years in preschool before attending first grade, why he'll be two years older before graduating from law school and before beginning his law practice!

But, she has it in her to be a good girl. She's been to Sunday School since she was three—that's two years now. We want to give her examples of the best to emulate. What better than those found in the *Bible?* Later, we intend to give her biographies of great people. She hears only the best English at home. I dismissed her last nurse because she made grammatical errors. We set her the best example that we can and see that she plays only with other children of the right sort—so, why did she say to me, "I will not do that" when I asked her to put away her doll dishes? She knows that her room must be in perfect order before she eats dinner.

My daughter, Deena, is a little lady, I am proud to say. Further, you exemplify the perfect teacher to us which is the reason that we chose this school. While I do think that everyone should have a chance, I do think that a boy like that one spoils your group. From what I have been able to observe, the children are fine and the group is perfect, but for that boy. I don't want to make trouble, but shall I ask the principal either to put him in another group or to drop him. He just seems neither to fit in nor to behave correctly.

The above are all based on real statements made to the writer at some time. A scrutiny of the remarks will indicate an underlying stress on good and right, as absolutes; on good examples; on elimination of the one who does not fit the pattern—usually preconceived—of the perfect group; on obedience or submission to parental design and pattern or behavior; on sequence and on preplanning for years ahead; on parental authority.

Many people carry about an implicit perfect pattern for certain, if not all, behavior. They speak as though there were a perfect child, a perfect sort of behavior, a perfect profession, group, etc. The ideal is literally most real—at least in times of anxiety.

The modern Idealist, in the philosophical sense, does believe in an orderly universe. Each part fits into its place, and one sets his aim or goal for perfection and takes the steps necessary to attain it. The proper examples, such as acceptance or acquiescence on the part of the child until he can assume his own controls, and removal of the imperfect—since it interferes with what is better—are all implied. There is an Absolute of some sort, and lower echelon absolutes, which are smaller wholes within the larger whole. These serve as ideals which are part of the Ideal, or larger, all-inclusive whole. Since the adult possesses greater maturity and actually knows more, it is his job to be sure that the young are set upon the paths necessary to achieve the goal. Deviations are frowned upon, and any kind of change should receive careful reflection and then only be undertaken gradually.

Horne said that "The individual is a whole and he is also part of a larger whole."[9] Butler has stated, "There is a natural basis, too, for conscience in the sense that something is right, that there is a right."[10]

"One important and valuable means by which student response is given birth is imitative activity, especially when given direction by worthy models of creative work and a noble teacher personality."[11] Thus the essential emphases in modern Idealism! This philosophy may be summarized briefly: the most real is the spiritual aspect of the self struggling toward the Absolute; the overall value is the nearest possible attainment of this overall whole or spiritual Absolute; the little whole of the self, or microcosm, should reflect the larger whole, or macrocosm; knowledge of the essentials is attained through setting one's sights on the perfect and seeking to attain it through rapport with other older, better selves, who should encourage emulation of examples of one's ideal person, learning all knowledge essential to one's chosen goal and life pattern; understanding of one's place as a smaller whole in the larger whole in a universe which is coherent or interwoven in such a way that each part fits into and is essential in the overall whole.

Idealism has a long tradition. Plato is known as the "father of Idealism." Much of what was said above has come down to us as a modification of his philosophical Idealism. The stress on the elite as fit to attain the highest, on selection or sometimes censorship for the good of the young, on the proper example for imitation, on pushing toward the best of which one is capable, and on little deviation from the right path have come down to some educators today as essentials for the sound education of children.

Each parent, in the preceding illustrations, implied some sort of perfection for his child. Each had a preconceived belief in the ideal for his child, and each expected rather direct implementation toward it. It should be noted that there is a kind of underlying compulsion for or toward certain things. These parents will keep urging each child to turn the A- into an A through greater effort, although they will rarely grant the child the satisfaction of believing that he has realized an A state of perfection. The child must keep striving to become ever more perfect.

Froebel is an important figure in preschool education, and he is an Idealist of a type between Plato of the past and Horne, Butler, or Hocking of present times.

> Froebel sought to turn the Kindergarten child to God by awakening within each a sense of the Greater Unity and the Absolute.[12]

> Education consisted in leading man, as a thinking, intelligent being, growing into self-consciousness to a pure and unsullied, conscious and free representation of the inner law of Divine Unity, and in teaching him ways and means thereto.[13]

By 1826,* this Ideal, through various additions and reinterpretations, had evolved into the Christian and especially Protestant concept of God or Absolute Being. According to the philosophy, each of us has a spark of the divine spirit, Absolute Being, or Divine Unity. This must be awakened and turned toward the greater perfection as each self seeks to perfect himself.

Froebel sought, through his use of "gifts" and symbols, to guide each child to a more perfect unity. Children formed circles to symbolize the whole. The "gifts" were used in sequence. Froebel believed that his "gifts" represented the outer world or macrocosm, that they satisfied the inner world or microcosm, that they represented a complete orderly whole, and that each "gift" contained the preceding and foreshadowed the succeeding.[14] The educator conducted "an orderly, sequential, and unified development of the child as a microcosm growing in greater likeness to Absolute Unity. Each should be a harmonious unity reflecting the greater Self"[15] (known as the coherence theory of the universe, each little spiritual self is part of the large all-inclusive whole).

Although Froebel's child was made cognizant of his surroundings and although he was active, this was all directed toward the Ideal, resplendent in the Absolute and attained only imperfectly by man—and child. This philosophy of Idealism with various revisions was rather carefully followed in many schools until recently, and, without its earlier specific accoutrements, is implied by some educators today. Although they might consider Froebel old-fashioned, they

---

*The Education of Man was first published in 1826.

do, by their teaching, imply with him that "In all things there lives and reigns an eternal law . . . The divine effluence that lives in each thing is the essence of each thing."[16]

Thus the teacher should have some insight into the modern Idealist parents and educators.

THE REALIST ESSENTIALIST

My son is living in a scientific world. Why do you have these stories here? I see that you have books about caterpillars and turtles, but why waste his time with these others? They are nothing but fantasy.

What special materials do you have for tactile development? Don't you think that education through sequential development of the senses will best fit Luci for this world? After all, there are a number of material objects that exist!

Do they learn some of the simple laws of science? If they learn these, they will have a solid base, won't they! Isn't scientific law our underlying reality?

Parents, like the above, are common in some schools. Their stress on science, on knowledge through sensory development, and on being fit for the present world reflects one kind of Realist philosophy.

After all, we are all a part of nature, aren't we? Can anything be wrong, if it goes along with what is natural?

But, why does he have to put his materials away? Won't he learn from falling over them? Does it matter, if the floors get dusty around them?

Why shouldn't he have nothing but meat? He has tasted everything at home. He doesn't like vegetables. Doesn't everyone live according to the underlying natural rules which he finds govern him? Isn't this a fact?

Some of these rather extreme individualistic manifestations of reliance upon an implicit natural order are couched in partial concepts of an implied Realism, or Naturalism.

In ancient Rome, Lucretius emphasized a universe in which atoms, space, and law were basic. If man attuned himself to these basic laws and accepted the fact that he existed because certain atoms came together, would remain together while he lived, and that when he died, they would disperse as "dust to dust," he would not be disillusioned. Lucretius sought to remove fear of the gods from the mind of man." At ease they sleep and dream, but affect us not!"[17]

Comenius, although God-oriented, did stress development of the senses . . . . "The child perceives that he sees, hears, and feels. Then the intellect comes into existence by cognizing the differences between objects; . . . ."[18] Sensory knowledge of the environment occurs during the first six years of the child's life. During the second six, his abilities to imagine and to remember what he has sensed come into existence, and this is followed during the third six-year period by the ability to judge the characteristics and relations of things sensed, imagined, and remembered—or the ability to reason emerges. Then during the six years from age eighteen to twenty-four, the will becomes strong and assumes the direction of one's life. There is an order and purpose in organic nature.

Comenius' stress on the senses clearly added to the realist stream. One cannot but laud his use of pictures in books for the education of children, even though small and even though numerous words were presented but once, devoid of repetition. The name accompanied the picture and the young child had to learn the names of what was around him. According to his philosophy, each of us should have a perfect language which is defined as follows: (1) each sensible thing would have no more than one name; (2) no name would be applied to more than one sensible thing; (3) every sensible thing would have a name; (4) each name would resemble the thing it names; (5) the names would be ordered in sentences. Students should see the things named or pictures of them.[19] Comenius left some valid prescriptions for education.*

John Locke, too, advocated freedom from the artificiality of the stuffy drawing room and from limb-confining clothing. His emphasis on sense-objects first, singly, then grouped, then compared for the sequential development of clear concepts does not differ too greatly from Comenius' stress on sense objects.

In more recent times, Rousseau's *Emile* illustrates much of modern naturalistic realism. Emile is to follow his own inclinations because "things are good as they come from nature." "Man spoils them."[20] Through his senses, Emile will learn about his surroundings. He will be free—from swaddling clothes as an infant; from the dictates of those who would bend him to their purposes as a child; from the artificiality of cities which destroy his natural inclinations. Many of the strands in so-called modern education came down to us from Rousseau.

The modern Realist holds that there are natural scientific laws in the universe and when we can attune ourselves to them, we make our lives correspond to what is there. Then we are living the good life meant for us! Heightened emphasis on the senses is stressed by some and adherence to past "objective" knowledge by others. Once a basis of natural scientific law is known, then one keeps abreast of the latest facts and adjusts his life and work pattern to them. The efficiency expert raising the best (bred by him) white leghorns complete with egg laying records, feed records, and cleaning time analysis sees life in terms similar to the man whose diet consists of the best basic foods known to be essential for the maintenance of basic nutrition. Each has discovered natural laws and made his living correspond to them.

---

*See Appendix 7.

The modern Realist may be in one of several subclassifications such as scientific realist, natural realist, mechanistic realist. Each, however, does stress sense learning and the gradual building of sequential knowledge from the senses. For instance, Martin holds that ". . . so sense experience of the existent world transcends conceptual experience. Sense experience is much more inclusive, and it is from such experience that conceptual experience is obtained by the process of abstraction."[21] As Kneller says, "The basic principle of philosophic realism is that matter is the ultimate reality."[22] The laws of nature give structure. When one's knowledge corresponds to what is there in the world, the child has true knowledge. Thus what the child knows should correspond to that which is the knowledge of the teacher or the accepted verified body of fact.

The realist stresses natural scientific law, the independent existence of matter, or the things of the universe, and the sensory intake of the person as he experiences these "things" as knowledge.

The child needs facts not frivolities! He thrives on information not informality! Thus the modern parent with a realist bent urges what appears to be based on science, on found laws, and on the necessary adjustments to so live and learn. If his child has "drives" to do this or that, these usually are explained as examples of Tim following his "natural" bent. The *whys* and *wherefores*, the effects following from their causes are fundamental to learning. If the child falls over his own blocks, he will understand the need to put them away—regardless of the seventeen other four-year-olds, eighteen parents, a teacher and an assistant, and the cleaning staff! Children who eat what they select will give themselves what they need—regardless of three-thirty visits to the local ice cream stand. Children told facts in sequence about whatever they question amass this information and continue to add to the store. The parent who is intellectually alert to the affairs of his modern society frequently has a hard time recognizing that Marie Elaine has lived but forty-eight months!

There are variations in the above pattern: learning through the senses is all-important; factual information given in sequence is education; underlying natural scientific laws are there, have been, and are waiting to be discovered, and, if we know them, we can live by them. However, certain emphases underlie the differences: impersonal law is of primary importance; matter exists independent of whether we know that it is there; facts are fundamental with little stress upon how or why they are learned because they must be acquired; emphasis on sensory learning is basic; although the child is to be given facts when he requests them, there is an underlying natural manifestation within each of his own law to which his actions must correspond.

THE PROGRESSIVIST

But, doesn't Bill learn from what he is doing? Shouldn't he, therefore, have as many kinds of experiences as possible?

Marilyn has been an individual from the day she arrived. Each thing she does seems to be carried out according to her own special way of doing it.

Burt does things for himself. We let him struggle with his own little problems because he does come through with his own solutions. Sometimes he tries out two or three possibilities before he does successfully what he is attempting.

Yes, Oscar went to the zoo on Saturday, to see the Indians in the Museum on Sunday, and next week on Saturday he will go to the Statue of Liberty, and then on Sunday to the animal farm. He is interested in animals and well— Indians, of course. The Statue of Liberty trip will enable him to see a number of boats. Yesterday he asked why a ferry boat has two fronts. We try to get him answers to his questions in some way. He seems to be learning from being constantly exposed to many kinds of experience.

Maria, take care of baby. She good! She changa pants, give bottle. She do thing lika me. She knowa what do now. He cry—she fixa him.

Stan went to Chinatown on Friday with Al. Mrs. Arnt believes, as we do, that our children should see many different kinds of people. If Stan and Al see only each other and others like themselves, how will they grow up? Mrs. Arnt thought that they should see a Chinese community. After all, they both know Mr. Lee, but all Chinese don't run laundries!

All of the above parents stated, or directly implied, certain emphases which are listed rather easily. These emphases may be summarized as follows: constantly experiencing; direct exposure to many aspects of the environment; pride in individuality; fostering of problem solving, questioning, and inquiry; "learning through doing"; nurturing of developing interests; being aware of differences in the social environment.

The above parents, who made these statements to their child's teacher, are all modern adults who believe in the Pragmatic, sometimes known as the Progressivist or Experimentalist, approach to life and education. They, too, represent an underlying philosophy of education which is well represented— sometimes implicitly and sometimes overtly—by teachers and administrators in a number of preschool groups today. Although the above parents were all articulate and had definite ideas about child-rearing, they probably were unaware—except perhaps vaguely—that they were expressing an educational philosophy. With the exception of Maria's mother, each was conversant with modern psychology but unaware of the deeper and broader implications of what they had said. Each implied that he/she was letting the child be active in line with his own choices and purposes (expressed as interests), that the child's active experiencing was central, and that the parents' role was to encourage and foster it. In this role the parent was aware but not dominating, cooperative but not the chief determiner.

Although John Dewey is the best modern exemplar of the above theory, he has had numerous followers and some real interpreters such as Kilpatrick, Childs, Axtelle, and Raup. Others have misinterpreted him, in small or large part. As the Progressivist philosophy has evolved, the present day pragmatist or philosophic progressivist agrees with Dewey's emphasis on the uniqueness or difference which makes Marian distinct from Maude. Both Marian and Maude are individual organisms, and each is interacting with her environment. Each subsequent experience is different due to what preceded it, and thus Marian and Maude are different. Their environment is one of things and people. The richer this environment is, the broader the child's exposure. Although Oscar was, undoubtedly, being overexposed, his interests were being used as foci for what his parents did. As interests develop, trips and special experiences feed each child with firsthand opportunities to observe and sometimes to manipulate. Maria was actively manipulative in her situation. In school in a free situation, fostering abundant choice through the doing of block building, creative expression utilizing music and art materials, dramatic play and general individual and group creativeness give Paul and Paula self-assurance. This is what Axtelle calls "knowhow." To a growing extent, each child becomes a controller of his own environment and thus of his life.

Dewey's so-called steps of reflective thinking are important bases for the learning that takes place. Briefly, these steps may be summarized as follows: (a) the experience—Jon is building with blocks; (b) the problem arises from this experience—as he builds, he wants to make a simple bridge in order to drive his small car under it. He sets up two uprights and the third to go across falls between as it is not long enough to span the distance between the uprights; (c) data collecting—Jon has alternative possibilities because he can look for a longer block, he can call his teacher, he can put another upright in the middle, he can shove one upright closer to the other; (d) choice of a tentative hypothesis or possibility for solution of the problem—Jon puts a third upright between the two existing ones and succeeds in placing the "bridging" block across the top; (e) testing—Jon succeeds in driving his small car under the bridge and continues on down the block road. If unsuccessful and his car does not go through, then Jon may try another alternative (thus returning to step b or to further possibilities c) such as making the whole bridge of larger blocks.*

The stress on experiencing for one's self in an environment of "relatives" rather than "absolutes," the use of an expanding surrounding environment, the encouragement to solve problems within one's level of possibility, the choice of alternatives, and the stress on interacting within a natural-social context are all important here. (Natural because the child is an active biological, organism and social because the informal environment fosters meanings derived from interaction with people as well as with things.) To a greater or lesser extent, the parents quoted reflected some of these concepts. From considerable experience with such parents, the conclusion may be drawn that although doing was almost constant, Dewey's stress on the undergoing of the results of the doing was not as apparent.

---

*See Appendix 4 for discussion of problem solving.

Although Dewey continued on the path set by William James and Charles Peirce, he neither imitated nor completely reflected them. Certainly James's emphasis on the individual finding out for himself, on collecting his own first-hand information, and on finding out what works are found in Dewey.[23] Also, Peirce's stress on utilizing ideas as instruments is in Dewey's philosophy of education.

Numerous early educators pointed the way *in part* to the thinking of the man born in 1859. In general, early indications are couched in methods which are usually but a part of a nonpragmatic, overall philosophy. For instance, Quintilian advocated knowing each individual, letting children handle ivory letters, and he had his young orators-to-be involved in problem solving. He did seem more modern in underlying psychological principles than many others in the intervening years.

Pestalozzi found "the highest supreme principle of instruction in the recognition of sense impression as the absolute foundation of all knowledge."[24] Pestalozzi's stress on having children discuss what they could observe shows forth in numerous instances. The orphan children were to talk about the cracks in the wall because they could see them. Object lessons were preferable because children could observe a bird's nest, etc. Stress was on sense impression as "the external object before the senses which rouses a consciousness of the impression made by it."

Although Rousseau was mentioned earlier—where he belongs philosophically—he did, in his stress on Emile's experiencing, also point to a *doing* rather than a listening education.[25]

THE RECONSTRUCTIONIST

Jim likes people. We hope that he'll want to be some sort of social leader. Of course, he'll realize himself in his own way, but, then, there is so much to be done in the world of relationships, isn't there?

Don wanted a large piece of paper on Sunday. Then he said, "You see, I am on strike. I need a sign!" I suppose he saw the pickets near our house.

Don't you think that everyone should have a real chance. We, Blacks, have gone quite a piece, but look at the long road ahead. Kathy wanted to know whether we had ever had a President with a face like her father's.

The world's problems among people won't be solved in an ivory tower. You have a mixed group here. I'm glad. Toni should have all kinds of friends.

We have a sponsored child in the Philippines. Sandy looked at her picture yesterday and said, "My sister."

Reconstructionism is a relatively new educational philosophy. It may be dated most specifically from Brameld's *Patterns of Educational Philosophy*, published in 1950.[26] The term had been introduced by Berkson in 1940 in *Preface to an Educational Philosophy*,[27] but it began to gain status in the fifties with publication of Brameld's books. As an outgrowth of a critique and reformulation of Dewey's Progressivism, the group which became known as Reconstructionists sought initially to reaffirm Dewey's stress on the social context as well as to continue to maintain his affirmation of the strengths of the individual. The group of theorists concerned with this problem believed that educators had fostered Dewey's emphasis on the uniqueness of the individual, but that they had tended to neglect the social context of the individual which also was emphasized by Dewey. Since its inception, Reconstructionism has incorporated many of Dewey's emphases, sponsored group process, and veered into an ardent support for cultural interaction. Stress on anthropology and the development of human relations education had some close ties with the Reconstructionists. What Brameld terms "culturology" is basic to this educational theory.* The problem of trying to keep a balance between the realization of the self and the realization of society has continued to be a problem in Reconstructionism.

The statements of the parents which precede the above paragraph tend to focus on some of the major emphases of Reconstructionism. Briefly, these may be summarized as:

1. social-self-realization as an overall goal and value orientation means that maximum development and achievement is to be fostered for all—for self and for other peoples;
2. social-self-realization can be utilized as a focus for secondary and junior college curriculum;
3. younger children are to be educated in a program which, while primarily Progressivist, develops certain overtones and the beginning manifestations of what is the Reconstructionist viewpoint of education for older students;
4. the group process which seeks maximum consensus concerning ends and means of attainment is a central theme in methodology;
5. stress on relationships as they arise from and reflect cultural allegiances and conflicts form numerous subthemes toward realization;
6. the strengths of groups such as societies and unions can be positive means to the desired goals;
7. prejudice and degradation of minorities has no place in a social democracy.

---

*"... by culturology we mean here a philosophy of mankind that is primarily governed by, and exerts profound influence upon, the life of members of culture, " in Theodore Brameld, *Patterns of Educational Philosophy* (New York: Holt, Rinehart and Winston, 1971), pp. 4-5.

After Dewey's methodology, exemplified in some notable progressive schools, had begun to produce some graduates, various theorists in the late thirties and through the forties found its human products to be too individually oriented. They turned back to Dewey and sought to reaffirm his convictions about the social context of the individual. They also reflected the coming interest in social groups and, in certain ways, in communal movement. Those most concerned about such matters spoke of the importance of *convictions* on the part of educators and began to reaffirm some of the points made by Counts earlier in *Dare the Schools Build a New Social Order?*[28] These theorists said that education should unify itself, work with others, and lead the way to social change.

We have seen that while Brameld actually developed philosophical reconstruction into Reconstructionism, Berkson utilized the term first.* Stanley moved a bit away from Dewey and emphasized some aspects, especially about the community, which were incorporated into this developing theory. Reconstructionism held, and still holds, that the school was to become a fluid center for communal activities and to be open every day throughout the year.

If man is defined as a natural-social animal spending much of his time in groups, then he must learn how to work in this context. Methodology must incorporate problem solving on a group level. Human relations techniques are stressed as Reconstructionism seeks to fuse the dynamics of persons as well as their as yet untapped resources into means for action toward agreed upon goals. The far reaches of the earth hold peoples in cultures which, in large part, also seek realization. Our recent communicative and technological innovations are fostering increasing contact with such groups. When they mature, our children will have to be able to work together effectively with those of far-flung peoples, if we are all to survive. Thus realization must be a balance between stress on the social and on the self. Loss of stress on either one will tend to work to our detriment.

> Reconstructionists also choose. But in the choice of commitment to the future of world civilization, they seek dialectically to strengthen this commitment, not by exclusions, but by whatever inclusions may be tenable and fruitful ... perceived in culturalogical perspective.[29]

Brameld terms Reconstructionism a transformative philosophy which seeks a convergence of powers to focus upon and to attain a future-centered world civilization.

Reconstructionism gives a voice to minorities and seeks to raise their contributions to effective action. At present this is focussed most directly on the culture which surrounds each group. However, UNESCO, for instance, is a rapid-

---

*In 1940, Berkson used the term Reconstructionists which he defined as the general point of view expressed in "The Educational Frontier," the Yearbooks of the John Dewey Society, and in the editorial position of "The Social Frontier."

ly growing international voice. The means and ends being utilized by underdeveloped countries are studied and manifestations of unity for maximum national growth, such as this writer found in Brazil for instance, are noted and evaluated for possible help elsewhere. In preschool education, parents are an effective means for furthering theories and practices of Reconstructionism. Preschool education reaches directly into varied manifestations of the culture and the theory holds promise as a way to meet the needs of children and parents. It gives focus on a future of fulfillment.

Now that we have met the children in chapter 1, considered some of the present educational centers for them in chapter 2, met some of the parents and indicated the foremost educational philosophies in chapter 3, it is time to turn to the present classroom. Some specific kinds of programs and how they are utilized will be considered in the next chapter.

Notes

1. Benjamin Jowett, trans., *Plato: The Republic* (New York: The World Book Co., 1946), especially Book 2.

2. See, for instance, Elmer Wilds and Kenneth Lottich, *The Foundations of Modern Education* (New York: Holt, Rinehart and Winston, 1961), Chapter 3.

3. Walter Farrell, O.P., S.T.M. and Martin J. Healey, S.T.D., *My Way of Life* (Pocket Edition of St. Thomas) (Brooklyn: Confraternity of the Precious Blood), p. 148.

4. Ibid., p. 316.

5. George Leckie, trans., *St. Aurelius Augustine Concerning the Teacher and On the Immortality of the Soul* (New York: Appleton-Century-Crofts, Inc., 1938), pp. 48-51.

6. Farrell and Healey, *My Way of Life*, p. 98.

7. Paul Nash, *Models of Man* (New York: John Wiley and Sons, 1968), p. 37.

8. Robert M. Hutchins, *The Conflict in Education* (New York: Harper and Brothers, 1953), p. 90.

9. Herman H. Horne, *The Philosophy of Education* (New York: The Macmillan Co., 1930), p. 37.

10. J. Donald Butler, *Four Philosophies and Their Practice in Education and Religion* (New York: Harper and Row, Publishers 1968), p. 195.

11. Ibid., p. 219.

12. Grace K. Pratt, "Ethical Imperatives for Head Start," *The Educational Forum* (January 1972): 216.

13. W.H. Haitman, trans., Friedrich Froebel, *The Education of Man* (New York: D. Appleton, 1902), p. 2.

14. Pratt, "Ethical Imperatives for Head Start," p. 216.

15. Ibid.

16. Haitman, *The Education of Man*, pp. 1-2.

17. H.A.J. Munro, trans., Lucretius, *On the Nature of Things* (Garden City: Doubleday and Co., no date).

18. Kingsley Price, *Education and Philosophical Thought* (Boston: Allyn Bacon, Inc., 1962), p. 207.

19. Ibid.

20. Barbara Foxley, trans., Jean Jacques Rousseau, *Emile* (London: J.M. Dent and Sons, Ltd., 1938).

21. William Oliver Martin, *Realism in Education* (New York: Harper and Row, Publishers, 1969), p. 168.

22. George Kneller, *Introduction to the Philosophy of Education* (New York: John Wiley and Sons, Inc., 1971), p. 10.

23. William James, *Pragmatism* (New York: Longmans, Green and Co., 1907).

24. Lewis Flint Anderson, *Pestalozzi* (New York: McGraw-Hill Book Co., 1931), p. 61.

25. Foxley, Rousseau's *Emile*.

26. Theodore Brameld, *Patterns of Educational Philosophy* (New York: World Book Co., 1950).

27. I.B. Berkson, *Preface to an Educational Philosophy* (New York: Columbia University Press, 1940).

28. George S. Counts, *Dare the Schools Build a New Social Order?* (New York: The John Day Co., Inc., 1932).

29. Brameld, *Patterns of Educational Philosophy* (1971 edition), p. 561 and last chapter.

CHAPTER 4

The Why's and Wherefore's of Programming

PROGRAMMING CONSIDERATIONS

A class of three-, four-, or five-year-olds should have a daily program which is flexible, but certain routines and activities should be carried out at about the same time daily. Given an anticipated basic daily plan, each child comes to expect that certain events will occur and take place. Within these expectations there is opportunity for considerable fluctuation. The general expectations lead to feelings of security. Security tends to foster calmness, whereas constant insecurity may lead to overstimulation or feelings of withdrawal and anxiety. The teacher whose children never know what to expect may breed patterns of deep insecurity. But this does not mean that the schedule is rigid! Some variations can and should take place. Children need to be able to adjust to changes. These should be explained. However, once routines related to *physical* needs are established, they should be changed only after careful consideration.

Most peoples, groups, and individuals tend to pattern their behaviors. When such patterns are determined and administered from outside of those involved, the needs and interests of the recipients of the externally imposed patterns are not always met. External motivations and controls should be the outward projections of internal motivations captured, clarified, generalized, and restated in ways acceptable to those involved.

Three-, four-, and five-year-olds manifest patterns of their own. Under conditions removed from anxiety, fear, and externally induced emotional pressures, the child can set his own patterns of food, toilet, and sleep needs, of quiet and active behavior, and of self and social actions. However, inasmuch as few children are fortunate enough to be in such tension-free situations, the adult should try to interpret observable needs, assess deviations from general group manifes-

48

tations of such needs, and acquiesce to the environmental determinants requiring acceptance. On these bases, the basic routines are established in the school program. For most children a short rest after active outdoor play seems preferable because as fatigue builds up, irritability and emotional upset tend to follow. Although one or two children may have their toilet needs met best after snack, most tend to enjoy the snack more after toileting. If the kitchen prefers to send in lunch at twelve because of its responsibility to other groups and their needs, then this should be accepted as a determinant in that particular environment, if it does not harm the recipients.

The preschool teacher, regardless of the kind of set-up, needs to keep certain other items in mind. Balance is necessary in regard to certain facets of preschool education. Five kinds of balance are especially important, and regardless of how they come to be established, the program should be analyzed in respect to whether they are present.

1. A balanced daily plan is important. Rest and activity should alternate. Outdoor play with equipment for large muscle activity, for instance, should precede or follow the rest time or follow the nap of the full day program. Activity itself should provide for alternation between blocks of robust playtime, utilizing large muscles, and shorter periods of time when attention is focussed primarily on activities which utilize small muscles or intermuscular coordination.

2. Regardless of his/her age or developmental level, each child needs opportunities to experience balance between individual and social play. For example, Pete and Linda, both three and one-half, built actively with the large blocks and drove their cars quickly through "streets" and beside "the house." After that, Linda went to the sandbox and made "pies" while Peter drew with crayons. Six five-year-olds ran and played very actively for over thirty minutes. Then Jean left the group and climbed to the top of the jungle gym and sat there quietly for ten minutes. Soon after, Ray and Al went off to ride tricycles. After five more minutes, the other three went to the slide. After three slides each, two went to swing and the remaining one went off to sift sand in the sandbox. The presence of equipment allowing for this balance of activity encouraged each to alternate what he did both alone and with his friends and to move freely from one to the other.

3. The same alternation should hold for individual and whole group activities. For example, when everyone has participated together in music and rhythmic activities for twenty minutes, there should be an opportunity for each to do what he, as an individual, chooses. Building on the table with one-inch cubes, looking at a book, or drawing might be chosen. Activities with others, especially at the beginning of the school year, can be overstimulating as well as physically fatiguing.

4. A balance between leadership and followership is important for the well-being of each child. This is a very personal and individual concern, and the wise teacher should make certain that Larry's keen and occasionally somewhat domineering leadership of Bob and Danny is followed, at some time during the day, with time for Larry to follow someone else's ideas and plans. Bob and Danny need to be engaged in activities where they can assert some leadership. No child should always follow or lead, even though many tend, primarily, to do one or the other. Some adults boast that their certain child is a leader. Fine! We need plenty of leaders! But, each leader has to work with others, and every leader should experience times when he also follows.

5. There should be a balance between child- and teacher-initiated activities. Choices by the child should be primary, but the teacher needs to make decisions, plan, and carry out necessary items for maximum development. The teacher usually initiates the class clear-up activity after a work-play time because lunch will come at 11:45 A.M. At times the teacher needs to be firm about initiating an activity for a variety of reasons. For instance, a shy child's cautiously voiced suggestion needs to be accepted and followed, if at all possible; when most of the children are overstimulated, due to an unexpected visit by the school doctor or a lively period of rhythmic activity, the teacher should lead them to a corner for a quiet story. A certain routine must be followed if the children are to have a rest long enough to be helpful to them after an exciting morning or before a party.

Teacher judgment must function at such times and child initiative, valuable and treasured as it is, does need to be rechanneled in these instances for the good of the whole group.

It is interesting to note that structured studies like the "Discovery Program"[1] claim to be concerned with "the total ecology in which the child is functioning and how the various parts of the ecological system fit together in a state of balance." In chapter 1 we stated the need for an overall view of the child. It was pointed out, also, how the developmental aspects of the child are interrelated. Later, the parental role and other out-of-school factors received further attention. In most of the above ways, the preschools have considered such items, though often without special terminology. Balance is necessary, and perhaps an *emphasis on balance* will preclude overemphasis on prereading and reading which has been noted in too many Head Start and kindergarten programs to the detriment of the factors listed above.

Other factors, over which the teacher has no real control, may also influence the scheduling. For instance, the toilet may be situated across the hall and be used by others, usually at a certain time; lunch may be sent in at a preplanned hour to conform with the kitchen schedules; use of the playground may be gov-

erned by the schedules of other classes who use it, the weather, or by the placement of large, movable equipment by maintenance staff. The time and place for
the after-lunch nap may be determined by factors of space used by others, availability of people to set up cots, relationship to lunch or toileting—to mention
but three of the most usual factors which preclude much deviation.

Although it is important that children's individual hunger patterns be considered, it has been noted through the years that given those three or three and
one-half hours of preschool activity after arrival and a small snack at about
the halfway mark, most children go from the table to the toilet and on into a
separate area to rest.

Adjustments need to be made, when outdoor play space is shared. The climate has to be considered. Whereas it is time saving to have children go outdoors upon arrival so that outer clothing need not be removed, if it is cold in the
early morning this is not feasible. If children go outdoors just before lunch,
this means that time must be set aside for a complete cycle of dressing and undressing. If they go out before going home, the extra undressing is eliminated,
but they usually do need to wash. Also, the play space may be cooler or shadowed
by then, at least during some parts of the year. A few fortunate preschool classes are situated so that the room opens out into an outdoor play space. Then, of
course, much greater flexibility is possible. The wise teacher keeps all of the
above factors in mind when planning the preschool day.

If one follows a half-day program, mornings appear to be preferable. For the
half-day afternoon programs, problems of lunch and rest at home prior to coming may cause problems. Parent cooperation is necessary. This type of problem
may require a meeting during which ideas are exchanged among the parents.
Usually individual conferences are necessary because household patterns vary.
Whereas Tim may rise early and be able to take a short rest at home before
a hardy lunch, Diane may get up later, not need a rest, and have a small lunch
before coming to prekindergarten.

The case of Charlie is to the point. Charlie arrived at 12:30 P.M. for a demonstration four-year-old group. These children had been given the afternoon
session so that the three-year-olds might have the morning. Charlie participated in the work-play activities until about one o'clock and then he disap-
peared. Until other plans were made, he was always found sound asleep in the
large chest in which the blankets were kept! Charlie's physical need for rest
dominated.

A full-day schedule, like those of many day care centers, has other problems:
sufficient personnel for the longer hours are required; beds or cots—in a quiet
place—must be available for longer hours; a nurse or physician should be on the
premises or immediately accessible for inspection and to provide for the child
who becomes ill during the day or sometimes to help parents plan how to
meet physical needs. A nurse or physician's presence is necessary for a longer
period in a day care center which opens very early in the morning.

Although a vast array of programs is possible and it is not the intent here to state that some one formulation is far superior to another, the samples that follow are presented because they have been found workable and satisfactory in many situations. If the teacher tries to set routines at times which seem satisfactory in answer to the needs of the majority and recognizes that some will deviate, a few specifics can be set down. Although work-play times usually permit use of all equipment, some teachers have found that special music and/or story times, for example, are desired in addition and that they seem preferable at certain times. These may be general and not rigidly adhered to events. Keeping these suggestions in mind, several sample programs follow.

These programs are general. For three-year-olds, the mid-morning rest on mats would be longer. The story and music time might be of five minutes duration, whereas for older prekindergarten and kindergarten children, the latter would be considerably longer and former shorter.

SAMPLE PROGRAMS

Half-day Schedule

8:45-9:35   Outdoors (work-play period inside, if the weather is inclement)

9:35-9:50   Going inside, removing outer clothing, toileting

9:50-10:10   Snack at table served by children insofar as they are able, discussion

10:10-10:30 Rest on mats

10:30-10:50 Stories, music, rhythms, special events, science and nature, trips about building. Activities are somewhat dependent upon what happened during the first fifty minutes

10:50-11:40 Work-play in the room. All materials available

11:40-12:00 Clean up, wash, getting ready to leave

Full-day Schedule

8:45-9:50   Outdoors (indoor work-play time if weather is inclement)

9:50-10:15   Going inside, removing outer clothing, toileting

10:15-10:35 Snack at table served by children insofar as they are able, discussion

10:35-11:00 Rest on mats

11:00-11:20 Stories, music, rhythms, special events, science and nature, trips, etc.

11:20-11:50 Free work and play in the room with all materials available

11:50-12:00 Preparation for lunch

12:00-12:45 Lunch

12:45-1:00 Toileting, quiet play

1:00-2:15 Rest on cots

2:15-3:00 Outdoor play (indoor work-play time in inclement weather)

DAY CARE CENTERS

7:30-9:00 Breakfast

9:00-9:45 Work-play time in room.

9:45-10:10 Clean up, toileting, snack

10:10-10:30 Rest on mats

10:30-10:45 Stories, music, rhythms, special events, science and nature activities, trips

10:45-11:45 Outdoor activity

11:45-12:00 Toileting, preparation for lunch

12:00-1:00 Lunch

1:00-3:00 Rest on cots

3:00-5:00 Work-play time in room or outdoors.
Go home, when called for, from 5:00 P.M. to 6:00 P.M.

The above programs are general and require qualifications in terms of age level, weather, special needs, and problems of particular concern. Younger preschoolers tire more easily and tend to be fairly calm, and although they are able to locomote easily, they are less active than four-year-olds. Four-year-olds are lively, changeable, and apt to try out the teacher about whatever rules and regulations are set up. They can control their physical movement better than younger children and thus are independent to a greater degree. Five-year-olds tend to be more calm and can do more together in whole class groups. They have tried out things earlier, and they have noticeably longer spans of attention and seem quite calm and self-sufficient in comparison to younger age levels.

INITIATION INTO PROGRAM

The child's initial school day can set the tone for several years to come. Many schools invite the child for a visit during the late spring preceding the fall in which he is to enter. This enables school personnel to observe him, to have a discussion with his parents, and to let the child find out something of what is to come. With four- and five-year-olds who are to enter school for the first time, it is advisable, when possible, to let them join the group in attendance. Three-year-olds are usually best when alone with the teacher or with one or two other visitors.

For three-year-olds, the first day in the fall should not be more than an hour and a half.* No more than six children should be present at a time. During this time, materials requiring no special supervision or assistance can be available. The toilet routine should begin. The second day can be the same unless the child is reluctant, in which case care should be taken to keep him for only an hour and to make it a satisfying one. The third, fourth, and fifth days can be extended to two hours. During the following week, all the children can be present for two hours on the first and second days and three hours for the remainder of the week. The program can be extended to include lunch during the third week and by the fourth week a very short afternoon nap may be started. By the fifth week, the children can go outdoors very briefly after rest. During the next week, the complete program can be followed. Needless to say, there may be variations due to climate, to particular school situations, and to the children themselves.

In individual cases where children are reluctant to leave their parents by the end of the first week, it may be necessary to keep their schedule reduced for a longer period. Children who play in their backyards at home and who have matured under secure and calm conditions tend to be under less tension than those from smaller living quarters in the heart of a metropolis.

Four-year-old children can be initiated into the full day after fewer short days. They may be following a program which is complete by the beginning of the third week.

Five-year-olds are usually ready for a full program by the end of the second week, or before. In fact, they may ask to stay all day by the second or third day.

An easy transition from home to school is important. If a child is hesitant about leaving his/her parent, the parent should stay and leave the room gradually—with an explanation to the child—for longer periods of time. This, of course, differs in a Parent Co-op Nursery. A few children, especially at age three, may require a longer period of adjustment, some will require less.

The above, of course, implies a situation in which the parent can stay. This is frequently impossible in a day care situation. In these cases, after the parent has gone, a few suggestions may help what can be a very trying situation.

If you know that the parent(s) cannot return until five o'clock for instance, say firmly "your mother/father will come back after she/he has finished her/his work." Say goodbye and have the parent say goodbye, repeat what you

---

*Several groupings can be planned for easily. One should allow about thirty minutes between groups.

have said, and leave immediately. If the child is upset, be firm but affectionate. Remove the child from near the door and sit down with him to play or look at a book. If he is very negative, remain near but do not force yourself upon him. If he cries, wash his face with cool water after five minutes or so. If he responds and you can be spared, put him on your lap to watch some active play or a pet. If he shows any interest in the class pet—if there is one present—have him help you feed it. If he indicates an interest in anything, have him use it, do it, or join it. If possible, bring out the snack a little early and/or let him pass the cookies. Speak gently but very audibly and say matter-of-factly, "there are some big building blocks over there." Or, "if you will draw a picture, we'll hang it up there," pointing to the spot. Play a record if he is sobbing and neither crying loudly nor yelling. Make no demands for routines, such as for cleanup, passing napkins at snacktime, etc. Sing a lively song with motions. Watch for a look of interest on his part. Be sure, above all, that you know his word for toilet functions and that he knows where it is. Tell him the names of one or two socially mature children and, if possible, take him to where they are. Let him look at what he has shown even a glimmer of interest in. Try to take him to the toilet so that he doesn't upset himself further by having an accident. Assure him that mother/father or both will come back after work. Try to make overtures to another child for him, if he shows any interest. Avoid having him near the door through which his parent(s) left and do not tell him that he is a "big boy" or anything equally nonsensical. Try to see that doors are not open unnecessarily. Again, be affectionate but firm.*

Now it is obvious that someone else is or should be present in the room so that one of you can be free to follow through on the above suggestions, especially since it is hazardous and often illegal to have only one teacher with three-, four-, or five-year-olds.

PREPARING FOR THE FIRST DAY

Acquaint yourself with each child's name, nickname, and any deviations from the usual family pattern such as a deceased parent, divorced parents, or the fact that the child is new to this area of the country. This should be functional knowledge, so that you will not upset the child unnecessarily, especially on his first day.

Try to plan the appearance of the room so that it looks inviting, partially familiar, and friendly. If possible, have some bright colors in evidence. A few books should be on the table, some open to an interesting picture. Have clusters of pictures of familiar objects grouped according to subject matter. In one corner,

---

*The treatment for temper tantrums is similar: a firm but affectionate approach; no show of anger; great patience. Later try to discuss the situation with the child. He may need to be removed from the group, if he is violent during the tantrum. When he is able to return, be cheerful with him.

pictures of farm animals and pets might be mounted on bright colored paper. In another, there might be transportation pictures with which a child can identify. Some sheets of paper can be placed near crayons on a table inviting some child to try them. Each child should have his own locker or cubby. He can choose it and label it with a picture sticker of his choice.

Avoid having materials requiring special supervision, such as workbench tools or fingerpaint, in evidence. You might have some goldfish, but for children under five it is wise not to have a warm-blooded pet until you are sure of your group. Make it very clear where the bathroom is and that it may be used freely.

If the children are to stay for an hour and a half, for example, meet each one at the door. Greet him and have him look with you for something that he would like to do. It is frequently easier for a four-year-old to look over a new scene seated at a table with paper before him and a crayon in his hand for use. He is holding a familiar object and knows what to do with it. This kind of activity could continue for forty-five minutes, permitting free use of the materials you have made available. Announce that "We have five more minutes and then we'll put everything away" (children of this age do not know what five minutes is, but some grow accustomed to the short time interval). In five minutes say, "Now it is time to clean up. Put everything in the place where it belongs." Help those who seem ready to cooperate. Others who need a little urging, can be asked again. The resistant ones can be told "Perhaps you will be able to do it tomorrow."

On this first day, if possible, enourage everyone to go together to wash and use the toilet. Then have them set the table for a snack. One mature child might pass cookies, while another gives everyone a napkin, and you take charge of the juice or milk. Keep a cheerful conversation going.

After that, have someone pass the wastebasket and establish the routine for milk containers or juice cups.

Then have the children go immediately to you "collection spot." It is important to have some such place, and its use should be established during the first day. For example, this can be near the piano, on a rug, or near the window. Tell a very short story. If this is successful, state that you would like to sing a song and that some may know it. Listen. Sing it alone and say "I'll sing it again. Sing it with me if you like." A rhyme or two may be said. Get the children ready to leave and when they are called for, say goodbye to them individually, and tell them "we'll see you tomorrow."

Three-year-olds may not group at a "collection spot." If not, try to keep them during these few minutes at quieter activities such as looking at books, drawing, using cube blocks, or puzzles. If they are moderately calm and quiet, a few may wish to have a book to read or join you in a song. A record may be a focal point of interest for a few minutes.

Four-year-olds are likely to accept a story, a few songs, and possibly one rhythmic activity, while five-year-olds may sit or participate for twenty minutes in stories, music, and rhythmic activities.

Remain calm, cheerful, lively, and ready to meet the child all of the way in order to establish good rapport.

AS THEY DEVELOP

During the course of the school year, programs for three-, four-, and five-year-olds change. As the children develop, as the teacher becomes better acquainted with each child, and as the routines that are necessary become established, revisions can be made. Many of these are for larger blocks of time to meet a longer span of attention and the extended development of interests. A few daily events will require less time. These include dressing and undressing, toileting, eating, and putting away equipment.

A number of changes toward longer time blocks in the program can be made to account for the following:

I.   At three:
   A. Increase in individual desire to verbalize which makes it necessary to plan for more time for discussions, children's "stories," etc.;
   B. A greater number of short trips about the building, or the immediate area, due to greater curiosity about their surroundings after the children are secure in their own area;
   C. Increasing opportunity to satisfy large motor coordination due to greater physical mobility and experience with simple materials and equipment;
   D. Added special events such as simple picnics or simple parties to meet the need for greater group cohesiveness and awareness of doing what other groups do;
   E. More time to solve individual problems as the use of materials and equipment incorporates growing skills.
II. At four:
   A. Added special activities out of their room and immediate area due to having "tried out" teacher and whatever necessary regulations have been established and thus being able to take new and different experiences without so much overstimulation;
   B. More time for talking to group as a whole due to greater need to tell stories and to relate "what I did"; (This frequently lengthens lunch time.)
   C. Necessary attention by the teacher to meet the desire to recognize his own name, rather than picture label, simple signs, preliminary math concepts, concern about the big hand on clock, and other indications of greater awareness of symbols;
   D. Provision for leaving block buildings up overnight, occasionally.

III.   At five:
   A. More *planned* time for activities of the whole group due to in-
      terest in each other, in planning projects, in exchanging ideas,
      and in greater interest in symbols, and in relationships;
   B. More space for keeping children's own items due to increasing
      desire to collect things, to bring them to school, and to show oth-
      ers such possessions as rocks, bottle caps, guppies, etc.;
   C. Greater blocks of time for conversations alone with teachers and
      as part of group in order to satisfy need for added verbalization
      and accompanying need to clarify meanings and associations such
      as antenna on a grasshopper and on the TV set, or Jim Smith
      and the gym;
   D. Greater necessity for understanding and trying out for one's self
      alone and with others in order to attain satisfaction through
      personal control such as building a house, that we can live in,
      with a chimney, or fastening a rope to the pulley so that it will
      lift a small chair.

The above indications are merely a few of the most obvious signs of the kinds
of opportunities needed for growing realization of the self as an individual and
a social being. The list, while far from inclusive, does indicate necessity for
greater relating socially, for being able to accept some change once routines are
well-established. As each child matures, he tends to reach out in all directions
at the same time that his own reactions to his outgoing activities tend to go
deeper and to be not only more lasting but also basic aspects of his representa-
tional life. For example, the three-year-old who originally resented his parents
going out at night, may at three-and-a-half still resent his mother putting on
her coat but will go into nursery school the next morning and play out the sequence. He will "put on" a blanket as coat, tell the doll what it can and can't
do, and walk out of the housekeeping corner in order to "go to the theatre,"
"visit Mrs. Jones downstairs," etc.

Toward the end of the year, the group should go together to visit the class or
classes, where they will be during the following year. Most children are well
acquainted with these other groups by late spring but may not be aware that this
is to be their new room. Even in a very open situation, each needs to know
where he will hang *his* coat, keep *his* belongings, and greet *his* teacher. To be
acquainted with the teacher and to be clear about the next fall's placement will
place the child in a state of anticipation.

PARENTS' FIRST DAY

Although most parents realize some of the reasons for preschool education, few
are aware of the breadth and depth of the expectations which are genuinely edu-

cational held by the numerous centers for three-, four-, and five-year-olds. Many preschool centers have procedures for parent orientation and thus mothers and fathers are more fully aware of what to expect.

The relationship of the parent to a preschool center will be discussed in a later chapter.* Now, however, an indication of what is done to orient parents is indicated.

1. A visit and/or interview is customary in a majority of centers after the parent(s) has applied and in advance of acceptance and of the first visit of the child;

2. A booklet or synopsis of the theory and practices of the center is given the parent(s) (in many day care centers these are in various languages);

3. A practical handbook including information about such items as snacks, a change of clothing, etc., may be a part of the preceding, or separate from it;

4. Upon application, a comprehensive information file is begun for the child which includes such items as family background, medical history, phone numbers of persons to be called in emergency, sometimes permission slips for short trips, special items such as allergies, fear of loud noises, etc., knowledge of which is necessary for working with this child;

5. The child visits and, if possible, his parents leave him with the teacher;

6. The initial interview held with the parent specifically about the child may take place before the child begins attending or shortly thereafter;

7. A meeting for prospective parents prior to the child's attendance, or shortly thereafter serves to let the teacher orient the parents to the program, to get parents acquainted, to encourage them to ask questions, and to request any assistance which may be necessary.

Although this is but a brief outline, it does indicate some necessary items for consideration.

At the time of the first conference with parents, anxieties may be allayed— many children do behave in similar ways although the parents may not be fully aware of this; questions which concern the parent may be answered—these cover a wide range; rapport should be established if possible—this is basic to establishing good working relations for the benefit of the child.

It is important to remember that it is sometimes as hard, if not harder, for a parent to leave his/her child with his teacher for the first time than it is for the child to adjust to the surroundings of the preschool.

---

*See chapter 10.

Now that general programming has been considered, it is time to turn to the specifics.

It is wise, perhaps, to digress for a moment in order to consider the reason for the use of the term work-play. The term activities does explain, partially, but is not precise enough. If play includes its purposes, then and there, in the activity in progress, certainly, as a term, it would be inclusive of much of the freely chosen activities of preschool children. Maria picks up a doll and cradling it in her arms begins to rock back and forth as she hums. Seeing a carriage nearby, she walks to it and puts the doll into it, and then pushes the carriage around the room. This activity is quite complete within its self. The doll and carriage functioned to fulfill Maria's immediate purpose or aim. Every item was present in the immediate situation and Maria moved from rocking the doll to pushing it in the carriage. In contrast, work has a purpose somewhat beyond the here and now activity being carried through by the child. Five-year-old Karl gets out a large pile of unit blocks on Friday and says, "I'm going to make a pigeon-hole garage." He builds his structure with care and as Tim joins him says, "Hey, Tim, help me finish. Monday we'll put cars in. Bring your helicopter. We can load it with people after they leave their cars. It will work good." Karl had a purpose beyond his immediate building. He projected beyond what he was doing then and was working toward a purpose to be fulfilled. He pushed from the present situation and projected into a future situation. The end was more remote and the time span longer than that involved in Maria's activities. Those, who say that play is children's work seem to be missing a point. Children put effort into both types of activity. Play brings immediate satisfaction and work, delayed satisfaction because it includes an anticipated aim or purpose which is not then present in the situation. A child in the realistic stage of painting,* for instance, says, "I'm going to paint my house" as he steps up to the easel. In terms of our definition, this is work. The line of demarcation is often rather "fuzzy" at this preschool age level. It should be noted, too, that Karl's aim or purpose was in the future. It was clear enough to serve as a focus for his means or action and for him to include Tim, who understood it, in his plan.

PROGRAM AREAS

It is important to consider a few of the program areas. Stories, music, rhythms, and science and nature experiences are all considered specifically in later chapters. During the work-play time, there is considerable dramatic play as well as the opportunity for using finger paint. Easel painting, collage making, the use of clay and dough, crayons, and opportunities for woodworking can be provided, also; these are discussed later in other chapters.** The work-play time, however, includes more than the activities just listed.

*See chapter 6.
**See chapter 6, especially.

A visit to a preschool group during the work-play time which also may be known as activities, chosen activities, or by some other name, is usually quite indicative of what is offered, of the underlying theory for so doing, and of the point of view toward children. The visitor should consider the following.

a) *How much choice does the child have in what he does?* If a child is to develop initiative and necessary controls over himself and what he does, he must begin early. When children know that this is "our" room and that this is the time we use whatever we want to use, it should mean just that! After all the children are together at the "collection spot," they may be told, "all right, we'll have time to get out everything you want to use now. John and Pete, do you know what you are going to do? Mary, can you start by yourself? Tina, if you want to finger paint, get your smock on and the paint will be ready right away. Don, if you are going to use the work bench, choose your wood and the nails. Yes, I'll help you with the saw as soon as Tina has started, etc., etc." Thus each starts, and those who need special help or items know that these will be forthcoming. If Ron, Bess, and Eloise do not start off on their own, "Ron, you were building yesterday. Do you want to use the blocks again or do something else? Why not take a minute to decide?" (After looking about for a minute, Ron gets his smock because he has decided to finger paint with Tina.) "Bess and Eloise, do you know what you want to do?" As Bess points to the housekeeping

"Don, if you are going to use the workbench, choose your wood and the nails." (Courtesy Department of Health, Education and Welfare and Dick Swartz.)

corner, "All right, Bess." If Eloise still does not know—perhaps she has been absent or perhaps she is overdominated at home—"Would you like to go with Bess or would you rather help me with the finger paint?" Thus Eloise has a choice, and once she begins some activity, the chances are that she will continue and then move on freely to the next. If Eloise seems incapable of choosing then, further suggestions can be made. "The clean sheets are in the dresser drawer." "Eloise, the rabbit's water dish is empty." "Have you seen the new books on the book table? One is about the circus and one is about a boy who lost his dog." If Eloise shyly shakes her head, a smile and a hand outstretched with "Won't you come with me while I go over there?" may help. If Eloise seems cheerful, perhaps, "All right, you sit there and watch for awhile. Then perhaps you can decide" will do for then. However, the teacher watches Eloise and, when she notes an interest on her part, encourages her. If Eloise continues to sit, a doll or a book may be brought to her. She may well be the kind of child, who prefers to sit, watch, and then decide.

This work-play time is quite different from a teacher-dominated one. If the teacher continues to decide who will paint, build with the blocks, and use the housekeeping corner, then most of the children will be passive and go where they are sent. Children need to be able to choose for themselves.

Shy children, especially, need warm, secure surroundings. (Courtesy Department of Health, Education and Welfare and Dick Swartz.)

Needless to say, a wise teacher will watch to see that children broaden their choices, try what they haven't used, and have a chance to find out what all of the equipment and materials have to offer. The children who repeat the same activity day after day need to become aware of new possibilities. Free choice when possible, suggestions when necessary, an additional supplementary item, here and there, and a watchful eye over the whole, indicate a functional room which is geared to choice, to furthering initiative, and to individual realization at the same time that the rights and opportunities of others are kept clear.

b) *How many kinds of activities and kinds of materials and equipment are available and how autonomous can the child be in obtaining, using, and clearing them up?* If materials have their own places, if equipment is durable, and if the teacher and class have set down a few simple regulations such as "We leave the saw in the drawer when we are not using it," at age four or "We only feed the guinea pig *his* food," at age three or "We tell me (the teacher), if you need to go into Miss Joyce's room (the nurse), or into the locker room," at age five then most of what can be used may be available. If records and rhythm band instruments, for instance, are on a low shelf near the record player, then children may have many rhythmic activities and musical experiences. If initiated by the children, they are often creative and indicate expressions for the teacher to build upon. If the instruments are in the top of the closet and brought out at a certain time by the teacher, much spontaniety and creativity may never be expressed.

If each item has its place, getting children to put it back becomes part of its use. If there are ample block shelves, for instance, putting blocks away is easier and two or three children can do it. The child who does not want to clear up is likely to do so if (a) he sees that others do and (b) he finds that "We clear up before we can have lunch." Group pressure may be quite operative in such instances. Choice is still the child's, but as he sees what follows, what he is missing, or what others are enjoying, he will tend to participate.

c) *How adequate is the space for the work of each child?* Every child is part of the group and has the right to see his picture or work kept, hung up, or saved to be carried home. To the visitor, some pictures may look better by adult standards, but four-year-old Jean's manipulative painting is just as important to her as Josh's bus with wheels is to him. If it is the child's room, then equal space should be kept for the work of each member of the group.

Some teachers make a frieze across one wall for large pictures. If Ted knows that his painting is near the door, then this place can remain his. Sometimes putting two or three of his paintings on top of each other—with the latest on top—is a worthwhile plan. Ted's parents then can see several of Ted's paintings at one time as well as those of other children. They learn, too, that Ted's work is accepted by his teacher regardless of the stage that it is in and that manipulative "scribble scrabble" is an early stage through which all children develop. If this plan is followed, several paintings may be carried home at one time.

Wall space, shelf space, a place for clay to dry, clips and a wire or a flat paper covered table for wet pictures, adequate water, sink space, soap, and towels as well as quiet places in which to sit and rock or look at a book are all conducive to self-help and to a sense of belonging because the child can put *his* there.

d) *How is adequate supervision planned for the use of equipment which may be dangerous?* Saws, for instance, do require supervision. If the teacher is alone in a large room with twenty-five four-year-old children, there may be times when she will have to say, "I'm sorry, Jody, but you will have to wait until Miss Ross is here to help us. Then you can saw."

Saws, for instance, do require careful supervision. (Courtesy Department of Health, Education and Welfare and Dick Swartz.)

A few routines are necessary, such as one to get children who have been finger painting to the sink without touching anything. An indoor ladder gym may need careful supervision, especially at the beginning of the year. Does it have a mat under it? The adult near it must stand so as to see as much as possible of everything else. The experienced teacher knows what to stand near and has developed a "roving eye" so that little escapes her attention. Are the blocks free of splinters? Are there glass or plastic objects for children to carry for watering plants and pouring juice? Are most of the things to be used within reach? In the three-year-old room is the knob of the door to the hall or outdoors high enough so that a child cannot reach it? Are the sinks low enough to reach? Is the playground fenced? Such items make for safety and independence. The teacher can work with the children and not need to worry if such safety factors are well planned.

e) *How are transitions made from one activity to another, from work-play, in general, to clean-up, and to whatever comes next?* Transitions should move smoothly so that children do not just stand waiting. If the work-play time is drawing to a close and is to be followed by toiletting and lunch, the teacher can warn everyone that "we have only a few minutes before we clear up." Those who are painting need to wash and may be warned first so that they will be out of the way of the others. Children who are building should be warned early because blocks take longer to put away than puzzles or crayons. As children finish at the toilet, they can begin to set the table for lunch or sit and look at a book at the book table until everyone is ready. If this pattern is established at the beginning of the year, it may go so smoothly that the visitor wonders how everyone knows what to do. It makes sense to the children and they understand. For example, we clear up, wash, set the table, look at a book while others are finishing, and then we eat lunch. If the table is all set, "We go right to the book table." The sequence is manageable by each child, and he knows what will follow. After lunch the following works well in some situations: dishes up to the tray, wash and toiletting, back to the room and choose an easy-to-clear-up material from the shelf, sit and use it, then go together or with a small group to the rest room. If the rest takes place in the room or in an adjourning one, the child can go directly to his cot from the bathroom. The shelf of easy-to-clear-up materials may hold puzzles, cube blocks, small snapblock sets, finger puppets, crayons, scissors, and paper.

The set-up of the room is not only conducive to choice and the use and clearing-up of materials, but there is a careful arrangement. Block building requires space, painting should not be too near the books, there should be space near the musical instruments, etc. Space management is a basic factor in a smooth-running room.

Materials are chosen to encourage the development of the child physically, socially, emotionally, and mentally. Thus there are materials to foster the development of large and small muscles and of hand and eye coordination. Other items tend to encourage social development because they are used to greater advantage by two or more. A telephone is fun, especially if someone else has one, too. Two doll carriages permit two "mothers" or "fathers" to go out with their "babies."

Materials to pound with like clay, punching bags, bingo beds, and hammers make outlets for hostility as well as for creativity or muscular coordination. Stuffed animals may be comforting to a three-year-old. A rocking chair sometimes provides soothing motion to a child who is upset.

The stimulation of materials that are durable, bright, and inviting adds to experience and provides problems for solving because children use them toward their own ends and purposes. Children at ages three, four, and five tend to think with things. Watch John carefully making his garage. He needs a roof, and it's a problem. Which block will bridge the space between the walls? He doesn't tell you verbally; he does it with blocks! If his choice (the block) does not work, the consequence is right before him, and he can change the building or choose another block. He thinks with the materials available to him.

Growth should be evident and work-play time provides an excellent opportunity for observing it. Greater coordination, such as the ability to button the doll's dress and the skill of hammering the nail straight into the wood, is readily observed.

Milly's active participation in give-and-take social relationships with Donna, Elise, and Patrick is right there in the ongoing experiences of the four children in the housekeeping corner.

Henry is able to wait for his turn now. He no longer screams or pushes another child off of the red tricycle. Alison leaves her mother at the door and smiles as she enters the room alone. Isabel pats the large rabbit and says, "I played with Aunt Mary's poodle." She was afraid of animals earlier. Floyd solves his own simple problems in building, in putting together the puzzle, and in getting his right boot on his right foot alone. All are growing and developing—in ways other than added vocabulary, weight, and height!

SOME SELECTED MATERIALS

There are materials which encourage certain types of development, and they are listed according to category.

PHYSICAL DEVELOPMENT

arts and crafts materials
balls of various sizes
beads of large sizes
beam for balance
bingo bed or knock out bench (name depends on manufacturer)
blocks of large size for outdoors and smaller unit size for indoor building
boards for use with outdoor blocks
bowling pin set (for five-year-olds)
boxes of large or packing box size
dolleys or platform trucks for moving blocks or riding
fasteners on doll clothing of large size
form boards for shape concepts
gardening tools which are durable enough for use.

jungle gym or other provision for climbing
kegs or small barrels
ladders
parallel bars
pasting
pegs and a mallet
punching bag (for age five)
pushmobile
puzzles of graded difficulty
rhythm band instruments (see music section)
ring toss
rocking boat
ropes (used only with careful supervision)
sand box and shovels, pails, strainers, etc.
saw horses for building and making seesaws
scooter (for age five)
seesaws (unless adequate saw horses and boards are available)
shoe for lacing
slide
snap blocks
sprinkling can for watering plants and sand

Tools foster physical development and hand-eye coordination. (Courtesy Department of Health, Education and Welfare, and Dick Swartz.)

step gym or set of steps or underside of rocking boat (for three-year-olds)
swings
tea set and other provisions for pouring
tires for rolling and perhaps swinging
tools of adult but small size such as hammer, saw, large headed nails, etc.
tricycles
wagons
walking board
wheel barrows

SOCIAL DEVELOPMENT

art materials
balls of various sizes
blocks of large and small sizes
books for participation and for ethnic awareness
book table and chairs
costumes or adult clothes for dress-up
dolls of different races and sex
dramatic play materials
family figures of plastic or wood
housekeeping equipment
jungle gym
kitchen utensils for "cooking and eating"
live animals
lotto games
mirrors for developing self-concept and seeing others
music materials
packing or ladder box
playhouse of solid construction for outdoors
picture sets for emotional development
puppets for fingers and hands
rocking boat (for three-year-olds)
sand box and toys with a place to sit either in the sand or around the edges
seat of solid construction and low and large enough for several children
seesaws
swings
telephones
trucks to sit on or to carry two children (for three-year-olds)
wagons

EMOTIONAL DEVELOPMENT

animals
aquarium
arts and crafts materials
baking equipment
balls of various sizes
blocks of varous sizes in sets
bingo bed or knock out bench for pounding
boxing gloves (for five-year-olds)
clay
colored lens for self-knowledge and development
dolls of various types
dough
dramatic play materials
dress-up clothes
drums strong enough for heavy pounding
"eating" equipment for housekeeping corner
family figures
hammers, nails, wood, saw, etc.
jump rope (for five-year-olds)
jungle gym
kitchen utensils
mirror
painting materials, especially finger paint
pictures for discussion, especially those depicting strong emotion
plants
punching bag (for five-year-olds)
puppets of various types, size, and appearance
quiet corner
records of various sorts accessible to children
rhythm band instruments
rocking chair
role-playing props
sand box and materials for sand and water play
scarves for rhythmic activity
seesaw
soft toys and materials to hold and fondle
stories and books
swings
textured materials such as wool, fur, plush, velvet

tricycles
walking beam
wash tub for washing doll clothes and dishes
water play materials such as soap chips and washable materials

MENTAL OR INTELLECTUAL DEVELOPMENT

animals
art materials
batteries and flashlight, bell and light bulb
bingo (for five-year-olds)
blocks and objects to use in building
clock with movable hands
dolls of various types
dominoes with large dots or pictures (for four- and five-year-olds)
dough
flannel board
form boards
games of a simple type (for five-year-olds)
graduated blocks, rings, and other items for size and weight discrimination
lotto cards (for five-year-olds)
magnifying glass
mail box with openings for forms (for three-year-olds)
measuring cups, spoons, etc.
number games of large size (for five-year-olds)
peg boards
pictures of many types and kinds for looking and discussion
plants, seeds, etc.
puppets for finger and hand
puzzles of graded difficulty
records for listening
rhythms and music materials
sand box and measuring cups, spoons, etc.
scales and balances (especially for five-year-olds)
self-help equipment for cleaning, for keeping clothing, etc.
shapes and form boards
stories
tape recorder
telephones
textured materials
thermometer (large)
toy money or chips

We return now to other important items in the program.

SNACK TIME

Snack time should be fun time. Children usually look forward to their milk or juice and cookie or slice of bread and butter. Sometimes fruit is part of the snack, and in some centers, vitamins or other dietary supplements are given. If children run and grab their snack and then gulp it down in the midst of their play, it is true that the play is not interrupted, but much else is lost.

Setting the table with napkins for all is something children can do. In some groups, they pour their juice and may wash their cups after one has passed the waste basket. Passing cookies to everyone is a step to social development. Sitting together with the teacher and other adults makes snack time an excellent opportunity for language development through the conversation, planning, and discussions which take place.

Sometimes, a visitor may be invited. For example, if the teachers are all female, a man teacher or other worker in the school should be asked to join the children for snack time, occasionally. This is not a time to show things—but a time to eat, talk, and to enjoy each other's company. In fact, a few teachers known to the writer consider snack time so important, especially for language development, that no one is permitted to enter the room and interrupt this time.

Snack time is a time to eat, talk, and enjoy each other's company. (Courtesy Brooklyn-Parma Coop Pre-school, Cleveland, Ohio and Lois Overbeck.)

LUNCH TIME

Lunch time can be a fun time, too! The children can help set the table. They can put their own plates on trays after finishing and get their own dessert, which should be dished out prior to beginning the meal. At ages three, four, and five it is best to have children leave the table after they have finished their meal. They can take care of toiletting needs and do something quiet such as look at a book or put together a puzzle at a specified table or other place while waiting for everyone to finish. If the rest area can be supervised, they can go directly to their cots.

Children can sit in small groups at tables with an adult. If the food is served "family style" by the adult at the table, each child should be addressed individually, and asked whether there is something he wants only a little of or a small portion of. Thus, if Jon dislikes peas, he gets only a few. However, a useful routine is that "We taste everything." If this is established at the first meal together, most children tend to accept it. The teacher knows about the children's allergies and may even discover new ones if a food which is new to the child is served.

There are numerous theories about food, eating, self-choice, and natural wants. Parents, too, may have theories. Without getting into a discussion of these and their strengths and weaknesses, the writer advocates the above system because of her past experiences. It is useful to get a written note if there is some food that the parent is willing to have the child omit. The teacher, too, must be aware of what foods must not be given children for religious reasons and, when possible, see that they are omitted from the menus.

Menus should be planned and sent home every one or two weeks so that the child won't be given the same food at home that he had for lunch. Large schools and centers usually have a dietician and/or others who do the planning ahead. The time of year, price level, and availability, of course, need to be considered. A balanced diet is basic, but different ethnic groups may have different staples in their diets with which the teacher should be acquainted.

Young children tend to dislike food presented in mixtures. They usually dislike creamed or casserole dishes. Unfamiliar foods, like Brussel sprouts in some areas, cause consternation. Young children like foods that ar. clearly what they seem. For instance, carrot and celery sticks are usually eaten with gusto, while either one presented in a creamed style is likely to be unpopular. Sandwiches are well-liked and, in one school, where lettuce produced problems, lettuce sandwiches were a hit!

Eating problems come to the fore during lunch. The writer has had children of age four who never had chewable food before, who did not eat any vegetables, or who had never eaten any meat. A child with a genuine eating problem should be seated near the teacher. Encouragement and a calm unemotional attitude are very supportive to the view expressed. If everything has been tasted, dessert is forthcoming. Dessert is not a bribe—it is that which follows the first part of the meal. Discussions of Popeye, becoming strong, and of curly hair should be omitted. Underlying psychiatric problems are for educated psychiatrists and not the layman unless the teacher has been part of the planning and carrying out process with parent and psychiatrist. Most children are quite hungry by noon and small portions help the reluctant eater to clear his plate, or at least to eat some of everything. The child who vomits in order to gain sympathy or to avoid eating may need to be seated by himself because "we are busy eating over here." Why he uses this behavior and how it was developed should be discussed with his parents and/or a psychologist or psychiatrist.

Conversation should be carried on during lunch, but overstimulation, long accounts, or the showing of objects are usually distracting. When four-year-olds are turning five they frequently become more verbal. Then lunch takes longer. Parties may be at dessert time.*

Conversations include discussion of many kinds of experiences, not the least of which are of trips, visits, and shared special times. These, when appropriate, add enjoyment and information to preschool life.

TRIPS, VISITS, AND SPECIAL TIMES

What constitutes a trip, a visit, or a "special" time? "I want to see the new rats in my sister's class." "Can we go in that room there and see those big lights?" "They have a big machine down the street and it lifts the girders." "Mr. Johnson said if we came, we could choose our own pumpkins." "My father has a new kitchen in his restaurant. Can we go to see it?" "Mrs. Jones' dog has four puppies. They're fuzzy. Could she show them to us?" "We could buy the package and then make chocolate pudding for lunch." "Mr. Ives is going to wash the whole playground. Can we watch him?" "Ira's uncle has a monkey. Could he bring it here?" "Pete's father is a fireman. He says we can see the pumper, if we go to the firehouse." Questions! Information! Positive answers and open attitudes toward possibilities provide opportunities for trips, visits, and special times.

Visitors can extend children's experiences in numerous ways. The visit should be planned with the teacher and the time chosen with some care. For instance, a parent coming unannounced into a work-play time or a rest hour with a basket of eight puppies would be less welcome than if the visit were planned for after nap time. The children could all sit in a large circle or oval, and everyone would be able to see and play with the puppies!

---

*See chapter 10, pp.182-83.

The teacher often plans visits, too, because she knows what may be available upstairs which will add to her children's expanding experiences. Visits within a large school building frequently provide numerous additional learning experiences, especially for three- and four-year-olds. These may be extensions to experiences in which the children are already engaged.

Trips in the immediate area are fine for three-year-olds. Older children can benefit from these and move gradually farther out into the community. A trip, several blocks away, to watch a new building going up or several fields away to see a new calf provides fine learning experiences.

Mature four- and five-year-olds may go in cars or in busses (preferably small ones) for short distances to visit a farm, an animal nursery, a fire house, or a boat basin. The location of the class, the area surrounding it, and the work of the parents and of those in the community will provide a number of interesting opportunities. The teacher may well be in the position of refusing gracefully rather than of seeking opportunities.

"I can feed the baby goat from my wheelchair."
(Courtesy Society for Crippled Children, Cleveland, Ohio.)

Regardless of where children go out of the building, *certain factors need consideration*:

1. Are there signed permission slips for each child (either one for the year or one for each trip) on file?
2. Does the office know where you are going?
3. Have you enough adults to help you—preferably one for every two or three three-year-olds?
4. Have you, yourself, been to the site to look for such danger spots as unfenced areas with a drop, or hole, or water near by?
5. Do you know the best approach in terms of streets with traffic lights, gates for entrance of groups, etc.? (It may be easier to go the long way around if traffic lights are located more advantageously.)
6. Do you know where the toilet facilities are?
7. If you are to eat there, what about facilities?
8. Does each parent have adequate insurance, if he is to drive?
9. If a bus is to be used, does it have seats constructed properly for small children?
10. If you are to eat there, has this been planned carefully in terms of where, what, any purchasing, and any needed money?
11. Does the neighborhood grocer or librarian, if they are to be visited, expect you?
12. Are there features making for overstimulation near, or are they part of where you are going and what you are to see?
13. Has the time been planned so that you won't have children traveling in a rush hour, expected to enjoy something without their naps late in the day, or feeling hungry?
14. Have you extra panties, sox, bandaids, more tissues, safety pins, and a few plastic bags for wet panties, for a child sick in the bus, or to carry home a specimen or two, etc.?

If the above considerations become part of the usual planning for a trip, after a time or two everything will go smoothly. However, if the teacher remembers them at first, the first or second trip can be a success, too!

"Special" times may be defined as almost any event out of the usual routine or not part of a daily plan or program. Cooking, for instance, might be so considered. Mature three-, four- and five-year-olds, if near a grocer's, can go and buy pudding, junket, or jello, prepare it, and then eat it for lunch or after the afternoon rest. This can be a successful "special" time! Popping corn may be another! Going to get a baby guinea pig from the sixth grade and fixing him a cage in "our" room might be another! Visiting a class to see their pictures or having them visit for snack time is very "special." Observing or participating in part of

Mary's grandfather and Jimmy's big brother came
on our last trip.

Eating the sauce they cooked from the cranberries
they bought at the store makes the whole experience more meaningful. (Courtesy Brooklyn-Parma
Coop Preschool, Cleveland, Ohio and Lois Overbeck.)

an assembly program for the school is usually remembered, and children derive a feeling of being part of the whole school or center by so doing.

Needless to say, health should be a primary concern, if children are to live fully through each preschool day. This, too, is a responsibility of the teacher.

MORNING INSPECTION

Every child should be inspected as he enters. Attention should be given to his skin and muscle tone, his eyes, nose, throat, and general mien. This inspection should be by a nurse, the teacher, or even another teacher. Schools differ and health codes differ, but each child has the right to receive daily attention about his health needs and the way he feels at that time. Regulations differ about notes after illness or contagious diseases, and the new teacher must find out about what is expected. She owes it to each child to abide by the regulations. Provision for adequate rest is a necessity, too, which is related closely to health.

REST AND NAP TIME

Most preschool groups have a short rest during the morning whether the session be a half- or a full-day one. Teachers and supervisors, used to older children, do not always realize the need for a quiet time during a busy and somewhat exciting morning. In most groups, children rest on washable heavy bath mats or small rugs on the floor in their own room. The teacher needs to be aware of heat and of possible drafts. The child's name should be at the end of the mat where he puts his head. If he folds it long ways first, after he rises, and then folds it crossways, the head end of the mat will remain clean. The child can manage to fold and to store such a mat himself. If the children in a day care center arrive before 8:30 A.M., they tend to benefit more from a thirty-minute rest rather than the fifteen or twenty minutes so utilized by later arrivals.

If possible, the rest area for three- and four-year-olds should be dimmed. Absolute silence is rarely insisted upon, but the children need to be encouraged to be quiet and may listen to soft music at the time. Five-year-olds may look at a book as they rest or listen to a story. Some three-year-olds quiet down more easily with a doll or stuffed toy.

Most groups, following a full day schedule, have a nap after lunch. This is usually on cots which may be covered with the mat used in the morning or with a small sheet. Thin, small, easily laundered blankets are necessary, and a wooden, beaverboard, or plastic screen should be between the cots so that one child's breath does not reach another. In a separate room, or in his own room, the teacher sets a quiet relaxing tone or mood with the voice or some soft music, darkens the room, and finds that a high percentage of the children go to sleep. Those, who are slow to accept this, may sit up quietly for a few minutes. If the teacher sits on the edge of the cot of a high-strung child, this helps him to relax and perhaps to sleep.

In a nine to three or three-thirty day, an hour and three-quarters is usually of sufficient length for three-year-olds, an hour and a quarter for four-year-olds, and three-quarters of an hour to an hour for five-year-olds. A longer day should be planned with ample time for a longer nap time.

Most preschool centers have provision, too, for a bed for a very tired or an ill child who cannot be sent home. This may be in the regular rest area or in the nurse's quarters.

The teacher needs to look carefully at each child when he arises. A long day means that the morning inspection was some hours before. Many a child has developed a rash or a cold by the end of his nap time!

Notes

1. Ronald K. Parker, ed., *The Preschool in Action: Exploring Early Childhood Programs* (Boston: Allyn and Bacon, Inc., 1972), p. 268.

CHAPTER 5

Communication
and
Literature

NONVERBAL COMMUNICATION

Feelings may burst out, reveal themselves slowly, or be sublimated. Sally, an exuberant three-year-old, "bounces" across the nursery room. After five minutes, she says, "Pony, pony, running, running. Pony, pony, running, running." She feels happy and shows it. Sally is expressing her feeling outwardly and communicating it by her "bouncing." This objectifies it. At first her feeling is within, then she moves spontaneously, and confirms her feeling in the movement. At this point she may, or may not, alter or change what she is expressing or communicating outwardly. She can interact with her objectified feeling—the "bouncing." She interacts with feeling and thinking. She changes her expression at times, for instance, and says, "Pony running. Now pony eat." Thus the initial expression may be changed *after* it is expressed outwardly.[1]

Feelings that are revealed more slowly go through the same stages, but the tears or other outward expressions of feeling may not come immediately. Once begun, these objectifications of feeling may be altered into sobs or howls of rage.

Young children also begin to sublimate their feelings. These may be expressed outwardly by "guilty looks." For example, Josh's feelings of guilt may come forth as screams while he dreams. Sometimes he alters his expressions after he has felt and thought about his feeling. Before lunch, three-year-old Josh takes a cookie which he has been told he may have *after* lunch. He smiles after he has eaten it. Josh suddenly stops smiling and looks solemn—five minutes after he has finished the cookie—and then he sucks his thumb. He cannot feel and think about it and so react, however, until *after* he has confirmed the initial feeling through communicating some expression. In this case, it is his smile. His al-

tered expression is his "overt" look and the sucking of his thumb. In another instance, five-year-old Dick bangs his clay as hard as he can to project—or communicate outwardly—his feelings of hostility about something which has happened at home before he came to school. At four, Dick screamed, "I'll kill the
baby." However, by five, once he has objectified his feeling to himself as he
watches his mother fondle the baby, he is aware as he reacts to his feeling of envy
and desire to obliterate the baby that severe retribution will follow. Thus at five,
Dick hides the feeling for awhile and then "beats" the clay.

The above are examples of nonverbal expression. Such expression may, of
course, reach a high level of form through the dance. The first rhythmic movements are feelings expressed overtly. As the dance continues, the actual movement is an objectification which can be evaluated and/or changed through additional feeling reactions and thought interactions. Four-and-a-half-year-old
Hildy, swaying in rhythm with a doll in her arms, becomes aware of her motion as objectified action and then perhaps rises and walks as she sways, thus
embelishing the original action-expression. (If an alert teacher plays Brahms'
Lullaby to accompany it, there may be further interactions.)

A group of people are sitting in a room when Ravel's *Bolero* is heard suddenly as a radio is turned on. Some part or parts of every anatomy move in
rhythm. This is a feeling response to the rhythm and as such is a reaction to an
outer stimulus. There may be a deep level of feeling stirred, but it is *induced* (or
in a sense motivated), rather than originating as spontaneous feeling pouring
forth from the individual.

Communication is outward. The individual feels and expresses. Thus he
communicates to himself in the sense that he confirms his feeling in his own
objectification. Once objectified, his initial expression may be changed by his
own feeling and thinking interactions, but it is likely to be repeated because, as
objectification, it has a pattern. The pattern may be repeated enough to become habit or it may be repeated and changed.[2]

All of the above nonverbal forms function as communication. The child
communicates deliberately to another when he expresses the pattern he has
created to this other. A high percentage of our art forms are nonverbal expressions which are communication media. After the interaction with the
initial objectification has taken place and the creator has confirmed his individual pattern, he has his picture, dance, sculpture, or cadenza.*

VERBAL COMMUNICATION

Verbal communication gradually replaces crying. Two-year-old Steve hits, but
five-year-old Alan screams, "Stop, you hurt." Inasmuch as words are comparatively recent attainments, Alan may still regress rather easily to hitting.

---

*See chapter 6 for further discussion.

Verbal communication is the use of sounds which develop into words with meaning. Verbal communication may be sound functioning as clarification of the self to the self and/or as deliberately directed toward another. Clear speech is clearer communication. The child communicates verbally for a number of reasons, but feeling usually underlies it. He communicates:

1. To identify himself or his possessions;
2. To request what he wants;
3. To ask questions in order to find out;
4. To tell some item of importance;
5. To explain what he has brought;
6. To state a choice between alternatives;
7. To experiment with and to share sounds;
8. To put feeling into words, more specifically for the sake of the feeling.

For example, he feels happy in number five and objectifies it by explaining about his new airplane which makes him feel happy. In number eight, his words come forth as objectifications of feelings which are clarified through this means of communication.

Children need talking opportunities! The child who knows where materials are, who cooperates fully, and who appears well-adjusted may need as much or more of a chance to talk to someone who is sympathetic, patient, and understanding than the child who through lack of adjustment is directed verbally, constantly. The latter *hears* constantly, while the former may have many fewer contacts with increasing, mature speech patterns. Self-confidence is embellished by increasing verbal controls and guided verbal communication.

As the Ego expands, accomodates the new, and is in turn accomodated, it expresses Mary or Tom. The Ego image of each child develops positively and confidently, or in unfortunate cases becomes an obliterative, self-effacing image of lack of confidence. Unfortunately, the non-English speaking child may be experiencing repeated reenforcement in such defeating image-making patterns. This too is the case with slow learners all too frequently. These children need the maximum number of "talking opportunities" in order to increase their confidence and ability to communicate verbally.

There are numerous ways to encourage language development in young children. These include:

1. being an understanding and sympathetic listener so that the child knows that you will "hear him out";
2. speaking clearly in order to let the child hear the correct pronunciation;
3. listening patiently so that the child feels relaxed and unhurried;
4. giving him feelings of freedom from pressure;

5. encouraging him to experiment with new words by using the new words he has used and by introducing a new one when it is appropriate and you have his full attention;

6. freeing him from the tensions which may cause stuttering by indicating that you have plenty of time to listen to him;

7. using new words in context or with simple explanations;

8. listening for mispronounciations in order to find out whether there is impaired hearing, the use of "baby talk" at home, or whether the correct pronunciation needs to be heard more often;

9. replacing an incorrect word with a correct one unobtrusively, yet in a meaningful context so that the proper word is heard and yet the child's train of thought is uninterrupted and his Ego remains in tact;

10. repeating the incorrectly pronounced word correctly in varied instances so that others will hear it correctly;

11. recording stories, incidents, chants, and rhymes originated by each child as well as group expressions and occasionally repeating them for the individual or the group either by reading, chanting, or playing a tape;

12. writing what each child says about his picture under it;

13. writing what is said by each child about his picture or clay work (which should increase as he develops into the symbolic stage at about four-and-a-half, or so);

14. clapping and sometimes walking, or otherwise moving, with rhythmic chants or verses as they are repeated in order to reinforce what is heard by giving it a rhythmic context;

15. utilizing books and stories for listening, participation, and to encourage discussion;

16. using attractive pictures to encourage identification, description, and/or discussion;

17. identifying pictures and some objects with labels;

18. beginning to utilize a few written symbols accompanied by verbalization at five, or so, such as "stop," "go," "exit," etc. in the context of dramatic play, block play, or outdoors.

Needless to say, these activities are all excellent prereading experiences, too.

Nonverbal communication should be retained in its more advanced forms such as the dance, rhythmic movements, pantomime, arts and crafts, puppetry (may be nonverbal and verbal) even after verbal communication is well established.[3] All children need both forms. The addition of the verbal should *add to* rather than diminish the nonverbal.

Speech Development

As we know, most children acquire nouns and verbs in their vocabulary first. "Baby fall" is used with certain inflections to mean: I, David, fell down; would

I fall; John (the baby) fell; did John fall? The toddler points a finger and says, "Dat" as a declaration or a question, depending upon the inflection given it. By nursery school, most children use short sentences. Plurals may not be clear as "Uncle Ned has gooses," for instance. The teacher can assume that more is comprehended than the child can state. Peter went home and said to his mother, "In school we stay in phone booths in the dark." The rest room had screens around each cot and the lights were put out. Peter did try to inform his mother! The teacher needs to try to attune her ear to the way the young children, in the situation in which she is, speak. Taping a few conversations and jotting down phrases is helpful. Use the nouns and verbs used by the children at first before trying to introduce new ones will get the teacher off to a good start!

The teacher working with a class in a neighborhood different from her own needs to gain a clear awareness of how the parents and children speak. The use of "Man," for example, with some inner-city groups or the use of "sucker" rather than "lollypop" in certain areas of the country are the terms which must be acquired. The teacher, who told the child to put his galoshes near the seesaw received a blank stare. What he would have understood was "Put your boots by the teeter-totter."

Children sometimes regress for a short time as they enter school. This may be manifested in toilet training, eating habits, and/or in speech! Given an easy transition to school and a secure atmosphere, if such does occur, the lapse to an earlier level of development usually will not last very long unless, of course, there are other problems in the situation.

BABY TALK

Baby talk is well known. In preschool, it frequently functions in ways detrimental to the child. Other children often refer to such a child as a baby. Although the teacher tries to encourage him to speak clearly, other adults are likely to make disparaging remarks within his hearing range. The teacher needs to confer with the parent at the earliest possible opportunity (a) to assure herself of cooperation and (b) to ascertain the parent's speech pattern.

Cooperation in speaking clear English to the child is necessary. While parents may consider baby talk cute, they must realize that it is likely to harm their child. Sometimes such a parent may become aware of this suddenly when the child enters school! He/she may try frantically to make the child change his speech then, or not knowing what to do, make numerous excuses for him. At a conference, a teacher may learn other possible causes for the baby talk. "Aunt Mary cared for her just as she was beginning to talk. Aunt Mary encouraged it," or, "Her father says, 'Let's keep her a baby as long as possible' and I don't want to upset him." In such a situation, the other person should be conferred with also. A high percentage of parents want help by the time their child is turning age four, if not earlier. When they want assistance, the parents need help in slowing down in order not to create a psychological problem where there may not be one. If parents and teacher work together and keep anxiety and tension at a minimum, the child will benefit. Once the problem has had consideration by the teacher, referrals can be made to a speech therapist if deemed necessary.

Parental speech patterns, on rare occasions, foster baby talk. A parent who lisps may have infantile speech patterns. A self-conscious adult sometimes promotes such a pattern in himself or herself in order to gain approbation. Cases of insecure and young second wives, for instance, have been known to do this. The mother's insecurity may be reflected in the child, who imitates his mother, and, as he senses her insecurity, seeks a closer identification. This is to indict neither young second wives nor parents with poor speech. It *is* used only as a sample to indicate that psychological problems are sometimes reflected in the children and may result in baby talk!

At times, the parents foster baby talk—not always too consciously—because the child was a late child, the only boy or girl, the youngest, or the only child who arrived late in their lives when they had nearly given up expecting one. The reasons for advanced speech and baby talk are often similar. In both cases, they *may* be reflecting pressure felt by the parents. A child may be kept "babyish" in speech and in other ways, too, at times when the parents are divorced. For example, Jimmy gives his mother some security and yet also may arouse feelings of guilt because she feels that she has failed in some way. Thus keeping Jimmy a baby gives her a sense of control over someone.

Underlying psychological reasons for parental behavior are not always clear. The average teacher is usually neither psychologically aware enough nor does she or he have sufficient education in this area to attempt any remedial treatment. If possible, a school counselor may help, but in many situations it is left to the teacher to work on her or his own as well as possible. Referrals to the family doctor sometimes cause the doctor to suggest a psychiatrist.

Speaking slowly and clearly to a child with whom you have rapport is the best beginning to encouraging clear speech. Children frequently give the "l" sound for the "y," the "w" sound for "r," and the "y" for "j," for example. Rhymes containing the sounds are helpful when said with the child. If there is a real disability and/or a hearing problem, a speech consultant should be recommended. The ways listed to encourage speech development in any child are helpful too.

Similar recommendations may be made for the child who speaks with an accent. Hearing correct English is what helps. The writer had a child of Italian parentage who spoke with a Finnish accent. When this was called to the parents' attention, they sought a new nurse. The child had spent far more time with the nurse than with her parents. This, too, was helpful because they planned to give more time to their children after they found out!

LITERATURE AND STORIES

We have summarized how communication develops in its nonverbal and verbal forms and how the growing child moves outward into the surrounding environment of people and things. As his experiences broaden so, too, do the number and kinds of problem-solving situations that he meets. He gives and takes in an ever-widening context. His learnings become a vast network of interrelated inquiries with requisite "know how" and goal attainments. The latter are, if recognized as entities at all, usually mere pauses on the way to further goal seeking and attainment. The child is constantly acting and increasing the number of means and kinds of ends he achieves as he gives and takes in the various situations requiring communication.

"Read this," "tell a story," "where's Mike Mulligan" are common place in any preschool group.

The vast field of children's literature is one source for facilitating goal seeking and attainment, "know how" and learning, and is a pleasurable accompaniment to dreaming and doing, to exploring and expecting, to probing and

Literature is a medium of communication to the child. (Courtesy Ethical Culture Schools, New York City and Celeste Muschel.)

proving, to seeking and to satisfaction. Literature is a medium of communication to the child which can develop, inspire, and add to information that he communicates outwardly. The variety of literature available at present far exceeds that of any period of the past. The array confronting one who is looking for a worthwhile children's book can be confounding. It includes choices of illustration, of content, of format, and of price. The three-year-old can *Ask Mr. Bear*[4] one hour and enjoy *The Snowy Day*[5] the next.

In order to ascertain just what is available, a few categories are helpful. When books are classified, they are easier to find and use. Useful classifications, which the author has worked out and found useful for the three-, four-, and five-year-old, are the following:

1. *Picture books* defined as those books in which the illustration is the predominating focal point. These may or may not be *picture books* in which the picture, though predominant, is accompanied by some very simple story, description, or explanation;*

2. *"Here and now" experiential* literature, defined as that which deals with what might well be seen as you look out of the door or step outside to the street, and which clarifies previous experiences and extends others;

3. *Transitional* literature defined as that which seems almost as though it could happen and yet, in some part, is just over the border into the imaginary, making it an easy "bridge" from the real to the make believe;

4. *Imaginative* literature defined as that which transcends the "here and now" experiential and moves us into the make-believe as it extends fantasy;

5. *Folk tales* defined as representatives of that vast body of stories handed down from earlier generations by word of mouth and then by collectors, editors, and/or translators which includes representation from any and all cultures and which represents the want and need fulfillments of various peoples. For this age, these should be selected carefully and used only in a simple form, depict healthful content, and be represented through psychologically and socially acceptable characters;

6. *Chants, rhymes, verse, and poems* defined as those expressions possessing a definable rhythm, perhaps rhyme, and usually a more intense way of telling about something. These may be classified under one or more of the preceding categories, but due to form, are given separate classification status. A brief discussion of haiku and of Mother Goose will be included in this category.

---

*It is sometimes useful to distinguish between picture and picture-story books.

THE PICTURE BOOK AND THE PICTURE-STORY BOOK

Picture books of our present period are usually colorful, clear as to subject, varied as to size, and of a wide span of content. They range from the clear pink, blues, and yellows of Françoise[6] to the predominance of brown, yellow, and orange found in the illustrations of Rojankovsky.[7] They catch graphically the feelings of a small boy in *Peter's Chair*[8] and the size and power of a fire truck in Zaffo's *The Big Book of Real Fire Engines.*[9] They range in size from the little volumes of Joan Walsh Anglund[10] to Bemelman's original edition of *Madeline.*[11] Content, depicted in ways to catch the eye, adds information for further learning and delights the child as he ranges from *Little Blue and Little Yellow*[12] to *The Park Book*[13] and from *A Tree is Nice*[14] to *Goggles.*[15]

Due to the variety which confronts one, a few criteria should be emphasized. We remember that Jimmy can keep books with care at home, when they are his own, and thus may have a pop-up or stapled together book. However, even though some books may be used most often on an individual basis, our major concern is for use by numbers of children in classes or groups. It is necessary to remember that although Jon and Mae each choose fine books, which vary greatly, there are certain standards which do underlie the appraisal of each specific book.

The *picture book* and *picture-story book* should illustrate its own major emphasis—namely, present a series of pictorial focal points. If the book is about a boy, he or his major concerns should be central in most of the illustrations so that attention is kept focussed on him. He is the unifying character, and other things should revolve around him. On each page, a center of interest should be the focus of the illustration. Although one cannot but welcome experiments with form and color, the author has found that most preschoolers want faces, especially eyes and mouths, on their people and animals. They respond to clarity and not to too much detail. They find little appeal in pictures that are too impressionistic. This does not mean that many details are necessary, but that the most familiar indications of a boy or a dog or cow or car should be depicted.

Many picture books invite participation, especially alphabet and counting books. No illustration should be so cluttered that it is confusing. Alphabet and counting books are especially prone to have too much on a page. Here it is especially important that the letter or number and the objects for which it is intended be especially clear. If "U" is for umbrella, then that, and not the drops of rain or the little girl holding it, should be central. If the picture is intended for a discussion of a rainy day scene, then the letter "U" had best be omitted.

Jon, age four, is going through a large book at a fairly rapid rate. He stops, smiles, and says, "Here. Here is—the big duck. I saw it. I saw it at the zoo. No babies." Excitedly, Jon was pointing at the picture of Mrs. Mallard leading her offspring into the public garden in *Make Way for Ducklings.*[16] Jon was adding to his learning experiences. The duck he had observed in the zoo reminded him of the one he had already seen in Robert McCloskey's book. Association and confirmation are learning experiences. At the same time, little Ben, who usually said but little, burst out with, "That's me. See." He pointed to Clancy, the cop, a few pages later in the book. "Yeah, I'm a cop, too," said Tony, who had come to the book table just in time to see the picture. "Come on, Ben, we'll look for bad people," he added. Ben slowly followed him away from the table. To Ben, identification with the policeman's picture had given him an ego-boost. To Tony, the picture was a suggestion. In each case, the clarity of the illustration added to the child's learning. For instance, in the picture of Mrs. Mallard's entrance into the Public Garden, the people are way to the left. The story is about Mrs. Mallard and her ducklings and they are the center of interest here. Clancy is important to Mrs. Mallard and is clearly illustrated.

If it depicts a story, the picture book should present its central theme continuously and not interject, parenthetically, an illustration of what someone is dreaming of or thinking about because it usually breaks the pictorial continuity and confuses a young child. Captions should be clear and very short. The children will make the association with the picture, and the caption should add to the entire experience. Simple, well-chosen, familiar vocabulary is best. If a word new to many children is included, then it should extend the child's informational experience a bit. For instance, "The fire truck is red. It is called a pumper." In this case, "pumper" is a new word, and its distinctions can be seen readily.

The caption picture book may contain a variety of subjects or carefully presented pictures about one area of information. If it is the former, the pictures should be clear and informative enough to be worthy of scrutiny. The child's vocabulary is important. Today, most children say "car." Therefore, "auto" may confuse them.

The written and pictorial content should be so interwoven that they move along as one. The pictures can carry the story and are in continuous sequence so that, although words may be read, a child could follow the story or experience from the illustrations.

The media and the size may differ considerably. However, the clarity of the communication is what counts.

Although children of ages three and four, especially, tend to prefer bright colors like those of Keats,[17] clarity of illustration like those of Françoise,[18] and clear outline like the figures of Lenski,[19] there are older children who like Wildsmith's *Circus*[20] which is not always clear to the younger child. Woodcuts, the use of sepia, and elaborate or technically different uses of color usually have no special appeal. The use of cotton, fur, and fuzzy material gives tactile pleasure, while the use of buttons and zippers gives challenge and satisfaction. Size which is clear, color which is bright, and media which looks real in a one dimensional sense are primary. Size in illustrations may not be in proportions which adults are accustomed to because the elements of major importance to a child can be, and often are, exaggerated. When the feather on a hat is important to the story, it is better to exaggerate the size of the feather than to reduce it to adult-conceived proportions.

The *Indoor Noisy Book*[21] meets the criterion of brightness. However, the partial pictures seem unsatisfactory to some children in the same way that the partial sofa used to confuse three- and four-year-olds earlier in *Angus and the Ducks*.[22] "Where is Muffin? Where do people sit?" have been asked of each, respectively. These questions indicate the child's desire for literal representation. If one presents something normally sat upon, then it should be depicted in such a manner that one can sit upon it. The charming and carefully depicted details in Barbara Cooney's[23] books delight the eye and seem to remain part of the whole scene which children recollect, especially at age five.

The beginning teacher should become acquainted with the divergence found in the form, color, and period of various illustrators for young children. The representative editions of Mother Goose, listed in the Appendix, give a cross section for these rhymes. A consideration of the following depict some of the variety to be found in other books: Marcia Brown, Virginia Burton, Barbara Cooney, Marguerite de Angeli, Rober Duvoisin, Marie Hall Ets, Françoise (Françoise Seignobosc), Wanda Gag, Ezra Jack Keats, Leonard Kessler, Lois Lenski, Leo Lionni, Robert McCloskey, Leo Politi, Feodor Rojankovsky, Maurice Sendak, Dr. Seuss (Theodor Geisel), Tasha Tudor, Leonard Weisgard, Brian Wildsmith, Eloise Wilkin, Taro Yashima, Ylla (photographs).

The format of the picture book should be sturdy—even more so than a story book. Children will look at it sequentially and will thumb through it in order to find a particular illustration. Thus the pages should be thick and easy to grasp. The cover should be attractive and colorful. It should give some indication of the content so the child can pick it out. Stitched pages last best, and the book should open flat and be able to remain open for all to see. Stapled, pasted, and spiral bindings are not serviceable for group use. Pop-up books are fun at home, but are short-lived when used by many children.

HERE AND NOW—EXPERIENTIAL

John Dewey published *Democracy and Education*[24] in 1916. Frequently said to be his seminal work, it is the book which most of his adherents quote as the source from which their own thinking received impetus or continued. William Heard Kilpatrick did the most to clarify and to illustrate how Dewey meant his Pragmatic or Progressivist philosophy to work. Many teachers in such schools as Ethical Culture, Horace Mann, Lincoln, Walden, the Little Red School House, the City and Country School, and the Bank Street School studied with one or the other of these men at Teachers College, Columbia University. Other educators were influenced by those who had studied with these men. Progressive Education, in the experimental sense, was in the air in various parts of New York City and other places in the twenties.

One teacher in the Harriet Johnson Nursery School, later the Bank Street School, now College, who caught and used Progressivism's tenets in her approach to children's learning was Lucy Sprague Mitchell. In her daily living with children, she exemplified in the twenties what many accept as commonplace today.

Miss Mitchell took her classes out for walks in Greenwich Village which is where the Bank Street School was then. When the children returned from their expeditions, they talked about the river, the wharves, the stores and fish-market, the horses and the cats that they had seen. Sometimes, she wrote these down word for word as the child told them. On other occasions, the account was a group story written down as told by various class members. Miss Mitchell kept some of these accounts just about as they were, changed others in part, and some, she wrote herself, in the same vein as those told by her children. This literature was first published in *The Here and Now Story Book*[25] and shortly after, more reached the public in *Another Here and Now Story Book*.[26] The stories are of the "here and now" as it was to the children at the time of the experiences related in their accounts. They described experiences in child fashion replete with full sensory effects. "Here and now"—experiential literature seems an apt term by which to classify such stories.

Little children aged three and four enjoy how Marni dresses in the morning, for instance, because they can identify completely with it. They, too, get up and dress! The four-year-old enjoys *The Story of Spot*.[27] The fences along which Spot "prowled, and yowled, and howled" are very real to many Greenwich Village residents. The "crickle and crackle" of the fire, the "pat, pat, pat" of the little boy and girl's feet, and the repetition all make this the kind of story which starts with the type of experience that certainly could happen to a child "here and now." Thus the listener finds such a story adds something to similar experiences which he has had or into which he could very easily project himself as having. Such simple, everyday kind of stories—accounts as some call them—make up these Here and Now story books.

Mitchell began a steady stream of such books. Some were close to the picture-story type, and others had fewer pictures and more story. Regardless, they began to fill the bookshelves and they are still coming. Early writers, whose books were in this here and now—experiential classification were Lois Lenski, whose Mr. Small series and Little Family group are still liked by three-, four-, and five-year-olds.[28,29] Examples like many of Margaret Wise Brown's books,[30] those of Charlotte Steiner[31] and Charlotte Zolotow[32] may be so classified. They utilize experience and call forth sensory participation. Muffin, for instance, may not be able to *see* with the bandage over his eye, but Muffin can *hear*. Children hear with Muffin and distinguish what can and cannot be heard.

These here and now—experiential books from a major portion of children's book lists, and the type of literature so-classified here is still fully utilized by the nursery, prekindergarten, and kindergarten teacher. Fire trucks, taxis, boys and girls, trees, and animals continue to find their way into books for young children and are seen and heard every day.

They exemplify Dewey's philosophy of utilizing current experience, interest, problem solving, and participation in learning. Animals are scientifically presented rather than phantasized. Seeds grow into proper plants, with care, rather than through the use of magic wands. Humans are humans and animals are animals and not humanized. Although some rather scornfully refer to the "pat, pat" school of literature as inadequate,[33] others sponsor it for the meaning they see that it has. It is psychologically sound because it deals with experience as the child does and social because it clarifies and interprets the world of people and things immediately surrounding preschool children. Chants and rhymes from these stories may be quoted with ease. Here and now—experiential literature helps simplify the environment. It interprets where Jim lives to Jim. Thus it is indispensable.

TRANSITIONAL

A usable classification for literature which bridges the stage between the Here and Now—Experiential and the Imaginative is the Transitional. There are stories which seem to be "here and now" and relate experiences which seem altogether possible until they introduce something just over the border, separating the real from the impossible. An animal seems to laugh or a goose speaks and does so in a way which does not interfere with the experiential context. For instance, "The big white swan came floating calmly down the stream. He . . . lifted the napkin . . . and looked in the basket, 'Oh, oh, oh! Won't Mother Swan be pleased with this nice lunch', said he."[34] Yet, with this, one realizes that he has gone beyond the here and now. This is a factor to note in distinguishing how relatively easy it is to move from one to the other. Fantasy is easy, as Seuss so well shows in *And To Think That I Saw it on Mulberry Street*,[35] and children can swing back and forth from one to the other with ease providing the transitions do not go beyond the possibilities of their projections. In *And To Think That I Saw It on Mulberry Street*, Marco moves from a horse to a reindeer and from a wagon to a sleigh with ease. The development is continuous and does not go beyond the imagination of a five-year-old. Now that the distinction has been made between the Here and Now—Experiential and the Transitional literature, the realm of fantasy and the imaginative literature, which it dominates, can be considered.

IMAGINATIVE

Betty told us that her parakeet flew about as she ate breakfast,

> He sat on the clock and then he came and sat on the back of my chair. I said,
> "Good morning, Bucky." He cocked his head and said "Hi, Betty." I said,
> "Eat some breakfast!" Bucky said, "I'll eat some breakfast with you, Betty."
> and—he did eat breakfast with me.

The listener takes the above quite literally up to Bucky's long sentence about eating breakfast. The transition moves the listener into a state which he knows is that of Betty's imagination.

Many stories start off in a way which leaves no doubt about what type they are. For instance, "Once there was a little old woman . . ." or "Once upon a time there were five little rabbits . . ." moves one to expect either a folk tale or a modern imaginative story. *The Night Kitchen*[36] is a modern fantasy or imaginative story as is Sendak's *Where the Wild Things Are.*[37] The imaginative story or book may begin with an everyday context and then move into the imaginative realm as does *Ask Mr. Bear* or begin in a setting which leads the listener to expect something beyond the here and now. A cumulative type of imaginative story or book often encourages the child to add something of his own.

The modern imaginative story should meet several criteria which are psychologically sound and within the bounds of stimulating literature. Over the years, the writer has found that these are

1. The story which purports to start where the child is now should not jump too abruptly away from its initial context;
2. The transition into fantasy should be gradual so that the child listener is moved from where he is to where the story is moving him in a way that follows (or could follow) the development of associations. Each association is stimulated by what immediately precedes it. This is admirably illustrated in *And To Think That I Saw It on Mulberry Street;*
3. The story which begins by assuming that you are elsewhere should commence in a way which makes this very clear. For instance, "In the great forest a little elephant is born";[38]
4. The story should not jump too abruptly from one realm to another. This, perhaps, is a positive restatement of one and two above;
5. The story or book should incorporate the child as participant or be one with which he can readily identify and/or participate;
6. The story or book should not expose him to fearful objects such as gruesome descriptions or perhaps illustrations of horribly depicted trolls which cause distress later.

Psychological well-being thrives on a supportive attitude. Thus acts not supportive of child ego, child safety, and child well-being should be eliminated. The monster, in one form or another, who eats little children can be frightening and diminishing. Jack, the Giant Killer, does not belong in the preschool, but he can be very supportive at an older age.

Remember that acceptance of a story with one's friends at eleven A.M. in prekindergarten does not preclude nightmares about ogres at eleven P.M.!

The imaginative story or book should depict happenings within the age range of interests, of humor, and of understanding of the three- through five-year-old. We have found that interests center about animals, people, and things that move in the environment. Moving things such as cranes, fire engines, and boats gain the interest and attention of this age level. Inasmuch as the three- through five-year-old's ability to distinguish the real from the unreal is being constantly clarified, imaginative stories should be introduced with careful consideration of just how well such distinctions between what *is* and what is *pretend* can be made. Inasmuch as the three- or four-year-old does not know that there are not likely to be four-footed wolves lurking off Broadway in Manhattan. the imaginative tale should not create them. It can create a subway which speaks, a mid-city talking dog, or a person with an unending supply of candy in his pocket because these are projections of the little child's here and now interests; they are psychologically sound and socially acceptable. Pursued fully, and associated with understandable wants and/or needs, the imaginative is an extension of the real. Mrs. Rabbit has four children, lives in a house, and goes off to market after she has put her market basket over her arm. *If* one wishes to present animals in humanized fashion and not in terms of science and nature, what better way to introduce an imaginative tale about rabbits![39]

Folktales are, of course, beyond everyday life experiences. They do, however, fall into a category of their own which is to be discussed next. Some of the criteria stated or inferred in the preceding paragraphs also pertain to folktales.

FOLKTALES

Authorities differ in their definitions of folktales and fairy tales. Some classify the overall group as the latter and subsume the former under it. Others try to classify them into two separate categories. Still others take the view subscribed to here. The writer agrees with those who hold that folktales are those stories handed down by word of mouth and eventually written down. They describe the problems, the dreams, and the aspirations of cultural groups. Within this plethora of possible kinds of tale is the fairy tale. It is one type of folktale.

There are two basic theories of the origin of folktales. One theory holds that they all originated from one source, probably in Asia Minor, and slowly spread forth into the rest of the world from there. The other view maintains that inasmuch as each cultural group has similarities because people have general needs, wants, and interests in common, the tales do tend to be alike as to theme. The particular theme is expressed in terms of the cultural context, and thus the Cinderella type varies as to background. It may be the French glass slipper version or "Little Burnt Face" which expresses the general desire for "a good marriage," specifically, in terms of the American Indian.

The latter theory seems most acceptable. Psychologists and psychiatrists have long debated over the possibilities of fulfillment and/or the sublimation of man's deepest drives as well as his everyday manifestations of them. In most cultures, striving to excel is important, a good marriage is sought, wealth has its place, and virtue is often rewarded. There is nothing uncommon here. Add the cultural context, the beliefs—often superstitions—of the group, and the realization that the travelling tellers entertained the poor as well as the courts and told about what they saw and heard. Also, remember that many tales arose among the peasantry and remained within the milieu of the hard working poor. They served as explainers and/or purveyors of solace. Thus you have a psycho-social basis. For instance, some kind of helper is often relied upon and, in terms of the culture, thomtes and trolls abide in Scandinavia, leprechauns and banshees in Ireland, or the Golem in the Warsaw ghetto. The wish or prophecy can't be fulfilled under ordinary circumstances, but the needs, hopes, and desires are there. Means are necessary to achieve ends in fantasy and as explanations, and so magic means are brought to bear.

Many teachers do not use any folktales because they are unreal today, are often cruel, and seem unfitted to a scientific age. Others point to the fears that can be aroused, to the trickery which prevails, and to the unloving portraits of stepparents. They did precede present day psychological understanding and thus perpetrate unacceptable acts frequently.

While the preceding paragraph is true and must be recognized clearly, there are a few simple folktales which can be used with three-, four-, and five-year-olds—especially the latter two ages. The types of simple folktales which after careful scrutiny may be acceptable usually belong in the following classifications: (a) simple talking animal; (b) cumulative or accumulative; (c) *pourquoi* tales; (d) humorous tales. A few suggestions about each follow.

Children should become well acquainted with animals as they really are. Simple scientific learning experiences should be part of their daily living. However, there is no reason not to tell *The Little Red Hen.*[10] If real hens are seen, it is evident that they do certain things. However, it is fun to hear a pretend story. Some of these contain simple social-ethical values which can be understood. Some animals talk to each other, and some talk to people in the tales handed down to us. With careful selection, there is no reason not to include *some* talking animal stories.

The (ac) cumulative tale almost tells us how it was created. Tellers added to it, as it was told and retold, and so the resulting versions differ. The cumulative tale invites participation, frequently has catchy rhymes, and often presents a fun sequence. *The Rabbit Who Was Afraid*[41] is not too frightening for most five-year-olds, especially as the lion takes the rabbit back "to see how large a crack it is." The children know from the beginning and so when the coconut is discovered, the children who are "in the know" often identify with the lion and nod vigorously when he says, "What a foolish, foolish rabbit you are." When *The Gingerbread Boy*[42] is told for the first time, it is wise to get a cookie gingerbread boy from the bakery. It can be introduced before the story is begun and then shared with the children after the fox consumes the one in the story. This keeps the gingerbread on a cake rather than a human level.

Most *pourquoi* tales are best for six-, seven-, and eight-year-olds. Yet, telling *Why the Bear Has a Stumpy Tail*[43] is a good yarn! Five-year-olds are able to connect cause and effect in a number of ways and can feel superior to the bear. When you say that this is how some people *think* that this happened, it adds to story fun.

Some tales are funny and five-year-olds can appreciate them. *The Musicians of Bremen,*[44] for instance, is funny if the children are mature enough. Children's humor does develop. For example, the author has found that *Susie Mariar*[45] meets with a rather expressionless response and rather literal acceptance by three- and young four-year-olds but that by four-year-olds turning five and five-year-olds, it is frequently considered uproariously funny!

To some, this will seem to be a rather restricted use of folktales, but Cinderella dreams of wealthy princes, the magic of mirrors on the wall, the cruelty of stepmothers and of woodcutters, the demands of Rumpelstiltskin, and the swaggerings of giants simply have no place in preschool groups. In almost any group, some children are insecure and fear can be provoked. In all groups, the reality of present day living experience should be predominant with only carefully guided trips into the other world of the folktale. Later, folktales will be cherished!

In many cases, the imitation folktale is preferable. While all tales are in collections bearing the name of the collector, they are often literal translations of the tale as originally discovered. The Grimm Brothers, for instance, were concerned with linguistics and wrote out the tales later. Then, they were read to children. Andersen did three things: the literal setting down of the tales, the refurbishing of some originals, making up tales. However, someone in Wanda Gag's category of the imitation folktale writer, uses a folktale style beginning with "Once there was . . ." and continues to hold interest with *Millions of Cats.*[46] Watty Piper's *The Little Engine That Could*[47] is another example of a popular imitation folktale.

As was mentioned above, one of the ways to transfer wonder to the young is through the chant or rhyme used in the tale.* Children chant frequently. Let's consider this next.

*See also chapter 6.

CHANTS, RHYMES, VERSE, AND POEMS

The baby chants most often in a definite rhythm. The three-year-old may do this, too, but is likely to use words in his rhythmic repetition. "Tum, tum, bum, bum, car go, car go." At four, he may repeat a word, the sound of which he likes, over and over. One little boy walked about a prekindergarten saying "Millionaire, millionaire" over and over. He said it in a definite rhythm 1-11-. He did not know what a millionaire was, but was enjoying the sound and rhythm of it. After his teacher read *Millions of Cats*, he changed his chant to "Hundreds and millions and millions and billions," and repeated this many times.

Expression of feeling is frequently rhythmic if there is no interference. It is creative but may make little or no sense to the adult. It is a rhythmic playing with sounds, syllables, and words. It is feeling objectified outward and may be repeated.[48], [49]

The teacher can note these chants, write them down, if necessary, and either repeat them with the child then or wait until the group is together. Then the chant may be repeated for everyone to join and perhaps with a clapping or drum accompaniment. It becomes the group's own created chant.

Many simple folktales contain chants such as, "On little drummikin, tum, tum, too."* The simple repetition of the accumulative tale is often chanted, too. "I've run away from the little old woman, I've run away from the little old man, and I can run away from you, I can, I can."* *The Little Engine That Could* seems most often remembered for the "I think I can, I think I can" which children delight in repeating. *The Big Tall Indian*, although in *Singing Time*,[50] is practically a chant, and one which lends itself readily to four-year-old learning.

Rhymes are usually longer and they make some sense. "Auto, auto, may I have a ride"[51] is a simple rhyme and is often chanted. In most such rhymes, children of ages three, four, and five are not concerned with the end as a rhyme, but with the rhythm. However, the fact that "hen" rhymes with "ten" encourages participation on the part of some children. Most teachers make up rhymes of this sort for use with their classes. For instance,

> "Snow flakes, snow flakes
> Falling all around,
> Soft and white, they're
> Cov'ring all the ground."

Teachers' rhymes, children's rhymes, and those of collaborated authorship can make a useful collection. Children like to repeat "my" rhyme and Tony's rhyme. These are a means to greater creativity too.

---

*See "The Story of Lambikin" in Bailey, *Once Upon a Time Animal Stories*.
**See "The Ginger Man" in Bryant, *Best Stories to Tell Children*.

Mother Goose presents the teacher with a number of choices. Which edition? Which rhymes shall be used? Briefly, while Arbuthnot is correct in saying that the rhymes possess variety, musical quality, action, story interest, humor, and illustrations which "bedeck his favorite book,"[52] and Huck and Kuhn are right when they state that "much of the appeal of Mother Goose is in the varied language pattern; the rhythm and rhyme of the verses; the alliteration . . . ," the viewpoint of this author is that the rhymes must be selected with extreme care, if used at all. The six points for evaluation as presented by Huck and Kuhn are useful. These are: consideration of coverage, the many and varied illustrations available, the period, the setting, the arrangement, the format.[53] We agree that children do enjoy *Jack and Jill,* but, should Miss Muffet be depicted as afraid of a spider? What about repeating, "What a naughty boy was that, To drown poor pussy cat?" Although I am well aware of the supposed origin of *Ding Dong Bell, Little Boy Blue,* and many other rhymes, the three-, four-, and five-year-old is not aware of the period of Henry VIII. He takes these for what they are and for what they say.

Mother Goose rhymes in groups of mid-socioeconomic level are fine to bring a group together during the first days of school because so many children know them. In other groups, they are unknown. The rhythm is catchy, the repetition is helpful, but many are completely meaningless to today's children. A high percentage of Mother Goose rhymes are frightening, cruel, and unrelated to present day living. The teacher and student are concerned about psychology and yet sentimental over Mother Goose rhymes! If use is to be made of them, *look* at the rhyme *objectively, evaluate* it in terms of *sociopsychological implications,* and then decide whether or not to use it. A more recent circle of criticism has grown up as a result of the Women's Liberation Movement. Miss Muffet is fighting back, and many women resent the implications and denigrating roles in which many females are pictured.*

Lear's Nonsense Alphabet[54] is fun. Mature five-year-olds often like to make up their own nonsense after hearing Lear's. For instance, "B is for Bobby. Boom, boom Bobby."

Dorothy Baruch's simple verses are enjoyed.[55] While all verse need not rhyme, many children seem to find it easier to learn those that do.

A simple poem like Polly Boyden's *Mud*[56] or Tippett's *Sh*[37] is fun, easy to say, and readily repeated. Criteria for poetry and verse should include (a) simplicity, (b) meaning, (c) ease in repeating, (d) be not too far removed from present experience. Judging by these criteria, one can decide what to include from the works of Robert Louis Stevenson, for instance. The discussion under the heading Here and Now—Experiential literature is apt here, too.** Rhymes, verse, and poems should clarify and extend experience, be easy to say, and be relevant to the child today.***

---

*See Appendix 3, Mother Goose Collections.
**See pages 89-91.
***See Appendix 3.

"Squat frog in noon sun
Silent, bulging eyes staring
Splash, fly's disaster!"

"Sparkling white sea gull
Spiral down the air current
Now, snatch the swift fish."[58]

With some definition—disaster, spiral, and air current—many five-year-olds enjoy hearing and repeating simple Haiku. Haiku fascinates older children, who like to try its pattern and form. A description in five syllables, painting a mood in seven, and finishing in five more is a verbal challenge. Some five-year-olds, especially those possessing a fine command of English, enjoy hearing these verses. "Chicken" and "Frog," for instance, in a related setting, from *In A Spring Garden*[59] frequently appeal to such children and it is wise for the teacher to be aware of this verse form. Unless there is genuine interest, however, these are best left for early and mid-grades.

ETHNICITY

Ezra Jack Keats has presented black children in simple situations which appeal to preschool children. *The Snowy Day*, for example, appeals to all children. Some of the verse in *Spin a Soft Black Song*[60] is easy for young children to relate to, regardless of color. We need many more books, poems, and verse in which various minority groups are presented as everyday children living their lives in our present culture. We must continue a growing trend to illustrate books with pictures showing children of mixed background in group pictures. Preschool is where this must be part of everyday life and regular literature.*

Creativity has been considered, briefly, in relation to communication—both nonverbal and verbal—and where it was appropriate in the discussion of literature. However, as a basic component in preschool education, it will receive justifiable attention in the next chapter.

Notes

1. The reader is urged to study Grace K. Pratt-Butler, *Let Them Write Creatively* (Columbus, Ohio: Charles E. Merrill Publishing Co., 1973), especially Chapters I and II for a discussion of this theory and the accompanying practice.

2. Pratt-Butler, *Let Them Write Creatively*, p. 8.

*See Appendix 3, Books.

3. Ibid., pp. 21-28.

4. Marjorie Flack, *Ask Mr. Bear* (New York: The Macmillan Co., 1932).

5. Ezra Jack Keats, *The Snowy Day* (New York: The Viking Press, 1963).

6. Françoise, *The Gay ABC* (New York: Charles Scribner's Sons, 1938).

7. Feodor Rojankovsky, *The Tall Book of Mother Goose* (New York: Artists and Writers Guild, 1942).

8. Ezra Jack Keats, *Peter's Chair* (New York: Harper and Row, 1967).

9. George Zaffo, *The Big Book of Real Fire Engines* (New York: Grosset and Dunlap, 1949).

10. Joan Walsh Anglund, *A Friend is Someone Who Likes You* (New York: Harcourt, 1958).

11. Ludwig Bemelmans, *Madeline* (New York: The Viking Press, 1939).

12. Leo Lionni, *Little Blue and Little Yellow* (New York: Obolensky, 1959).

13. Charlotte Zolotow, *The Park Book* (New York: Harper and Brothers, 1944).

14. Janice May Udry, *A Tree is Nice* (New York: Harper and Row, 1957).

15. Ezra Jack Keats, *Goggles* (Toronto: The Macmillan Co., 1969).

16. Robert McCloskey, *Make Way for Ducklings* (New York: The Viking Press, 1941).

17. Ezra Jack Keats, *The Snowy Day.*

18. Françoise, *The Gay ABC.*

19. Lois Lenski, *Papa Small* (New York: Walck, 1951).

20. Brian Wildsmith, *Brian Wildsmith's Circus* (New York: Franklin Watts, 1970).

21. Margaret Wise Brown, *The Indoor Noisy Book* (New York: Harper and Row, 1942).

22. Marjorie Flack, *Angus and the Ducks* (New York: Doubleday, 1930).

23. Barbara Cooney, *Chanticleer and the Fox* (New York: Thomas Y. Crowell, 1958).

24. John Dewey, *Democracy and Education* (New York: The Macmillan Co., 1916).

25. Lucy Sprague Mitchell, *Here and Now Story Book* (New York: E. P. Dutton and Co., Inc., 1921).

26. Lucy Sprague Mitchell, *Another Here and Now Story Book* (New York: E. P. Dutton, 1937).

27. Mitchell, *Here and Now Story Book.*

28. Lois Lenski, *Cowboy Small* (New York: Henry Walck, 1949).

29. Lois Lenski, *Davy's Day* (New York: Henry Walck, 1943).

30. Margaret Wise Brown, *The Country Noisy Book* (New York: Harper and Row, 1940).

31. Charlotte Steiner, *Kiki and Mufty* (New York: Doubleday and Co., 1943).

32. Charlotte Zolotow, *The Park Book* (New York: Harper and Brothers, 1944).

33. May Hill Arbuthnot, *Children and Books* (Fairlawn, New Jersey: Scott, Foresman and Co., 1957), p. 393.

34. Margery Clark, "The Picnic Basket" from *The Poppy Seed Cakes* (New York: Doubleday and Co., Inc., 1924).

35. Dr. Seuss (Theodor Geisel), *And To Think That I Saw It on Mulberry Street* (New York: Vanguard Press, 1937).

36. Maurice Sendak, *The Night Kitchen* (New York: Harper and Row, Publishers, 1970).

37. Maurice Sendak, *Where the Wild Things Are* (New York: Harper and Row, Publishers, 1963).

38. Jean De Brunhoff, *The Story of Babar, the Little Elephant* (New York: Random House, 1937).

39. Beatrix Potter, *The Tale of Peter Rabbit* (New York: Frederick Warne, 1902).

40. *The Little Red Hen* (Racine: A Whitman Book, 1963).

41. Carolyn Sherwin Bailey, "The Rabbit Who Was Afraid" in *Once Upon a Time Animal Stories* (Springfield, Mass.: Milton Bradley Co., 1920), pp. 100-105.

42. "The Gingerbread Man" in S. Bryant, *Best Stories to Tell Children* (Boston: Houghton Mifflin, 1912).

43. "Why the Bear Has a Stumpy Tail" in Carolyn S. Bailey, *Once Upon a Time Animal Stories* (Springfield, Mass.: Milton Bradley Co., 1920).

44. "The Musicians of Bremen" in Jacob and Wilhelm Grimm, *The Traveling Musicians* (New York: Harcourt, 1955).

45. Lois Lenski, *Susie Mariar* (New York: Henry Z. Walck, 1967).

46. Wanda Gag, *Millions of Cats* (New York: Coward McCann, 1928).

47. Watty Piper, *The Little Engine That Could* (New York: Platt and Munk Co., 1930 and 1954).

48. Pratt-Butler, *Let Them Write Creatively.*

49. Grace K. Pratt, "Whoopee, I'm a Tree" *Elementary English* (October 1966).

50. Satis Coleman and Alice Thorn, *Singing Time* (New York: The John Day Co., Inc., 1929).

51. Mitchell, *Here and Now Story Book.*

52. Arbuthnot, *Children and Books,* pp. 81-87.

53. Charlotte Huck and Doris Kuhn, *Children's Literature in the Elementary School* (New York: Holt, Rinehart and Winston, Inc., 1961), p. 104.

54. Edward Lear, *Nonsense Books* (Boston: Little Brown and Co., 1934).

55. Dorothy Baruch, *I Would Like to be a Pony and Other Wishes* (New York: Harper and Row, 1959).

56. Polly Chase Boyden, "Mud" in May Hill Arbuthnot, *Time for Poetry* (Fairlawn, New Jersey: Scott, Foresman 1952).

57. James Tippett, "Sh" in *I Live in a City* (New York: Harper and Row, 1927).

58. Grace K. Pratt-Butler, Unpublished Haiku.

59. Richard Lewis, ed., *In a Spring Garden* (New York: The Dial Press, 1965).

60. Nikki Giovanni, *Spin a Soft Black Song* (New York: Hill and Wang, Inc., 1971).

CHAPTER 6

Creative Expression

FEELING

Feeling is awareness which may be observed in the expressed behavior of young children. It may be separate from or interwoven with overt sensory responses. Warm milk relaxes Mary, and she smiles as she feels more secure. The bunny is soft and Mike pats him, murmuring, "Fur, fur." Pete claps two blocks together expressing the march rhythm his feet pound out. He appears to feel the rhythm with his whole body as he expresses a definite patterned beat. His expression is overt, and thus he is communicating outwardly what he feels inwardly.

The baby develops from his head and bodily axis downward and outward to his extremities. The cold or frightened three-year-old will pull in and seek to shrink into himself or to get as tightly up to the adult as possible. However, when he feels happy he skips on one foot, jumps, hops, or trots—his expression of feeling is turned outward. In a sense, he appears to be expanding all over.

Secure children tend to express their feelings externally. In a relaxed situation they develop a pattern that is repeated in basic form. The pattern is the child's own. Some children repeat over and over as though to assure themselves that it is their own. In general, Molly and Mona have like patterns of response. Given freedom to develop, Molly's specific pattern differs from Mona's particular mode of expressing her way of doing. Individual embellishments are added to the general pattern developed by each child. Initial feelings quickly become habits, patterns, creative expressions communicated outwardly as children feed themselves, build with blocks, or "fly" about the room to the music coming from the record player.

*A few handy scarves can add to the joy of flying.
(Courtesy Ethical Culture Schools, New York City
and Celeste Muschel.)*

Nicky and Nora in the four-year-old group liked to play the piano. Nicky's
exuberance brought forth loud bangs. He was expressing definite feeling. Nora
kept saying, "Bang softly Nicky." Nora liked to tap the keys softly. She would
smile and say, "My baby's sleeping." Nora would often cradle a doll in her
arms. Then she would walk over to the piano, lay the doll down, and then
"play" and repeat the phrase over and over. It became more rhythmic, and she
usually nodded her head in time to her own rhythm.

Tomas reached over and softly patted Clarida's hair. "Hair, hair," he
chanted. At age three-and-a-half, he was not only reaching out to another and
enjoying the texture of her hair, but he was also expressing some feeling in his
limited English. The teacher clapped as he said it and joined him, "Hair, hair,
Clarida's hair. Hair, hair, pretty hair, nice." He had changed his rhythm as
he added the words. "Clarida's" was emphasized on the second syllable, and
the beat accompanying "pretty" was shortened on the last syllable. Tomas repeated this six times. Going to the instrument shelf, he took a tomtom and beat
the same rhythm as he smiled. He stopped chanting but was emphatic as he beat
the rhythm on the tomtom. Tomas was expressing his feeling about Clarida's
hair. His feeling was expressed rhythmically. It was his own pattern objectified
in his clapping and beating the tomtom. Given a less alert teacher he might
have done no more than pull Clarida's hair! The teacher imitated Tomas'
rhythm. It was his pattern. Repetition added to his confidence and the tomtom
accentuated his pattern. His feeling was clearly objectified.

Rhythmic Responses to Feeling*

External responses are natural to young children. At ages three, four, and five, they are frequently accompanied by overt movement. Close observation reveals an individual rhythmic pattern as we have seen above. The rhythmic expression of each is *his* particularization of the general overt response. Thus, each five-year-old may skip, but the variations of expression can be equated to the number of children skipping. Danny still skips with his right foot only but does this freely with a sweeping motion as he moves his left foot. Tina skips lightly tossing her arms into the air, while Alan skips precisely, his hands moving slightly. Unless someone says, "You must skip this way," each child can establish his rhythmic expression. Granting that these may develop more fully, Tina and Alan will, if not given someone else's model, each tend to build on his own rhythmic expression as he has created it up to this time. While this special kind of expression may be the developing potentiality toward far greater creativity for Tina but not Alan, each should be encouraged to continue to respond in his *own* way. Each has a right to his own response providing it is neither detrimental to that of another nor restrictive to his own development. The expressed response is the objectification of each child's feeling.

Feeling Communicated

Children's feelings when communicated in overt behavior express the children's individuality. In a certain special way, a child is creating himself. He tends to place in overt pattern what his inner feelings are.

The modes of creative expression are varied and numerous. Here are a few instances.

Chanting is a typical expression which often follows or accompanies nonverbal expression. While Jimmy's

"Bang, bang,
Bangetty, bang.
Bang, bang,
Bangetty, bang."

may sound like meaningless repetition, it usually has a definite rhythm. Pete, Tim, and Joan quickly join—later others may! The teacher can join in with clapping, rhythm sticks, or drums. Children building with blocks or using clay frequently initiate such chanting, which may arise at any time.

Al could never put the blocks away at clean-up time without tapping them together in rhythm. Miss Lawrence frequently used Al and his blocks to initi-

---

*Responses through language have been considered more fully in chapter 5. This is combined with dramatic play and with dramatization as well as nonverbal and verbal response.

ate a rhythms session. If she did not, other children did. With a record player and a record collection available on a convenient shelf, rhythmic activity becomes an integral part of dramatic play, as well as of classroom living in general.

Elise is putting the guinea pig back into his cage. She pats him gently as she says,

> "Go to sleep,
> Go to sleep,
> Piggy, piggy, Joe,
> Go to sleep."

Then running to the record player, "I'll just play you a sleep song, Little Joe."

The observant teacher reminded Elise, and the other children, of this later. Then, she said, "Here's another sleep song." She sang, "The Animals Go to Sleep."[1]

Although all rhythmic and musical activity need not be so initiated, a high percentage of rhythms, rhythm instrument playing, and songs can grow right out of what the children are, or were, doing. Then it extends the experience, adds breadth to the activity, and increases what the children are learning; it is creative learning.*

The child will use almost anything handy to augment his expression. However, various media are designed especially for child use.

MEDIA FOR EXPRESSION

SIMPLE RHYTHMS AND MUSICAL ACTIVITIES

Rhythm sticks are easy to hold and to find out how to hit together. Most three-year-olds are successful after a few attempts. The experimental hitting usually develops rather quickly into a pattern. Given music to accompany this, the child happily hits the sticks with increasing skill. He may then experiment more fully. Jingle sticks, bowl drums or tomtoms, various types of bells, and triangles should be accessible. By age four the child is usually adept at moving while beating rhythm sticks and by age five may begin to orchestrate a simple tune such as *Frere Jacques*.[2] In the latter case, sticks may play the first two measures, triangles the third and fourth, and drums the last.

This approach starts with the child. He feels and plays. Once he has established some pattern—after various experiments—he then begins to think about his overt expressions of feeling. At this time he can decide how to coordinate his playing with that of his friends or that of his teacher.

*See also chapter 5.

This is the direct opposite of a teacher-dominated session, when the teacher says, "Here are the instruments. Now we will all play a march." There are times for accompanying the teacher's playing, but these should neither be the only time for playing the rhythm instruments nor be completely dependent upon the teacher's choices. The teacher needs to try to catch the child's rhythm. Her accompaniment to the child's expression of his overtly turned feeling keeps his focus on his feeling. The accompaniment can be on the piano, with the drum, or with rhythm sticks, or it may be just with one's hands or arms.

There may well be times—and there should be—when the teacher says, "Let's listen and hear what the music is asking us to do." This helps children distinguish, "It's asking us to run fast," from "It's asking us to go to sleep." Such times can be interspersed with child-initiated overt expressions of feeling. By this means, the teacher is extending the breadth of possible responses.

Responses do vary, and some children seem unable to respond freely at first. For instance, there may be a Ruthy! Whatever anyone does, whatever anyone hears, Ruthy aged five, skips with one foot. Fast, slow, loud or soft—Ruthy skips. Ruthy's hearing was fine although some children, who can't hear, often do re-act as Ruthy did. Ruthy had been praised when she learned to skip with one foot during the preceding year in prekindergarten. The praise made Ruthy glow! In her life, there had been little praise. She needed praise for other things, and her kindergarten teacher gave her this. She also had Ruthy listen and move her hand with slow music. Then they walked to slow music. Ruthy began to find other bodily movements possible. "Rowing" on the floor with Rita helped her, too.

A varied record collection should be available to the children. Favorites can be marked with a tiny picture so the choice is made more easily. A small number for selection is best to begin with at the three-year-old level. This can be added to, and unused records can be removed for a period of time. Four-year-olds need more variety and five-year-olds can utilize an extensive collection. It is wisest to have fifteen or twenty available at a time, to bring out additional records occasionally, and to remove the less popular ones for a few weeks.

Rhythm instruments can be kept near the records. There should be enough rhythm sticks for at least half of a three-year-old group with bells, jingle sticks, triangles, cymbals (to be struck separately), and drums enough to allow a total of at least three or four more items than the total number of children. Thus, eighteen or twenty playable instruments should be accessible for fourteen to sixteen children. All will not play together often until the fourth year. But children need to experiment and to play out how they feel alone and in small groups. By the time they approach age four, there can be occasional short times for all to play together. If a teacher observes four children beating sticks and a triangle and marching, she can accompany them. This may bring most, or all, of the others to the group. They may all join together and march for five minutes. The teacher may continue this group-initiated rhythm and music session if interest is high.

As children mature, they may ask for "bird music." Their expressed desire is usually the result of a feeling which becomes intensified. Thus there are occasions when children request some particular music. There are frequent rhythm and music sessions initiated spontaneously by the children which may be during the work-play time, for instance. There also are times initiated by the teacher which are frequently in conjunction with singing and stories. Whereas these "music times" are likely to last five minutes for three-year-olds, they may extend to twenty-five minutes by five years of age.

Rhythms and the use of rhythm instruments have been discussed as part of the overt expression of feeling. Such activity is usually part of general rhythmic and music expression which does, of course, include singing.

The three-year-old may chant, "Janie goes boom, boom. Janie goes boom, boom," over and over. The alert teacher will clap the rhythm and chant with Janie. She may repeat Janie's song later. Others may join. What do you do Mikey may bring "Mikey goes choo choo, Mikey goes choo choo." This chant may include four or five children before it ends for that day.

Elissa, age four, was swinging. Her teacher pushed her a time or two and sang in rhythm to the swing. "Swinging, swinging, Elissa goes up, Elissa goes down."[3] Later, when the group had gathered together just before lunch, Miss Albert sang "the song I sang to Elissa when she was swinging." Thus songs are most frequently introduced and related to an activity. When the first snowflakes fall, the teacher may sing a snow song. Thus, chanting and singing come when they are a natural part of preschool living.

The shy three-year-old may happily follow the teacher and some children when the teacher leads the group around the room singing, "Let's Go Walking."[4] This kind of activity is important for getting shy children to participate.

Needless to say, the teacher needs to know a variety of simple songs which she can sing readily when the situation is appropriate. After a few years, the average teacher finds that she possesses a broad repertoire and that she has added to it from all sorts of sources. Simple songs mean, for the most part, short and with easy notation. For example, most children can sing from sol to mi to do, but not easily from ti to fa to do! Songs include those about animals, children, people doing things, and they are usually action-oriented in what they say. Thus, they sometimes encourage children to move without a word being said about it.

The teacher can introduce a song by singing it. After it has been discussed, she can sing it again. Then, she can say the words and invite the children to join in singing it. Short songs with simple repetition are easiest, although a long song with a simple tune and repetition can be sung gustily by five-year-olds. The song may be introduced because it is related to the immediate expressed interests of all or some of the group because the teacher believes that it will extend experience, or it may be introduced to the whole group after she has sung it to a child or a small group earlier in the day.

Clapping is appropriate accompaniment to many songs. The piano, auto harp, or a guitar accompaniment is helpful with many of them. At the piano, it is frequently easier for the children to learn if the teacher plays the tune first with the right hand only and adds a chord accompaniment later. For the action type of song, the teacher can move about singing with the children following. This is especially helpful for three-year-olds who may be more hesitant about participating. Response songs usually delight young children, whether or not they are able to sing their response. Rhythm instruments are sometimes the best accompaniment. The teacher must be careful to sing softly enough to hear the children and should pitch her voice high because the children's voices are high.

It is important to remember that children show individual differences in musical activities as well as in other areas. Rena sang *Home on the Range,* at four, in perfect tune while Dick at five was whispering huskily whenever the kindergarten sang together. However, Dick fully appreciated the record player and was often to be found listening intently to it.

As we have indicated, singing and rhythmic activity go together. And if we consider singing and rhythmic movement to be natural expression, we find that they are central or peripheral many times during a school day and are accepted as part of daily living.*

PAINT, FINGER PAINT, AND CLAY

Paint, finger paint, and clay should be readily accessible to the four- and five-year-old. Once three-year-olds are accustomed to the daily routines and understand such simple rules as wiping your brush on the side of the jar, wearing a smock or apron when finger painting, and keeping the clay on the clay board or oilcloth, these materials should be available.

An easel with large sheets of newsprint, large mouth jars or cans securely held in the easel tray, and large brushes—either blunt or pointed at the end—are inviting. At first the three-year-old manipulates paint onto paper. As he experiments, his "mess" of several colors begins to clarify itself and colors are separated, lines may be made with precision, and dots can appear. His feelings are being expressed and his lines may swirl gaily and alone. For instance, the aggression which he can't turn onto his father becomes "bang, bang, bang" as he taps the brush vigorously each time. The new song partially remembered, such as "Swinging, Swinging," is chanted as the long swirl goes downward and

---

*Singing also is considered in chapter 5; see also Appendix 3, Music.

the loop at the end is done in rhythm to the chant. Usually, between three-and-a-half and four, Diana gazes at her manipulative swirls and remarks, "These are my stairs at home." Thus Diana's work has entered the symbolic stage. The marks themselves symbolize something about which she has strong feeling.*

The next, and more realistic stage will be when Dickie says decisively, "I'll paint my father and his car." His creation of his father varies in numerous ways in terms of what his self interests are. If neckties are of strong significance, he may paint them large and bold, thus indicating the significance attached to them. While Tom makes large neckties, for instance, he may neglect shoes. The flower may be larger than the apartment house, if it is the center of interest. Tim is expressing his feeling about that flower and that house. It is usually a specific house even though Tim may refer to it as "a house." He is more likely to be expressing how he feels about *my* house or *Aunt Rose's* house. As he paints things and when he decides what he will paint before he begins, the child's feelings become more objectified. "I will paint the rain" means that I have a feeling about the rain. (I can't go into the playground). In saying what he will paint, John has objectified his feelings. He may then think about just how best to paint what he is feeling.

It has been said that children begin manipulating paint on paper or clay on a clay board. As they do so, the shape may remind them of an object and the symbol is named. Later, the child decides before he starts what he will paint and proceeds to paint a house. The latter is the beginning of the realistic stage. All children appear to go through these stages in their use of art media. However, feeling is involved in each stage. At the first stage, the child is expressing feeling with his pounding of clay or brushing of color. If he is feeling happy, his movements are free and less restricted. However, if he is aggressively upset they may be large and free, but with a hard impact. The anxious, timid, and apprehensive child cautiously puts one finger into the clay or makes a small mark with a paint brush. When he reaches the symbolic stage, an experience of pleasure leads to swirls and dots, and his feelings of the steady beat of the rain may be associated with this as he calls it, "Rain falling down". Now he has felt it, expressed it, and named it. The spots on the paper become objects to him. Then he thinks and feels as he reacts to his own objects. Thinking and feeling are combined when he says, "I'll paint my dog." This does not imply that from now on he will paint nothing but objects. Mathew, aged four-and-a-half, said, "I'll make me and my Daddy." He made recognizable figures. Looking at them he suddenly laughed and said, "They are happy. They had ice cream." At this point, he took yellow paint and obliterated the figures in masses of yellow and red. He turned to his teacher and said, "See they are all over happy. Ice cream makes you feel good."

---

*There are often intermediary stages between the manipulative and the symbolic, such as keeping the colors separate, painting stripes, etc.

"I am painting rain." (Courtesy Ethical Culture Schools, New York City and Celeste Muschel.)

The same general stages of expression are in evidence in a child's use of each of the media. Children need the freedom to try out and to explore. Their feelings become overt as they use materials. Their experiences add to the objectification which causes them to label the symbolic stage. The feeling is usually clearly objectified and combined with thinking reaction at the realistic stage. Once he expresses what he wants to paint or make in clay, the child's response is usually a combination of how he feels and what he thinks. "The snake is too skinny." John has the clay snake in front of him as he says it. He decided to make a snake, he made it, and now with the clay object before him he is judging it. When he remodels it, it will be due to his combined feeling-thinking responses to the clay object before him.

COLLAGE MAKING

Collage making usually begins as pasting a shiny paper or two onto a piece of paper. It tends to follow the same pattern—manipulative, symbolic, and then more realistic.

A child's feelings become overt as he uses materials. (Courtesy Ethical Culture Schools, New York City and Celeste Muschel.)

Parents are usually happy to bring or send things for the collage box. Smocks, old shirts, or pieces of material with a hole for the head are necessary to protect children's clothing. Pieces of oil cloth or plastic can be worn but tend to be hot. Procedures for washing one's self and for putting away and cleaning up materials are necessary. Several large sponges should be handy for the children to use.

WOODWORKING

The two-year-old pushes a piece of wood along the floor with satisfaction. Looking up, he says, "Car," and goes on his way. Movement is natural, Symbolization, too, is a stage of development. The baby pokes, pats, sucks, and shakes what he can reach. When he walks or crawls actively, he pushes things in front of him. At age two, the block is associated with car, while by age three, the child wants more semblance of a real car. Shiny objects for lights, wheels, and perhaps a round-ended peg for a driver have been added by most equipment companies serving this age level.

Also at age three, a mallet and peg bench, called by various names depending upon the manufacturer, are useful equipment. After some experience most three-year-olds are able to hit the pegs with the mallet. Arm coordination as well as hand-eye coordination functions better and better.

By age four, providing there has been plenty of opportunity to use peg bench and mallet or similar materials, the child is ready to hit large headed nails into a block of soft pine with a lightweight, large headed hammer. He has developed coordination and at the same time is demanding more real features in the materials used.

Most four-year-olds begin with the expression of a simple felt need. Two pieces of wood placed across each other are an airplane. An upright small piece of wood on a larger piece is a boat. At first the nail must be started for the child. As he grows more experienced, he can drive his own nail into the wood.

Soft pine scraps, shiny large headed nails, and the large hammer mentioned above are soon supplemented with a small (adult) crosscut saw, button molds, which serve as wheels, and dowel sticks. The teacher should have an awl in order to make a hole in the dowel stick. Dowel sticks are usually hard and the hole makes it easier to hammer in the nail. Water-based paint can be used if there is a real desire to paint the object.

By age five the child who has worked with wood for a year or more is quite adept at carrying through his plans with this medium. Small tables, chairs, and benches; boats of several types; trucks and wagons may be made. Screw eyes, washers, sandpaper, occasionally a brace and bit are additions to the workbench equipment. Nails of various sizes and occasionally screws, staples, small cleats are added. The child of age five needs guidance in keeping his preplanning down to proportions which he can carry out. Grandiose plans which require too much skill as well as long periods of time lead to frustration. At age five, shellac can be used to paint over poster paint. This prevents the color from rubbing off. With enough space and an adult who can be spared for this activity alone, experienced enough children can use regular paint.

Needless to say the workbench or work table must be firm and steady. A vise, preferably made as part of it, and drawer space are preferable. While a workbench and tools do require careful supervision of the girls and boys using them, they are excellent and worthwhile pieces of equipment. Wood lends itself to dimensional form and is superior to clay in that it is a firm, solid medium with definite texture. Sensory development, coordination, and expression objectified through a solid dimensional medium which encourages use make woodworking an important activity. The limits of expression through paint are overcome in wood. "I need a plane," said Tom. The four-year-old hammered a nail through two pieces of wood and was "zooming" around the room within ten minutes. He wanted it, made it, and used it. The shortness of the time span be-

By age five, the child who has worked with wood for a year or more is quite adept at carrying through her own plans. (Courtesy Ethical Culture Schools, New York City and Celeste Muschel.)

tween start and finish is typical of four-year-olds. The reaction the child has to the object he has created is interacted with on a physical plane. He may feel and think about what he has made, but this can be actively done with the physical object. "See my table," said Sue, "I'm going to eat my snack cookie off of it." Thus woodworking approaches block building in certain ways, especially in being dimensional, movable, and usable.

The teacher will find that scraps of soft wood are usually available for the asking or for a small amount from a lumber yard. Some schools have shops which have leftover scraps. Needless to say, the teacher must be skilled enough to encourage woodworking. Added experience on the part of the teacher may be necessary to develop self-confidence.

Thin weight cans of various sizes with no rough edges, heavy cardboard boxes and cartons, and some plastic and styrofoam materials are useful supplements to woodworking activity. Short pieces of wire may be kept handy by the teacher. At times larger boxes and cartons may be utilized for some activity. These can be made ready at the workbench.

Satisfaction from the use of all of the above media in the preschool should continue throughout school life. When it does it may grow into a lifetime hobby. Whether or not this happens, creativity expressed through various media should be a part of every three-, four-, and five-year-old's experiences.

PUPPETS

Puppets are a fine medium for self-expression and communication. When made by the children, they can be expressions of individual differences or part of a group-planned project. When bought, they are media for creative expression through language. In either case, they encourage the child to create and provide release, often for pent-up feelings. Children may use puppets in relation to dramatic play. Thoughts and feelings are projected readily through the puppets. The following is such an example.

> Jean, Lisa, and Ben, aged four, were busy in the housekeeping corner. "Now," said Lisa, "we must set the table. Company is coming."
>
> "What's coming?" asked Ben.
>
> "Company—you know—people. Put all the cups on the table."
>
> Jake, who was standing near by, dropped the little car that he was carrying and ran to the shelf where the hand puppets were. Quickly, choosing the dog, he put it on his right hand and ran back to the housekeeping corner. Jake got down on his knees behind the end of the doll bed.
>
> As he put his right hand up over the end of the bed, he moved the puppet up and down saying, "Woof, woof, I'm comp'ny. I'm comp'ny. Where's my dinner?"
>
> Jean said, "Go away, Jake, you're bothering us."
>
> "Woof, woof," said Jake.
>
> "No," said Lisa. "Be a quiet dog." Going over to where Jake was, she took him by the right wrist, and as she patted the puppet, said, "Nice doggy, nice doggy. Come in for supper." Lisa reached over and took a plate. As she held it under the puppet's mouth, she said, "Nice doggy, eat your supper."
>
> "Woof, woof," said Jake.

In prekindergarten and kindergarten, especially, puppets can be used as children spontaneously dramatize a story. They may repeat only one or two parts of the original, but these parts hold the most meaning for them then. Family puppets and animal puppets lend themselves readily to many stories. Anita and Jack each took a hand puppet one day. It was during the work-play time after they had heard *The Taxi That Hurried*.[5] Anita chose the mother puppet and Jack, the father. They went to the ladder gym, climbed it, and sat on top. As they sat facing each other, the following took place.

Anita: "Turn around and drive."

Jack: "Drive what?"

Anita: "The taxi, Silly."

Jack: "Oh. Brrrum, brrrum."

Anita, (as she moved the right hand of her puppet): "Turn around."

Jack: "O.K. Brrrum. Brrrum."

Anita (moving the puppet up and down): "You have to hurry. We're late."

Jack (as his puppet nodded): "O.K., lady. Brrrum. Brrrum."

Anita: "Hurry, the train is late. We're late for the train."

Jack: "Doing what I can, Lady. Truck is in the way. Beep, beep, off we go!"

Anita: "Off we go. Off we go."

Jack: "We're not slow."

Anita: "Hey, hey, listen, Jack. Off we go. We're not slow."

Jack: "Ho," (as he turned back to face Anita and putting his puppet up to face hers), "Off we go. We're not slow."

Pleased at the rhyme they had created, both children continued to repeat it.

Children may take the puppets from the shelf and create their dialogue as they go along. Joan and Don, young four-year-olds, chose puppets. Don took the father and Joan, the little girl.

Don: "Go to bed."

Joan: "I won't."

Don (in a deep voice): "Get to bed," and raising his left puppet hand "this instant."

Joan (laughing): "No."

Don: "You hear me? Get to your bed."

Joan: "No, I wanta watch TV."

Don (practically roaring): "To bed. No dessert."

Joan: "I won't, wah, waaahh."

[Loud laughter from both, attracted Jill, Dora, and Ella.]

Ella: "Hey, what you doing?"

Dora: "Me. Me, too."

[The three newcomers rushed for puppets.]

Ella (with the cat): "Meow, I don't like Don."

Don: "I'm father. I'm mad."

Dora *(with the fireman)*: "I'll get a ladder."

Jill *(with the dog)*: "Why?"

Dora: "Joan can climb."

Don: "Get to your bed. Up to your bunk bed."

Joan *(moving her puppet up and down in the air, as though to climb steps)*: "O.K., I'm going."

Jill: "What's that?"

Don: "Climb into your bed."

At age five, when a child's drawing often has reached the realistic stage, the teacher may suggest cutting out the face, or face and legs, or figure that the child has drawn. If the child talks about the figure, "This is my father. He's big," the teacher may ask the child if he would like to make a puppet.

Several quickly made, simple types of puppet may result:

1. The face or figure may be mounted on oak tag for added strength and stapled, pasted, or taped to a tongue depressor;
2. The figure can be stapled to a finger-sized roll of oak tag or corrugated paper for a finger puppet;
3. The face can be pasted or stapled to a cotton sock for a sock puppet.

All of these are quick and simple. It is important that they be so because when a young child is caught up in creating something spontaneously, a quick means of achieving the chance to use it is necessary. Suggesting that he wait until tomorrow may cause him to lose the feeling of the moment and shift his attention to the creating of the puppet rather than to a speedily constructed medium for expression.

Other puppets simple enough for preschool children include:

1. a sponge or styrofoam ball (for a head) on a tongue depressor or blunt stick;
2. a clay head on a pencil or blunt stick;
3. a potato with thumb tack features (five-year-olds only) on a blunt stick;
4. a cotton* sock stuffed lightly enough to allow for fingers or hand, with painted, crayoned, glued, or stapled on features;
5. glove fingers with similar features for finger puppets;
6. a figure made on oak tag with an indented waistline. The figure is placed up against the back of the child's hand and an elastic is put around the hand and the waistline of the figure.

---

*Cotton is cooler on the hand than nylon or wool.

Ready-made hand, finger, and stick puppets lend themselves readily to spontaneous use by preschool children, and they may give the teacher added insights into a child's feelings, background, and homelife. Needless to say, speech becomes clearer as the role, played through the puppet, is verbalized. Thus puppets have a variety of value ranging from the purely creative to being media for psychological insights. When two are worn—one on each hand—interesting and informative dialogue may result!

Paper bags deserve special attention. Small ones make fine, though not too sturdy, hand puppets. They can be stuffed lightly and stapled to a tongue depressor or blunt stick. Worn directly on the hand—or one on each hand—they are almost immediately available. Facial features can be painted, pasted, or crayoned on. Large bags can be used for costumes when cut out a bit. Bags are not substantial enough for three-year-olds, but they can be used occasionally with four- and five-year-olds.

Creative expression through sound, bodily movement, and materials is necessary to well-rounded growth and development. Through such expression John becomes John more fully and Alex develops more fully as Alex. John is not Alex. Although there are general modes of expression, each has his own particular developmental pattern.

Widmer, in discussing the creative arts area states aptly, "Too, there is a special spirit. All who enter here may express themselves in their own unique way. A very personal self-expression is at the heart of these individual creations. The adult who observes must have understanding and respect for the child's product or at least enough sensitivity not to demand "what is it?"[6]

SUGGESTIONS FOR THE TEACHER

The teacher's own attitude is of primary concern when planning for creative expression through the arts. If she enjoys her children's enjoyment, this is readily conveyed to them. If her concern is primarily for a spotless floor, she will be so fussy about how the children paint or use clay that her anxiety feelings will be readily conveyed.

The place for use of material should be as convenient as possible. However the easel should not be so near to the blocks that those building become spattered. Clay balls or blocks, ready for use, can be in a crock next to clean clay boards.

The teacher must respect the child's feeling. Once expressed, it may be regarded as objectification. The child can then react to it on both a feeling and a thinking level. At this time, he may think through how to solve his own problem of more satisfying representation. When he has attained the "realistic" stage, he has already acknowledged his feeling and decides on the basis of feeling and thinking that "I shall make a dog." Even though all children make dogs, this is a particular dog created by a specific child.

The teacher's own attitude is primary. (Courtesy Mary Jane Townsend, Cleveland Heights, Ohio.)

Rhythm instruments and the record player with some records can occupy a low shelf. Paper and crayons should be handy. A box containing collage materials and paper, paste, and scissors can be near the paper and crayons. While it is wise to keep finger paint, and saws, and hammers put away, the latter can be kept in workbench drawers or hanging on peg boards near the workbench.

Finger paint requires a few regulations—usually more than other media. Most children accept a few basic rules which they may have helped to formulate and which, regardless of formulation, are clearly understood as, "The way we do it here."

The teacher needs to encourage the cautious child. Such a child is likely to place one index finger carefully on the finger paint or clay. If the teacher or someone else can have another lump of clay to pummel or finger paint to spread with wide, vigorous motions, the cautious child may manipulate his medium more freely. He often needs to take his time and should be neither hurried nor told how to do it. The adult's finger paint and clay should be manipulated only, and then removed. It is not meant to set a pattern or to be a model; rather use of it by an adult encourages such a child to plunge his fingers and hands into the media.

Above all, the teacher's own enthusiasm and sincere regard for the child's expression is essential. It's contagious!

Although most teachers are fully cognizant of the interrelationships between various types of learning experiences, it does help sometimes to consider them separately in order to emphasize and to highlight items of importance. For instance, communication through language, music, and painting may utilize science information. Jim tells us, "my cat has four new kittens. Two are black, one is gray, and one is black and white." Janey wants hopping music so that she can "be" Peter Cotton Tail. Five-year-old Ilsa makes a realistic painting and says, "This is a big tree. It has a nest for birds." Pointing, she adds, "This is the mother bird going to her nest. She has a worm for her children."

In order, however, to give *emphasis* to science and nature learning experiences, we turn to chapter 7.

Notes

1. Satis Coleman and Alice Thorn, *Another Singing Time* (New York: The John Day Co., 1937).

2. "Frere Jacques" in *Music Through the Year* (Chicago: Follett Publishing Co., 1956).

3. "Swing Song" in Satis Coleman and Alice Thorn, *Singing Time* (New York: The John Day Co., Inc., 1929), p. 37.

4. "Let's Go Walking," in Coleman and Thorn, *Another Singing Time*, p. 13.

5. Lucy Sprague Mitchell, *The Taxi That Hurried* (New York: The Golden Press, 1946).

6. Emmy Louise Widmer, *The Critical Years* (Scranton, Pa.: International Textbook Co., 1970), p. 119.

CHAPTER 7

Exploring the Environment Through Science and Nature Experiences

Science* is a broad and ever-changing area of concern. It cannot and should not be avoided. Evidences of its formulations surround us, and advances in learning in one scientific study or another protrude from every newspaper. Formulations or causes and effects shift as new explorations and discoveries add to our constantly growing stockpile of information. New frontiers beckon and the curious scientists follow! Others pause to reflect upon the changes being wrought in constantly reformulated life patterns. The "good old days" are gone! "Good" they may have been—less complicated—more simple! Old they were! The new encircles us. We accept it, or we turn our backs, *but* it is impossible to ignore what surrounds us on every side. Children are the recipients of scientific change and progress. More importantly, they are the questioners, explorers, and future discoverers in the world of science and nature.

Jim asks, "Why does the button make light?" as the light is pushed on. Gina remarks, "A stick can't grow. It has no root." Tony says, "I saw my guppy lay a baby. It was a ball. Then it was a fish."

Questions, observations, facts! The young child wants to find out. He probes and explores for himself when he can. Do we encourage him to find the answers to his own questions and problems and develop the beginnings of reflective thinking? Do we lead him through further experiences or do we give him abrupt answers and turn our backs because we do not know? No one knows all of the answers anymore, if indeed, they ever did. We can explore with the children, help with what we know, and develop our own information more fully as we go!

---

*Learning experiences in science and nature are considered in this chapter. "Science" is used for brevity.

The young child wants to find out. He probes and explores for himself when he can.

THE INCIDENTAL

"Look at the fuzzy worm," called Kent.

The caterpillar was walking on the fence at the edge of the playground. After Kent's announcement of its presence, six four-year-olds crowded around it. As Mr. Bain approached, the following questions came in rapid and eager succession:

> "Will it bite?"
> "Where do you think its going?"
> "Whose baby is it?"
> "Did it come out of an egg?"
> "What is it named?"
> "Will it live in a bottle?"
> "What does it eat?"
> "Can I hold it?"
> "Is it tickly?"
> "Is it a worm?"
> "Can we keep it?"
> "Where are its brothers and sisters?"

Mr. Bain *could* have said, "It's a caterpillar. Come children, back to what you were doing."

Mr. Bain *did* say, "Let's see if we can find out more about the caterpillar. Ingrid, you go in and get a paper cup from the supply cupboard. Be sure that its a new, clean one."[1], *

As Ingrid sped toward the door, Mr. Bain said, "You must pick up a caterpillar very carefully in order not to squeeze it. Tim, can you be *very* careful?"

Tim removed the caterpillar from the fence carefully and put it into the cup which Ingrid had brought. After the children had returned to their room, the caterpillar was placed in a small aquarium with wire screening over the top. Some twigs were poked into the gravel at the bottom so that they stood upright. A few drops of water were sprinkled on the gravel and some of the twigs, and the class watched and awaited developments.

The presence of the caterpillar on the fence was incidental. It was unrelated to the children's activities at the time it was discovered on the playground fence. It could have been ignored completely. Even if Kent had seen it, talked about it, and even picked it up, Mr. Bain could have merely acknowledged Kent's exclamation. However, he took the incident, which was incidental to what was transpiring, and began to develop it into a science learning experience. In the course of the several weeks that followed, the complete life cycle of the cabbage butterfly was observed. It was a rich experience for the children. Kent and four other children pursued their concern about the one caterpillar into additional and broader fields. They added to Mr. Bain's supply of books, too. Their interest spread to nightcrawlers—discovered one morning after a rain—and to earthworms soon after, and, still later, to grasshoppers. Possibilities for such incidental experiences abound if teachers are aware of them, open to the possibilities for developing them, and ready to decide, on the spot, whether they are worthwhile for the children.

Other incidental experiences which might be developed into worthwhile science learning experiences could include (depending upon the location of the school) the following:

1. watching a bird as it flies nearby and alights and then planning how, where, and what to feed birds;
2. catching three crickets found on the sidewalk behind the school and placing them on an inch of soil in an old fish tank with a few drops of water and a string bean and a few kernels of corn;
3. carrying a worm found on the sidewalk into the room and watching how it moves down into the soft dirt in a jar;
4. catching milk weed seeds, as they float by, and then collecting seeds from nearby plants, shrubs, and trees;
5. collecting leaves in the fall, identifying a few, and putting their fruit with them such as acorns with oak leaves, horse chestnuts with chestnut tree leaves, etc.;

*See Appendix 4.

6. taking a cutting, with permission, from the ivy on the building and putting it into water to root;
7. watching an approaching storm from the window and then noting how the wind blows the rain against the window and how it turns the weather vane on the roof;
8. carrying the ice found in an old sand box pail inside, melting, and then refreezing it;
9. observing the rust on a sandscoop, sandpapering and painting it, and then watching whether rust forms when it is placed outside in the rain.

The incidental beginning of all of the preceding can be ignored, but each could be developed. Alertness to the science learning experiences possible from the incidental happenings and situations which lie around one requires from the teacher a minimum of the following: interest; a desire to find out; a few handy, simple reference books or knowledge of the location of them in a near-by library; some handy jars with covers (some with holes punched in the covers); an old small fish tank or two; a few clean cans of various sizes.

THE UNEXPECTED

Sandy walked proudly into the kindergarten. "What do you think I have?" he burst out. "It's in my pocket. It's live and its my own." As his friends drew near, Sandy reached into his pocket and carefully brought out a small black and white mouse. "Look," said Sandy, "His name is Columbus. I got him on Columbus Day." Seeing Mrs. Bonham coming over to him, he added, "Mrs. Bonham, it's Columbus. Isn't he *beautiful?*" Mrs. Bonham smiled and said, "Yes, Sandy, Columbus is *beautiful.* Come everyone, come over and sit by the piano. Sandy can tell us all about Columbus better there. If you all sit down, you can see him."

The children ran and sat down on the rug near the piano. This was their usual "collecting spot." Within two minutes everyone was seated except Sandy. He stood before the group with Columbus in his hand. As he began to tell how his Uncle George had taken him to a pet shop where Columbus had been purchased, Mrs. Bonham looked quickly across the top shelf of the closet. Finding the large pickle jar and the piece of screen wire that she wanted, she returned to the group, just as Alicia was asking, "Please Sandy, can you let us all hold him?"

This was an *unexpected* situation. Mrs. Bonham had to acknowledge the arrival of Columbus, whether she wanted to do so or not. It would have been deflating to Sandy, if she had just said, "Let's put him in this jar on top of the piano until you go home." The other children would have missed a series of fine learning experiences. As it was, Mrs. Bonham's response opened the way for further learning. Columbus was placed in the jar and fed a piece of lettuce and a bit of hard bread from the center's kitchen after everyone, who wanted to do so, had held him. Columbus was observed in the jar as he ate, washed his face, and curled up to go to sleep. Teachers can make or lose many opportunities for valuable learning unless they are ready to accept such unexpected events, to evaluate them quickly in terms of learning potentialities, and then to act positively, if it is deemed wise.

Such possibilities are frequent in the preschool. Among the number which can and do come about unexpectedly, and which must be acknowledged because the teacher is confronted face-to-face with the situation are events such as:

1. Elaine bringing a colored leaf to school and wanting to keep it there for everyone to see;
2. The serving of broccoli, a new food, for lunch at noon;
3. Doris carrying in an African violet leaf with the request "to plant it for a flower";
4. Al's dog, which had followed him to the day care center door, barking to be admitted;
5. The birth of baby guinea pigs to Puff, the class guinea pig, during lunch;
6. Henry's arrival with a chameleon in a cardboard box announcing loudly," I need a cage. I have to show my circus animal;"
7. Peter's grandmother stopping in at noon with an extra sweater for afternoon play outdoors on a day during which it had become colder and looked like snow;
8. The refusal of the bathroom light to go on and Jonathan's request to watch the man fix it;
9. Jack's request for some light "so we can see inside our block building";
10. The sudden breaking of Alice's balloon and Jean's question, "Why did it break and then fly?" (after Alice had released it still partially inflated).

Unexpected situations also can be dangerous such as Alma's package of matches which she had brought "to make a cigareete burn" in nursery school, and Danny's large sharp knive which he was brandishing as he arrived at the door of his Head Start group.

However, the majority afford the teacher ample opportunities for the development of valuable science learning experiences. As in the case of those defined as incidental, the unexpected situations require the teacher to have quick judgment, the desire to find out, and a few handy containers.

THE PREPLANNED

Many teachers hesitate to deviate from preplanned science activities, although their children are having experiences constantly, asking questions, and/or solving problems or difficulties. Whether the questions or problems arise from incidental or unexpected experiences or whether they arise from the preplanned activities which are taking place as part of the daily program, the child should be guided to find ways to further his learning through finding out his answers and through problem solving of his own. At times the teacher needs to preplan a learning experience because it extends present learning, adds perspective to what has been taking place, or it may open up a new area of possibilities.

The preplanned experiences are numerous and may be extremely varied. Science concepts can be *developed* if the teacher is willing (a) to clarify the initial experiential situation, (b) to note the underlying problem, (c) to find out just what the children know about it already and to get any speculations which they may have, (d) to try out feasible suggestions, and (e) to keep the results from such trying out clear. For example, (a) "Peppy, our guinea pig is very fat." Everyone looks again at Peppy. (b) "Do you know why she may look this way?" (c) Elaine: "Maybe she ate too much." Dick: "My cat looked that way before she had baby kittens." George: "Maybe she will burst." Dorothy: "She doesn't act sick. Is she?" (c) Miss Thomas: "I'll hold her in my lap. Watch her side" (As the pregnant guinea pig settled down in Miss Thomas's lap, her side moved.) Miss Thomas: "Patsy, give me your hand." As Patsy did so, Miss Thomas laid it against Peppy's side. She did this with each child's hand. (d) "Dick said that his cat looked this way before she had kittens, didn't you Dick?" Dick: "Yes. And I felt Peppy's babies move. I know I did. She has babies inside." Dora: "I felt them move, too." "Me, too" rang out from several of the other children. "Peppy will have babies very soon," said Miss Thomas. "We need to be quiet near her and not to pick her up any more for awhile."* "Oh, boy," said Dick. "Just like Spotty, my cat." (e) In this case, the results, namely the baby guinea pigs, arrived the next day.

Despite the value of the two preceding kinds of science learning situations, the incidental and the unexpected, most teachers overdo the preplanned because they do feel more secure with it. With added experience, they should use all three and not over use the latter.

THE IMMEDIATE

Three-, four-, and five-year-olds are present-centered. What they are doing "here and now," what they see before them "then and there" is of the greatest

---

*In this case, Miss Thomas wanted to protect Puff. In other, less vital situations, she might say, "Let's see whether this happens." After it did, the results could be summarized.

importance. This is why incidental and unexpected situations both have high learning value for these ages. Interest is, or can be, caught by what is there, developed on the spot, and extensions to learning are made. Children have only lived a comparatively few months. They have been plunged into a world full of ongoing situations peopled by adults who have had years of experience and learning. Children need learning experiences which make sense to them about what interests them and about what can be selected as of immediate interest and concern from all of the items surrounding them. The incidental and the unexpected both provide such instances. They provide understandable explanations for the events in the environment which surround the children. The preplanned does have a definite place, but it should not be the only type of learning carried through by the teacher.

THE MORE REMOTE

While the future and the "not fairly immediate present" mean little in any organized sense to young children, there are ways to extend, to connect, to clarify. One of the ways to accomplish this is through the preplanned science learning experience.

In the preceding illustration, the teacher waited until Peppy's babies were nearly due because two or three days were long enough for four-year-olds to anticipate them. Clarifications and extensions of separated experiences can also be connected by the teacher's preplanned learning experience. For example, if the coleus plant looks fine, is watered by Tommy, and then on Monday, looks limp, this can be called to the attention of all of the children. The need to water it becomes clearer as well as the necessity for an especially big drink on Friday. Learning is extended to "What happens, if it is not watered?" If the same coleus turns to the light, this can be considered and observed changes watched carefully after the plant has been turned. This should be done deliberately and when all the children are there watching and aware of what is being done.

The Halloween pumpkin was being scooped out by the children, when Harry asked, "Can we plant the seeds and get more pumpkins?" Having explained the need for drying them, Mr. Tabor got a dish and Harry put the seeds into it. The three- and four-year-olds remarked about them, occasionally, during the next few weeks. When they planted the dried seeds in a large window box in February, various references were made to the pumpkin. As the growth of the seeds was watched daily, the growth cycle became a concept which the children could understand and express. Teachers of preschool children need to consider demonstrable connections. "Demonstrable" is a far cry from merely telling or explaining! If children must wait for results, time spans are best kept short, or the object may be left in sight, as was done with the pumpkin seeds. Inquiring, questioning, discovering, trying out tentative projections are all necessary for real scientific exploration. Children benefit from this approach for the rest of their lives.

ANIMALS, PLANTS, AND THE INANIMATE

Wʜᴇʀᴇ, Hᴏᴡ, ᴀɴᴅ Wʜʏ

Animals, plants, and the inanimate aspects of science are best taken care of in the classroom where the child feels at home and can take time to examine and reexamine, and to use what is available over and over again. Three-year-olds, on the whole, benefit least from science and nature activities outside of their own familiar surroundings. An occasional visit to see a baby rabbit in a nearby room, to watch the electrician down the hall, or to gather leaves in the park are worthwhile additions to what is available to them in their own room. Four-year-olds can go further afield, and occasional visits to the science room of the school—if that is where they are housed—to a local park, or nearby pet shop are usually taken in stride, but should be considered peripheral to daily ongoing activities in their room. Five-year-olds can go much further. More specific references to trips will be made later in the chapter.

The more experiences with animals, the better it is for children. (Courtesy Ethical Culture Schools, New York City and Celeste Muschel.)

The more experiences that children can have with animals and plants, the better it is. Understanding grows rapidly as classroom pets are cared for, observed, and when possible handled *in prescribed ways*. Plants watered and tended by the children gain added stature in their eyes.

Inanimate science materials should be where they are easily accessible if they are objects for handling such as magnets or sets of batteries with wires and a bell. When objects such as a bell are first brought out to fill a need such as a bell for the house "so we know when company is there," to solve a problem such as "how can we tell when to go," or to answer a question such as "why does that buzzer buzz?" they can be kept in a place accessible to all.

All science and nature materials which can be held, cared for, or manipulated with educational justification should be in a preschool room at some time. Of course, no room can accomodate too much at once or the children may become confused! If there is abundant material, it can be rotated with that of other classes. To many preschoolers, though, a rabbit or guinea pig is one of them, belongs to *our* class, and should be a permanent pet.

Plants need adequate light unless they are among the few varieties requiring little such as a philodendron or sansevieria. Most animals need to be able to sleep occasionally as well as having their food and water requirements met. Safe cages and/or containers need to be considered for the sake of the animal as well as the child. Inanimate science objects may be brought out and exchanged occasionally with other groups. After major interests have been met, they can be put away for a time. However, some objects such as flashlights, bulbs and batteries, and magnifying glasses are usually utilized enough to keep them available as part of permanent equipment. Three-year-olds have a shorter interest span than four-year-olds and usually considerably less than five-year-olds. Three- and four-year-olds should have enough space available to keep such equipment so that it is readily usable; five-year-olds can keep their own in usable order more easily. Jumbled materials in a box or cluttered on a shelf are not conducive to use.

Children learn through their own experiencing and through undergoing the results of it; through guidance from their teacher; through having time enough to explore available possibilities; through encouragement; through "talking out" what they have seen and/or done afterwards; through constantly broadening experiences about which they may ask questions, solve simple problems, undergo the results of what they do, and be able, when possible, to repeat what has been done. The child who sits watching the fish swim for ten minutes may be trying to decide whether water comes out of their gills. He may want to pat the guinea pig so that the guinea pig "won't be lonesome" when he, himself, feels upset or rebuffed. He may want a can of water in order to try several times to see whether the toy boat will sink. Children need time to undergo the results of trying out, to repeat in order to establish the concept for themselves, and to find out for themselves. Concepts develop in this kind of environment. Children need a place and materials and equipment that they can handle. Science learning experiences form the means and the ends for much of this kind of doing, experiencing, and learning.

WHAT TO HAVE IN THE CLASSROOM[2]

ANIMALS

Science learning experiences are part of a developing continuum. If Larry had a pet guinea pig when he was in the three-year-old nursery, for instance, he may well have a guinea pig when he is in the five-year-old kindergarten, also. What he found out about the guinea pig at three is expanded and reconsidered. A considerable amount of further learning results from a more experienced mature consideration of the animal, its habits, needs, and characteristics. Larry's learning is refined, more detailed, and he can make simple comparisons. He knows some of the characteristics of the guinea pig, his diet, and needs, and how he differs from some other pets. To take another illustration: at age three, Maggie learned how and what to feed the white mouse. She learned the best way to pick it up and was able to explain how it washed. At age five, Maggie learned about baby mice—how they were born, what they looked like, and *their* needs. She knew the differences between mice and some other rodents and could tell you that Minnie Mouse learned to use the wheel in the mouse cage before Spotty Mouse. By her observations, her questions, and by finding out some answers to problems for herself, Maggie had the beginnings of scientific method. Children benefit from caring for living things. They do the feeding and are responsible— under their teacher's guidance.* They gain a great deal of information and many begin a lifelong interest in animals, their care, and their welfare.

Some of the animals which can be kept successfully in the three-, four-, and five-year-old classroom include rabbits and rodents such as guinea pigs, hamsters, gerbils, domestic mice, white and hooded rats; reptiles such as slider, box, and spotted turtles and amphibians such as green frogs, Eastern and Western toads, spawn and tadpoles, native Eastern and Western salamanders (either the eft or newt form of the Eastern depending upon the stage of development); fish, preferably goldfish and guppies; insects such as grasshoppers, crickets, ants, caterpillars, and cocoons or chrysalids and the resulting moths and butterflies; birds such as canaries and parakeets can visit providing there are no drafts or sudden changes in temperature and fowl such as chicks, ducklings, and pigeons providing proper facilities are available; earthworms and mealworms; puppies,

*See Appendix 4, Requirements for Various Animals.

dogs, kittens, cats as temporary visitors. Several of these provide a rather fast life cycle. For example, spawn, tadpoles, and small toads or green frogs can be observed in fairly rapid succession. The mealworm goes through the larva, pupa, beetle, and egg laying stages rather rapidly.

The teacher must take the responsibility for considering:

1. the amount of care required and the readiness with which children can participate in it;
2. whether the animal is safe—sufficiently used to being petted and handled—and not likely to harm children;
3. the hardiness and adaptability of the particular animal to classroom living;
4. the ease with which the animal can be observed and/or handled to provide the children with firsthand experiences;
5. the accessibility of necessary information about the animal (if the teacher is not too well informed);
6. the possibilities for *continued* and *varied* science learnings about the animal, especially for five-year-olds.

The teacher also *must* consider the following possible problems:

1. overheated rooms and drafts;
2. availability of reliable weekend and vacation care;
3. possibilities and results of overfeeding;
4. the extent of parental understanding and possible need for education about the values of living things;
5. negative cultural conditioning;
6. the teacher's own continuing and developing interest.

PLANTS

Plants, too, offer a number of worthwhile learning experiences. Seeds, leaves, roots, slips, fruits, and nuts are part of each child's daily living. Mildred says, questioningly, "Stone, stone here" as she takes the seed from the tangerine she is eating. At age three, any hard object is likely to be designated as a stone!* By age five, however, Mildred has found out that fruits contain seeds. She points to a shiny leaved green plant and says to the visitor in her improved English, "Here's our orange tree." Four-year-old Peter, looking at the beans sprouting in the plastic container of vermiculite asks, "Why does it have whiskers?" The "whiskers" are referred to as *roots* before very long.

Planting, sprouting, growing, watering become daily activities. Simple problems are solved and answers found to questions: the coleus plant did not have

---

*Although the seeds of some fruits such as a cherry are referred to as stones, it is wise to use "seeds" consistently with preschool youngsters.

enough light; the ivy vine needed a stick to climb on; roots hold a tree in the ground; Christmas trees stay green and birds live in them; this spider plant is a baby spider of that spider plant; moss feels soft; a rose has stickers and so does a cactus; a seed from an apple needs dirt to grow; apple seeds don't grow in your stomach; pumpkins grow on a vine and the vine grows from a pumpkin seed; a tree's coat is called bark like dog talk; a tiny green spot in the onion will grow a new onion plant. And so it goes! Information is amassed as experiences give answers to questions and solutions to simple problems.

Some of the plants which lend themselves rather readily to classroom life and care include the following:

1. upright growing potted plants such as coleus, begonia, geranium, impatiens;
2. hanging and vinelike potted plants such as ivy, philodendron, pothos, nephthytis, tradescantia, spider plants;
3. potted plants such as cactus, crown of thorns, snake plant;
4. African violet;
5. Chinese evergreen;
6. birdseed;
7. grass and oats;
8. flower seeds such as dwarf marigold, zinnia, cosmos, calendula, morning glory, sunflower;
9. lima bean seeds;
10. other vegetable seeds such as radish, carrot, lettuce;
11. vegetable tops such as carrot and beet;
12 sweet and white potato;
13. onions;
14. bulbs such as narcissus, hyacinth, tulip, daffodil, jonquil, amaryllis, crocus, grape hyacinth, scilla;
15. some ferns;
16. some small trees;
17. terrarium plants.*

The teacher's responsibilities in selecting plants for the classroom include the following considerations:

1. the ease with which the plant can be grown in the classroom;
2. the tendency of the plant to grow quickly and be sturdy;
3. the knowledge that the requirements for growth be ordinary rather than "exotic";
4. the ease of obtaining the plant and its resistance to disease and insect pests;

---

*This listing places together plants with similar needs and/or those with which similar learning experiences are possible.

5. the resistance to excesses of temperature and lack of optimum growing conditions;

6. the clarity with which it exemplifies a specific type of growth and propagation;

7. the readiness with which the plant lends itself to firsthand experience in care and handling by young children.

If the plant is delicate, prone to insect pests, or needs eight hours of sun or light, for instance, it is probably not a good choice for a preschool classroom.

The teacher must consider problems of poor air such as that caused by the chemicals in the air from a nearby inner city factory; little sunlight, and little space. Then plants able to meet these conditions can be obtained. The teacher must either possess adequate knowledge of plants or be willing to obtain it. Knowledge about a few simple basic requirements is easily learned about the plants listed. The most common problems are

1. those related to lack of attention to such growth basics as proper soil, adequate light, water, drainage;

2. indications of disease or insect pests;

3. how to judge a healthy looking plant and good grade bulbs upon purchase;

4. awareness of the dangers of a hot radiator or a drafty window;

5. provision for weekend and vacation care;

6. the need for a growing interest and understanding on the part of the teacher.

INANIMATE

Inanimate objects surround us. Many of them lend themselves to the early simple scientific explorations of very young children.[3] Teresita touches the ice in the old pail on the playground. "Water, no—no water," she says. By age five, in her improved English, she can tell you that water freezes into ice when it is cold enough and that the ice will melt when taken into the warm room. She has seen water turn to steam, watched it caught on a large cool spoon, and seen and touched the resulting droplets of water. Science concepts develop rapidly when time and attention are directed to this. Ford is heard to say to four-year-old Alan, as the two were running small metal cars into their block garage. "That thing came down. It stuck on the old squashed car. The car went up in the air." The teacher overheard and gave Ford and Alan each a small horse shoe magnet and a piece of string. Alan, "Let's not squash our cars." Ford, "O.K., but let's lift them." Magnets were tried out, discussed, and tried out some more by all the four-year-olds later in the day. Although possible experiences in inanimate science abound, some lend themselves more than others, to the science learning experiences of preschool children.

Suggested science learning experiences in the inanimate area for three-, four-, and five-year-olds include those related to the following: air and wind; water; snow, sleet, and hail; the sun; clouds; the seasons; balls; wheels and gears; levers; pulleys; magnets; mirrors, magnifying glasses, and prisms; gravity; rockets and space craft; sound; static electricity; simple electricity; mixtures and compounds; sugar, salt, and flour; metals such as gold, silver, copper, iron; rocks such as quartz, marble, and sand and coal (rock to a child); shells; fossils; erosion; conservation.*

The teacher needs to be selective in what interests, questions, and problems are followed because the possibilities are numerous. Responsibilities which need to be considered in relation to science learning experiences possible with the inanimate include giving positive answers to the following:

1. Does each item clarify some aspect of the nonliving portion of the young child's world?
2. Is each item of material readily obtainable or can it be experienced in the child's immediate environment?
3. Is each important enough in the young child's experience to warrant further examination and understanding?[4]
4. Are the usual learning experiences, undergone with each, comparatively safe?
5. Does each lend itself to simplicity of management and to sensory experiences?
6. Can each experience be clarified in language comprehensible to the young child?
7. Is the required equipment inexpensive?
8. Are supplementary materials available to assure clarification and further development of the experience?
9. Does each lend itself to the continuing science learning experiences of three-, four-, and five-year-old children?

There are so many possibilities available that the teacher should, under usual circumstances, tend to focus on and encourage the children to utilize those items which receive a positive answer to each of the above-listed criteria questions.

Problems or difficulties which require the teacher's consideration are:

1. to keep the language relating to the experience simple enough for ease of understanding;
2. to meet parents' fears about safety;
3. to gauge the number and variety of experiences possible in order to avoid confusion;
4. to consider ease of obtaining equipment;
5. to present opportunities for safe experimenting;
6. to keep the experiences with living and nonliving in balance.

*Conservation, of course, may well include consideration of inanimate *and* animate.

A pulley can be used to help solve a problem. (Courtesy Ethical Culture Schools, New York City and Celeste Muschel.)

ECOLOGICAL CONCERNS FOR THE YOUNGEST

John walked solemnly into the four-year-old prekindergarten. After he had been greeted by his teacher, he said, "Do you know what I saw? A man threw two bags of stuff on the sidewalk."

Mickey, age three said, "Papers go in the can."

Jean said, during the time when the five-year-olds were all gathered together, "My grandfather says he has to go to Canada to go fishing now. He says the water is too dirty around here, now."

Joan said to the other four-year-olds, "A lady planted a tree in her yard. She said it was for the birds. They need a place to live."

Five-year-old Don said, "It sure stunk by our house last night. I think it came from Eiman's factory."

Peter, to another three-year-old as the children walked over the bridge to the other side of the creek, "Fish swim in clean water. Don't throw cans in."

Becky said to her four-year-old friends, "My mother paid some money to have a tree planted in Israel. It will make Israel pretty."

Peter, age five asked, "What do you think I saw in the garbage can in the alley?" Without awaiting a reply, "Two big wild rats."

George said to the other children, "The sawmill sawed up the trees. My father says that the men will plant more."

Layne, to the five-year-olds' teacher, "We can save aluminum cans for recycling."

Joan, to her kindergarten friends, "My father says they are going to make a bus that won't have dirty smoke coming out of the back."

"We found pretty flowers named Lady Slippers. We only picked one. We want them to grow there," said Diane to the other five-year-olds.

Ecology, conservation, and pollution problems are current. Despite attempts earlier by interested adults, America had to wait until pollution was general before taking any genuine action for rectifying it and the ravages against nature. In terms of their own understanding, children make observations, have experiences, and hear the opinions of the adults around them.

A beginning toward pollution prevention, environmental controls, and ecological studies can be made in preschool classes.

The child begins to connect the cause and effect of one thing on another, to understand simple relationships, and interrelationships. The understanding of simple interrelationships can be developed into concepts of simple conservation. If we define conservation as "wise use,"[5] this too is related to ecological systems and relationships. For instance, the writer has found that if a vacant lot is suddenly depleted of trees, children can understand how this has interfered with some simple interrelationships: the squirrels did not dig up all of the acorns that they buried and so little new oak trees grew and became big trees until they were cut down; the squirrels have no home and no nuts now; the birds have no trees in which to live and nest; the insects, some of which were eaten by the birds, may go into neighboring gardens; the trees which "broke" the wind are gone; there is no shade; our swing is gone.

"Wise use" does not mean "no use." The necessity for planting new trees after the big ones are cut is usually understood by children in the Pacific Northwest, for instance. Four- and five-year-olds may not, and need not, know the term resource, but they can understand: (a) that we will have more sun and air tomorrow even if we breathe air today and do not see the sun tonight; (b) that soil can be fed fertilizer for its plants and that fresh water can be kept or dirty streams cleaned up; (c) that we dig up coal and silver, but that it does not come back; (d) that scientists are working on new things for us to use. These are versions of types of resources that can be used with young children. Blough lists them as: (a) inexhaustible resources such as air, sun, and water; (b) renewable resources such as soil and fresh water; (c) nonrenewable resources such as coal and metals; (d) new and to-be-developed resources such as further uses of the atom.[6] Children can understand the particular instances which have been listed above and, eventually, the underlying concept or generalization.

All the children cited above had some awareness of environmental problems and difficulties. The particular experience of seeing the lot decimated of trees held meaning, and they were able to share it. In certain localities, Smokey the

Bear, for instance, has been an important particular character. While children should not be made afraid of fire, they can find out about Smokey. Planes fighting forest fires can be watched if this is going on in the locality. In some parts of the Northwest, this is an all too real experience, and emphasis should be placed on fire spotting by plane, on forest rangers, and on fire patrols as well as on the fighting of the actual fires. Later, concepts of reforestation can be introduced.

In other areas, clear versus polluted water can be considered. Children can watch fish in one creek and understand why they are not to be found in another.

The plight of birds and animals in winter in the class's own area is readily comprehended as a problem and may be solved in *their* area by the children's own actions. These actions may be the provision of food, nesting places, protection from cats, and the general interest which they display. The latter often makes parents take a second look or concern themselves more fully than they might otherwise have done.

Littering is an experience—the consequences of which can be developed into clear concepts even with the youngest.

Among the related learning experiences understood by three-, four-, and especially five-year-olds, the following may be listed:

1. A few simple cycles such as the relation of a depletion of trees to birds and insects, of clear water to fish, of forest fires to wildlife, and of human dependency. Children usually like animals. They can feed animals and birds during the winter, understand what one or two conservation groups such as the National Wildlife Association or the National Mustang Association are doing, find out about the American Society for the Prevention of Cruelty to Animals (and other such groups which may bear different names in other states) as well as more inclusive animal protection groups.*

2. In relation to plants, young children can understand what protected means, how to pick flowers, why we walk on paths, and why trees, for example, are needed.

3. Children usually do, and can have more experiences in the inanimate area. For instance, picking up papers, participating in recycling drives and collections, helping to keep school surroundings attractive, putting out lights to conserve energy, and such other simple things as not wasting drawing paper or paper towels. Children of age five will work industriously on some of these projects. Three- and four-year-olds gain a growing awareness of the importance of man and his environment, their interrelationship, and what can be done to preserve "the best possible" for all concerned.

To many, science means scientific method. Children utilize this method quite naturally when care is given to fostering experiences from which problems can

*See Appendix 5.

arise, from stating the problems or questions, and from gathering together related possibilities or other relevant data. Children will choose a possibility or possible solution and test it. This is discussed in detail in the article which is reproduced in Appendix 4.

TAKING A SHORT TRIP: WHERE AND WHY

Three- and four-year-olds explore their own and adjacent areas first, and then move gradually into the larger environment of the center or school, and then into the neighborhood or community. Five-year-olds, on the whole, are more experienced and knowledgable at the beginning of the year and can go further, stay longer, and learn more from broader and a larger number of varied experiences. Although trips may be taken for a variety of reasons, many can and do serve primarily to enhance science learning experiences.

"That cow is looking at us!" (Courtesy Brooklyn-Parma Coop Preschool, Cleveland, Ohio and Lois Overbeck.)

As long as the teacher is aware of the needs and interests of the children as well as of their particular weaknesses and capabilities and of the special concerns of individuals and the group, short trips function as additional sources of information to answer questions and solve difficulties and to encourage constantly developing enquiry. For instance, Jack, a four-and-a-half-year-old arrived one morning with a grasshopper in a covered jar. He said, "I brought it from home." Len said, "Let's look for some." This was the beginning of a daily insect hunt which took place in a nearby field. Grasshoppers, crickets, sow bugs, and beetles were housed in jars and old fish tanks for the duration of the special session.

Additional adults, of course, should accompany any group off of the premises. All of the usual plans and precautions necessary for any trip should function on trips related to science and nature learning experiences.

Actual trips, depending upon locality and specific situations, may well include trips to the following.

Animals	*Plants*	*Inanimate*
Animal Nursery	Arboretum	Airport
Animal Training	Botany Department of	Bakery
Center	School or University	Boat Basin
Animal Farm	Christmas Tree	Building Site
Aquarium	Farm	Car Assembly
Chicken Hatchery	Farm	Plant
Farm	Flower Show	Cargo Loading
Fish Hatchery	Garden	or Unloading
Game Preserve	Greenhouse	(ship, truck,
Kennel	Maple Sugar House	train)
Neighbor's Kennel,	Market	Health Museum
New Litter, or	Neighbor's Special	Kitchen of Large
Special Pets	Plants or Garden	Home, Hotel, or
Pet Fair	Nursery	Other Institution
Pet Shop	Orchard and/or	Machine Shop
Pond, Lake, or	Vineyard	Milk Plant
Stream	Park	Museum
Stable (Police, Riding)	Plant Store	Science Department
Zoo	Sawmill	of School or
	Wooded Area	University
		Signal Tower or
		Station
		Steam Engine
		Truck Depot
		Water Wheel or
		Water Power
		Weather Station

It is to be remembered that children should have experiences to which they can relate, which hold meaning for them, and which neither overstimulate nor overfatigue them. Each teacher needs to judge her/his group in terms of how much and how far and to consider just what may be gained.

"We saw the lamb drink some milk from his mother, and then he walked on his little feet." (Courtesy Brooklyn-Parma Coop Preschool, Cleveland, Ohio and Lois Overbeck.)

Through all of these experiences children are developing socially. In the next chapter, a careful consideration of social growth and development will be presented.

Notes

1. Grace K. Pratt, "Developing Concepts About Science in Young Children" *Science and Children* 1(December 1963): no. 4.

2. Readers should consult Grace K. Pratt, *How to Care for Living Things in the Classroom* (Washington, D.C.: National Science Teachers Association, Pamphlet Number 471-14288).

3. Pratt, "Developing Concepts About Science in Young Children."

4. Ibid.

5. Glenn O. Blough and Julius Schwartz, *Elementary School Science and How to Teach It* (New York: Holt, Rinehart and Winston, 1964), p. 361.

6. Ibid., pp. 363-64.

CHAPTER 8

Social Development and Understandings

SOCIAL DEVELOPMENT

The social aspect of growth proceeds in developmental patterns which, while similar in general, may demonstrate wide individual distinctions. In terms of similarity, social development may be summarized as the gradual extension of an interactive relationship. This relationship has two facets: (a) it serves to distinguish and identify the child as an individual self and thus clarifies his self-image; (b) it serves to increase the every-widening concepts of the social world which surround the child and thus clarifies his social-cultural context. As he acts upon things and projects himself toward others, he is in turn acted upon—thus the *inter*action. The interactions differ and result in a tremendous variety of individual distinctions. Thus, although general in developmental pattern, interaction is quite particularized as it functions in each individual. Although this has been discussed in part in chapter 1, it is necessary to look more carefully at this interactive aspect of growth and development because it is of essential importance in the whole preschool program.

Sam, like other biological organisms, can move, is equipped with senses, and is able to respond to stimuli. His earliest motions seem to be such biological necessary behaviors as sucking. His random movements, so-called, appear to develop into controlled motion. Early motions are frequently imitative, although since Sam is Sam and not Bill, he makes an individual movement and his replication varies from Bill's. First movements are random, but they soon become directed and purposeful. Early locomotion on the floor with a toy, for instance, once under control is soon accompanied by "chugs" and "zooms," and Sam and car seem to be an almost completely identified unit. The play of the toddler is often transposition of toddler and object. Projection with simple, available objects rapidly changes toddler into car—and later, driver. As car, Sam and his activity seem to be one autonomous unit. Later, usually by the time he enters nursery school, Sam *runs* the car and thus *controls* at least in part that which he *chooses* to manipulate and/or direct.

Underlying the above is the natural desire to move and the development of self-extension through feeling and object. Inasmuch as Sam is not only acting but reacting, his behavior is termed interactive. The more varied his experiences, the broader his interactions. The more interactions, the more he stores up as "input" for the next active or interactive experience.

Independent play is an important precursor to later social relationships. (Courtesy Department of Health, Education and Welfare and Dick Swartz.)

As we saw earlier, the child's social relationships usually develop in the following sequence: individual play; processional play; parallel play; interactive play with one other; "fringe" play; interactive play in a small group; interactive play in a large group. Later, he develops some relationships to those at a distance whom he may or may not ever confront. These stages overlap, and the child's activity may be in more than one stage simultaneously. For instance,

Don may play positively in a small group but at times abandon this completely for parallel play at the sand box where he has neither nonverbal nor verbal exchange. In transitional periods of development, Don is especially likely to move back and forth between stages as though he is unable to enter into a new developmental phase all at once.

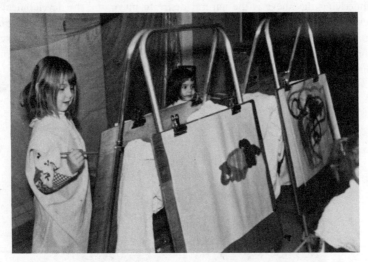

Each child is doing her own painting but enjoying the parallel activity. Activity may be in more than one stage of social development simultaneously. (Courtesy Brooklyn-Parma Coop Preschool, Cleveland, Ohio and Lois Overbeck.)

The child's self-identity evolves from a completely dependent baby in a family to a child who becomes increasingly more independent. The child may be passive, neutral, or aggressive. Thus Alex may assume a leadership or a followership role, or interchange them. As we said above, this assumes the underlying biological nature of the child which gives him such fundamental bases as physical growth and abilities, mobility, and some social proclivities. Thus one facet of social development is the natural or biological self. Alex as an active unit interacts with his environment. As initial instigator, or actor, his motion outward touches upon the environment surrounding him. Part of this is social. It is people—small, large, friendly, and unfriendly. Alex's early perceptions of these people are of profound significance. His actions, their reactions, and their actions in reference to him are foundational to Alex's self-image as it evolves its own distinction.

When the self-image is positive, the child accepts himself. He gradually builds his own assessment of what he can and cannot do. As his experiences widen and deepen, he develops assertiveness, initiative, and abilities. These become part of his developing pattern of self, and each means growing powers to maintain some measure of control over his movements outward and to regulate in what measure he reacts to actions directed to him. Interaction is action and being acted upon. It is important that this be fostered as two-way give-and-take. Continuous acting leaves no time for reacting or undergoing the consequences of the acting, while steadily being acted upon develops no individual initiative in acting. Interaction accounts for both.

The more restricted the child is and the more he is "talked at" as a passive being prior to give-and-take of his own, the less individual is his behavior. The preschool which fosters individuality also fosters choice. Choice by a child develops him as a more distinctive individual. Choices are social as well as material. Social interaction, while based on choice, to a greater or lesser degree is displayed in overt behavior. The young child behaves openly and fully. Even verbal interchange at three-and-a-half, for instance, is likely to accompany overt demonstrative behavior. "Go 'way," may still not stand on its own verbal power. Sally, who says this, is likely to push or to raise a hand because she is not yet entirely confident or dependent upon language. Physical control slowly gives way to verbal control. By four-and-a-half, verbal control may be dominant in a smooth situation, but regression to hitting or physical control is easy—and will continue to be so for several years.

Sally's concepts of the social environment, too, develop as she interacts. Conditioning of various sorts impinges upon her. For instance, she finds out what is *our* church and *our* neighborhood and understands the positive tone of voice used in reference to them. *Their* church can be understood much as she understands her own undesirable behavior. Not wanted, different, unacceptable are communicated easily, as tone of voice indicates underlying attitudes to her. At the same time, she asserts herself. *My* friend is a later concept. It replaces earlier give-and-take with another child over toys and equipment. Doing what she is doing at the sand box in parallel play which develops gradually into give-and-take focusses on the activity or object; *who* is doing it comes later. With negative adult intervention, however, *who* and *what* may be joined early. For example, "Jan, don't take his sand" in a gruff voice indicates negation, while "Let's give Mary some of Sally's sand," is positive. Thus, if Jan is a black child who is shoveling sand, she may slowly become a negative object, while Sally who is white and who also is shoveling sand, is maintained as part of an acceptable picture. Prejudices and stereotypic responses come as conditionings from adults. Repetition of a response indicating a unified adult attitude can develop prejudice in the child. Young children function together in terms of what they are doing until outside factors, e.g. parents, older siblings, enter. This kind of learned response will be considered later in greater detail.

SOCIAL UNDERSTANDINGS

The important topic of social understandings as they develop in the young child may be considered under the following headings: the child in his immediate family (in preschool, his room, class, and teacher may be a kind of surrogate home and family); the child in his community; the child as part of the larger world.

It is as though the child lives interactively within three circles. These overlap and he ranges at will, *as he matures,* from one circle to another. He is in the small home circle and then pushes out to the larger community. Here his interactions are slowly developed by the nature of the community. If John is black and the community is primarily white, John's initial interactive experience may be as the recipient of "such a cute baby." However, as he grows and is no longer so cute, he may be the recipient of prejudicial and otherwise negative actions. His interactions are affected and his give-and-take reflects what he feels.

The larger world, outside the immediate community, usually does not come to the child in the same gradual way. What does come are "fits and starts" of people and things from the experiences surrounding him. However, each leaves its mark, and if he can interact, so much the better in terms of his own future.

A story can provide great vicarious experience. (Courtesy Department of Health, Education and Welfare and Dick Swartz.)

However, the child interacting with the boy next door is a direct experience. The child reacting to a story is removed from the experience and undergoes it vicariously. The child, who gives and takes in the community understands, while the child who is told about the Japanese, who receives a lei, or who sees a movie about an Indian boy cannot react at firsthand. However, vicarious experiences do add to his awareness of the larger society.

Generally, preschool education has sought to develop the child's relationships from an understanding of his experiences in his immediate social surroundings. Then he is introduced to what has meaning for him in the larger community. This is a gradual process from home and school to the corner grocery, the zoo, etc. The larger world has been peripheral with the inclusion of an occasional interjection about Florida, Puerto Rico, or Japan, for example. In areas with a large transient population, children hear about and may experience not only greater mobility themselves, but also be more aware of the comings and goings of family and friends. With the increasing "shrinking" of the world, the child can vicariously experience a starving child at the other side of the world on television or see newly arrived Oriental or African nationals in native dress on the street. Uncle Bill was in Korea while Cousin Alan was in Thailand. Each has pictures and possibly some artifacts. These, too, become part of the child's expanding environment. When they impinge upon the daily lives of Jim and Joan, they must be acknowledged.

Thus we have the vital firsthand experience versus the passively received experience, or vicarious experience. The child can react to the second and may be very much a part of it as when he listens to a story which involves him very much. However it is primarily a passive experience even if he expresses himself about it, and thus it is less dynamic than the first. Children learn best from what they do as actual firsthand activity.

The teacher needs to guide each child into an understanding of his enlarging environment. "We are going to see Mr. Smith. His house is near the bakery." Understanding the enlarging environment may mean trying to simplify an overwhelming experience, or it may mean that interpretation is necessary. On a busy street with a rumbling elevated overhead, the bustle and noise can cause apprehension. "My it *is* noisy. We are going down this street to the supermarket to get the candy." Or, "The man in the store will help us, but we may need to wait. It is a very busy store."

When we look about, we realize how many things surround us. Many of these are specifically ours. They are neither Japanese nor Dutch. "These apples came from the country. They grew on an apple tree on a farm. The farmer put them in a basket." "Those cans are for the garbage from that store. Here comes the garbage truck now. It will take the garbage away." "Johnny's Daddy is going to fly in an airplane. He will carry that little blue bag on the airplane with him."

Social understandings derived from early interaction may be: positive or negative; expanding or contracting; exciting or frightening. As the child's environment expands socially, his interpretation of himself and others begins to be set in his own individual patterns. The more free interactive experiencing of his own that he has, the more definite the patterns are, providing that the experi-

ences come slowly enough for him to assimilate them. The development of social understandings in terms of the self and in terms of social reflections in behavior in the preschool is clearly revealed in the dramatic play of the three-,
four-, and five-year-old. In fact, dramatic play is an excellent laboratory for
child study.

DRAMATIC PLAY

Dramatic play is learning experience inherent in the development of children.
Although specific situations vary, there are general characteristics discernible
in most such play. Parten verifies what most preschool educators have found
out. She states that in the social play of most children from two to four years and
five months, play of family, house, and dolls was observed as the most popular
activity following play at the sand box. It was the most popular activity at the
three year level and was the most highly cooperative play at these ages.[1] As
each child matures, his dramatic play becomes more complicated and detailed,
although the context may remain similar. For example, simple house play at
three-and-a-half which includes mother, father, and baby and is of very short
duration may expand by age five to include grandparents, who are visited, a trip
on a bus, and a "movie." The latter play may last thirty or forty minutes.

To the experienced preschool teacher, dramatic play represents a major
means of extension of the self outward and of response to outward experience. It
is giving and taking, or interaction, and it is purposeful. To the writer, it also
has a third aspect. This is the result, or product of the process, namely undergoing or reformulation. This reformulation is likely to be included in the next
doing or playing out experience. One instance should make this clear. Mary
has been the grandmother in house play involving Angie as the mother, Lisa
as the baby, and herself. The next day, in a similar situation, Mary announces,
"Angie, I'm the grandmother. Lisa will visit me. She'll stay over. Then, I'll
cook, too, I'll cook on that stove." In this case, Mary, who was not as aggressive
as Angie, had played out her role as grandmother. The consequences, she found,
omitted a chance for her to use the stove, previously presided over by Angie.
Hence her recommendation or reformulation permitted her use of the stove,
but did not challenge Angie's role. This was problem-solving activity, but it
utilized the previous experience in a reformulation.

As the child organism grows, it extends itself in various ways. It undergoes
the results of its doing as Mary did in the preceding illustration and thus adds
dimension to the next interactive experience.

Danny pursues five-year-old Vince across the playground. "Bang, bang,"
he shouts. "You're dead. I got 'cha."

Snow Bird rocks her corn shuck papoose as she smiles with a four-year-old's
sense of possessiveness.

"I'm the mother," said Lynn. "You be the father." As the two four-year-olds began to set the table, Lynn added, turning to Clara, "Clara, you're the baby. Go to bed."

David looked down from the jungle gym smiling. He said, "Swish, switish, I'm in outer space." No one was near and no one said anything. David was so absorbed that he was oblivious to anyone. His teacher approached and said, "David, let's land your spaceship now. It's time to go inside."

A jungle gym is useful for large muscle development as well as dramatic play. (Courtesy Ethical Culture Schools, New York City and Celeste Muschel.)

IMITATION

Imitation tends to add to the experiential funds of the children and what is observed may be played out at first with or without embellishments by the player. Some imitation is meaningful because it helps the child to relate cause and effect and to understand the connection. Thus play gains greater vitality. For instance, four-year-old Peter who was delivering the milk from his basket of bottles looked up and when asked where the milk had come from said, "Moe's Market." Several weeks later, Peter was again delivering milk. However, he had been to a farm and had seen cows milked by machine in the interim. When asked, "Where did you get your bottles of milk?" he replied, "From the farmer out in

Hennersville. I helped him. We put the machine under the cow and they squirted milk into the pails from down the hoses. We put it into pails and I filled my bottles." The next day when wedgie cows, some small baskets, and pieces of rubber tubing appeared on the block shelf, Peter spied them immediately. He stood two cows on the floor, held a piece of rubber tubing under each in turn, and put the other end into a small bucket. He then poured his "milk" into his bottles and again delivered the milk. His imitation was not exact, but the connection of the activities he had seen flowed in sequence and made his whole play more rich. His understanding had expanded. The experience at the farm was imitated in part and reformulated as part of Peter's dramatic play.

The following dramatic play lasted nearly twenty minutes during the work-play time in the four-year-old group. This took place in the housekeeping corner.

Mary (as she put small plastic plates and a cup and saucer on the table): "Peter, come to the table. Your dinner is ready."

Peter (as he sat down): "How's our baby?"

Mary (as she picked up a doll from a chair): "She's better. I think she's 'lergic—she's got a rash."

[Both children "ate" a meal. Tom and Betty appeared.]

Mary: "Hey, Betty, you can be Aunt Molly."

Betty: "No, I'm the mother."

Mary (emphatically): "No, I'm the mother."

Betty: "O.K. What does Aunt Molly do?"

Mary: "Wash the baby."

[Tom picked up a small iron and began rubbing it across the stove.]

Peter: "Hey, Dopey, that's the stove. Ha, ha, iron, iron, iron the stove."

[Tom began to run the iron across the table, knocking the dishes to the floor.]

Betty (as she bent to gather up the dishes): "Go 'way, Tom."

Jack (from across the room): "Tom, Tom, Dopey Tom."

[Tom slammed the iron down to the floor and stalked over to the block shelves where he took out a stack of blocks.]

[Tina and Nancy approached the housekeeping corner.] Tina: "Can I play?"

Mary: "O.K. You can be the sister."

Nancy: "Me, too."

Mary: "Get out, Nancy, you can't play."

Nancy: "Why?"

Peter: " 'cause you cry."

Nancy: "I won't."

Mary: "Go wash the baby. I'm going to the supermarket."

[With that, Mary stomped out of the housekeeping corner and went to the shelf where the cube blocks were.]

"Hey, Mary," (shouted Betty). "The baby got the mumps."

Tina (went to the doll which Betty held and said): "Call Dr. Schwartz."

"Mike, Mike," (called Betty). "Come fix the baby. She's got the mumps."

"Oh," (said Mike from the book table) "does she have red spots?"

"No," said Betty, "only bumps in her neck."

The above dramatic play situation took about twenty minutes during the freely chosen and initiated work-play activities in the four-year-old group.

A variety of individual and social developmental elements were in evidence. We mention but three of these factors and several related questions which may be raised in connection with each of the three items:

1. Individual initiative and assertions—To what extent does individual initiative expressed as assertions in roles reflect social-emotional desires and longings or needs? To what extent are individual interpretations exact replications? To what extent is there a combination? Incidentally, these point up the necessity of considering the child as an individual and as a developing social being.
2. Self-projection, social conditioning, and possible causes of confusion and conflict—To what extent is social conditioning understood? To what extent do various kinds of social-cultural conditionings conflict, often for the first time, as they are played out in such dramatic play situations?
3. Individual-social constructions—To what extent does self and social construction take place? To what extent is it a creation of different and new patterns and/or of social accomodation?

A brief examination of these will indicate their importance. These questions underlie the more common concerns raised by questions of distinction of self and self-image, leadership and followership, acceptance of dominant and passive roles, learning through playing out and thus interpreting what each child experiences around him. Consideration of the three factors stated above should clairfy some of these concerns.

INDIVIDUAL INITIATIVE AND ASSERTIONS

The roles of the mother and father as played out by Mary and Peter were in large part replications of what went on in their lower middle class homes. These are primary roles and sought most frequently. Both children were articulate and well adjusted. They had no apparent frustrations and at age four were re-living a "here and now" type of situation. They asserted themselves individual-ly and showed initiative in taking the environmental situation given by the housekeeping corner and projecting themselves into the primary roles which they had created and which they played out as leaders.

Betty did express a desire for the dominant role—that of mother. While she did accept the role of Aunt Molly, she was not very clear about what was expected by Mary, whose leadership she accepted, and thus placed herself in a more passive role than the controlling role taken by Mary. The extent of her acquiescence in-to a followership role to someone else's pattern setting would determine eventual-ly whether she needed guidance into occasional leadership or dominant roles. Each child needs to experience both leadership and followership roles.

Tina did not play a prominent part. However, she arrived near the end of this particular incident. Her initial role was somewhat like Betty's. Her rela-tionship to children in other such situations as well as to Nancy should be consid-ered carefully by her teacher. In the above situation, her role was rather neutral. She was accepted and began to play out what was assigned. Although she pro-jected herself easily into what was expected, she showed no real initiative.

SELF-PROJECTION, SOCIAL CONDITIONING, AND
POSSIBLE CAUSES OF CONFUSION AND CONFLICT

Nancy was judged by others, as was Tom, in terms of past behavior. Neither child's past behavior appeared to measure up to the "we" of the others in this particular group. That standard that "*we* don't cry" (Nancy) and that certain behavior (Tom) is not accepted was a consensus expressed by Mary and Peter and seemingly accepted by all but Tom. Thus one social control had been con-structed, doubtless through considerable conditioning, by these children, and it functioned in their freely chosen activities. While the teacher was keeping an educated eye on this, along with various other activities, at no time was inter-vention necessary. Each child was adding to his own image of himself as he pro-jected himself into the role accepted by his friends. What was done was a re-flection of the kind of daily experiences which went on in their homes. The chil-dren had been conditioned socially to eat, to care for the baby, to consider dis-ease and doctor in ways acceptable to their particular family groups. Expecta-tions had been determined and although there was initiative in starting the activity and in assessing and accepting or rejecting the ongoing factors, the actual roles into which each child projected himself indicated social condition-ing rather than individual initiative.

However, confusion and conflicts in social-cultural conditioning are notice-able at times. Although none appeared here, it is entirely possible that given a few different elements, such conflict might have been apparent. Some conflicts are superficial, although they do not seem so to the participants. For example, two days later Betty and Tina both wanted to put the baby into the doll car-riage at the same time. Betty had a doll. She walked over to the carriage, took the handle, and placed the doll inside, saying, "I want the doll carriage." At the same time, Tina holding another doll, grabbed it from the front and said, "I want the pram." A tussle ensued, during which Betty maintained loudly her need for the doll carriage and Tina for the pram. The teacher's intervention settled the struggle at the same time that she said, "Some people call this a doll carriage and some people call it a pram. We can say either one." She did not want the somewhat passive Tina to feel that her English background was in-ferior. Similar struggles ensued over "napkin" versus "serviette" and verbal conflict over "lift" versus "elevator." These were settled in the same way. If Tina had been a dominant positive personality, the teacher would have said then, instead of some weeks later, that most people here say "napkin" and "elevator."

Other cultural differences may affect behavior more deeply, and the conflicts they raise can cause real confusion to the child. Examples of a few such situa-tions from preschool groups should suffice.

> 1. Charles, who was black, and Paul, who was white, were friends in the kindergarten. Their activities during work-play time tended to center around transportation. One morning both were "driving" small trucks when they halted for the STOP sign. Paul looked at Charles and said, "Your face is brown."

Cultural conditioning had not yet built up majority-minority standards. White faces predominated in this group. While Paul had not as yet developed a prejudice for or against skin color, he needed immediate intervention by his teacher in order to carry his factual exclamation into an area of acceptance. Paul's mother had been careful to see that Paul played in mixed groups. She had exposed him to racial and ethnic differences from birth. Fortunately, Paul's teacher overheard and said immediately, "Yes, Charles' face is brown. Your face is white. Dina's face is brown and Tom's face is white. You have blue eyes. I have blue eyes. Jean's eyes are brown. Charles's eyes are brown. You have blond hair. Charles has black hair. Rosie has red hair." She stated these facts slowly and Paul looked at each as it was indicated. "So," said his teacher, "some people have brown faces and some white. Some people have brown eyes and some people have blue eyes. Some people have blond hair, some black, and some people have red hair."

The teacher tried to answer the question of difference by immediately extending it to other items and thus removing the question from immediate racial distinctions of skin color at the same time that she did answer the question implied by Paul. While young children do not need a lecture when they make a single remark or ask a question, Paul's teacher did not want the matter of distinction to remain one of face color only!

This was very different from a situation observed in a park playground where three white and one black child were observed as they played house. The dominating white child was seen pointing at the black child and was heard to say, "You got to be the laudress 'cause your face and hands is all black." Unsupervised play can develop into a reflection of the adult attitudes of prejudice accepted and confirmed by the children who have been conditioned by what they have seen and heard at home.

> 2. Fanny and Nikki (both Jewish) and Tess (Catholic), all age four, were busy claiming dolls for babies. Finally, each child had one to her liking. As they settled down in the housekeeping corner, Tess said loudly, "I'll be the mother." "No," said Fanny, "I have to be the mother, you can be the Aunt, and Nikki, the sister." "I'll be," insisted Tess. "No," said Fanny very emphatically, "You can't be the mother 'cause you can't speak Yiddish."

Fanny came from a Jewish section of town while Tess came from what was referred to as Irishville. Fanny was a leader in a group which was composed primarily of Jewish children. Fanny's teacher said, "Some mothers speak Yiddith, some speak English, and some mothers speak Italian." When Fanny announced, "My mother speaks Yiddish, and so does Nikki's, and so does Sarah's," her teacher repeated what she had said. Later, when the group was all together, she repeated again what she had said. Then, "Miss Spano speaks Italian. Let's ask her to come in." Miss Spano, one of the secretaries came in, and said a few things in Italian to the children. Later, all of the children learned to say, "Good morning" in Yiddish and in Italian. Here again, the teacher tried to acknowledge difference without prejudice for or against either language. She turned the situation into a valuable learning experience for the children.

One week later, the teacher was pleased to hear Fanny and Tess in the following dialogue:

Fanny: "Let's play house. Come on."

Tess: "O.K. Let's get some babies."

Fanny: "I want two. And . . ."

Tess: "I'll be the mother."

Fanny: "No, I'll be . . ."

Tess: "I'll be today. The baby is sick. You be the doctor."

Fanny: "O.K. Maybe you could say "good morning" in Yiddish." Then, after a pause, "You can be a mother who says, "Hi, good morning, —like we're doing."

3. Joan (white) and Shelly (black), age four, were busy drawing. Joan was making the kind of figure that many four-year-olds make—a large head with features, a round body with arms and fingers, and legs and round feet. Joan carefully made two such figures while Shelly made what she later termed "swings in the playground." Joan colored in the face and body of one figure all bright green and filled in the other with bright red. When the teacher came near, Joan turned, and pointing to the green figure said, "This is Shelly," then pointing to the red one, "This is Joan."

Research differs somewhat about children's behavior in relation to color difference. For instance, in discussing studies of racial discrimination and segregation, Clark draws two general conclusion that black children from three through six tend to have an uncritical preference for white skin color[2] and Levin and Wardwell claim that black and white nursery school children appear to be well aware of racial physical differences.[3] However, it is one thing to perceive difference and quite another to prefer white. Joan, too, seemed aware of difference, but her matter of fact statement gave the teacher no need to concern herself about Joan's attitude. Joan saw and through her crayon stated a fact.

Parental influence is blamed usually as the cause of prejudice in young children. Parents of three-, four-, and five-year-olds who are consciously trying to foster equal rights tend to have children like Joan, who note skin color as a fact as they would color of dresses or eyes or hair. The writer has found that a child with long red waistlength hair caused considerable more comment in one group than did anyone else even though the group had two black and one Chinese child in it.

Mary Ellen Goodman summarizes generalizations by Gordon Allport, which she claims are supported by every relevant study, that the development of race awareness and attitudes is a continuous process through childhood, but that three essential and overlapping phases are distinguishable. She lists these as (1) *Awareness*, the beginning clarification of consciousness of self and of others in terms of racial identity. Children of two or two-and-half are likely to begin to give evidence of consciousness of own and others' racial characteristics; (2) *Orientation*, the learning and relating of race-related words, concepts, and values; (3) *True attitude*, the stabilizing of full-fledged race attitudes. Awareness of racial identity is one factor in the consciousness of self which is achieved gradually during the first three or four years of life.[4] *Awareness*, we can agree Joan had. How it would develop depended upon many factors, but the attitude fostered so far had developed an accepting outgoing child whose "best friend" was accepted happily.

Joan indicated that she and Shelly looked different, but insofar as anyone could determine this was an objective observation.[5] Research, in various instances, shows that children tend to play together without prejudice based on color when, and if, their cultural surroundings have been conducive to it. Children identify with adults and with each other. The child is accepted because he appears equal in terms of the processes in the situation—he can run, climb, participate in what others do, and thus proves his preschool acceptance on a physically adequate basis. Numerous instances can be cited of black and oriental children who have been leaders in mixed three-, four-, and five-year-old groups. Children think and do primarily with *things* at these ages. This appears to be a basic standard for acceptance at these ages. When acceptance is maintained and developmental factors for the judgments of older children are asserted, early acceptance is built upon.

> 4. Tyrone (black), age five and Sam (white) age five, went across the hall to the boys' toilet together. This was during the fourth month of school. Tyrone had just arrived in New York from South Carolina. It was his first day in the "inner city" school. Sam was mature and at home in the situation and thus his teacher had asked him to accompany Tyrone. When both had finished, Tyrone immediately ran down to the end of the hall. Sam went slowly after him, and when Tyrone went out the exit door, Sam turned and went back to the kindergarten room. "Miss Jones," he said, "Tyrone's gone." As Miss Jones' student teacher hurried to the door, Tyrone reappeared around the corner from the opposite corner of the hall. Walking up to Miss Jones with a puzzled look on his face, he said, "I can't find it. Where is it?" "You went," said Sam. "Miss Jones, he found it—he went." "Yes, but," said Tyrone, "when I was in my other school, we always ran around the pasture after we went. Then after we ran around the pasture, we came back inside. I can't find the pasture."

Tyrone was conditioned or habituated to what his southern teacher had done. Understanding of this pattern was needed. Fortunately, Tyrone, himself, had explained why he left the building. Behavioral patterns from one set of surroundings cannot always be transferred. Fortunately, Tyrone had spoken up about what he was trying to find. His teacher understood and began to try to explain to him that there was no pasture here.

The Puerto Rican child, for instance, who is used to playing freely outdoors in a rural area is also accustomed to having his bumps and bruises attended to by the parent who is near, at the time. This expectation would probably not be met on a crowded New York street.

> 5. Taro (Japanese-American) and Tim (white American), both five, were busy building in the block corner. They had made a garage and decided to name it after themselves. "What is your last name asked Tim. "Sachimoto," answered Taro. "What's yours?" "Snow," answered Tim. "What a funny name," said Taro.

Names may sound "funny" to children if they have grown up accustomed to those of a similar sound. The first time that a child's name, which has other associations, is heard may sound "funny," too. Snow fell from the sky in Taro's experience. "Funny" is the usual term for that which differs and it may not be associated with humor at all in the minds of young children. In the above situation, Taro made a statement. Since no one laughed and no one made any negative remarks, his statement stood as fact for him and the two boys continued in their activities. The teacher remarked to the group later that people had first names and last names. Some last names were long and some were short. Some people had the names of things like wood or snow. Thus she tried to broaden the children's concepts and to help Taro and Tim to expand their understanding.

> 6. Nancy and Mike, both white and both five, were placing chairs around the mat under the jungle gym. "This here's the jail," said Mike. "What's a jail?" asked Nancy. "Its where my father puts bad people," said Mike. "Why?" asked Nancy. "'Cause they're bad and he's a cop," said Mike. "When Uncle Pete got drunk, my father said he'd go to jail—and I guess he did," said Nancy. "Then my father put him there," said Mike. "No," said Nancy, "Uncle Pete's too big."

Nancy and Mike were engaged in talk involving the prowess of their relatives. Bragging is an early form of competition. "*My* father is bigger than yours," is common. It may be backed with "and he can beat up your father." Four- and five-year-olds frequently gain security in this way. The policeman—in some localities—is looked upon as THE strongman. Children, to whom he is a friend and a positive figure, often identify their fathers as a policeman even though their fathers may be real estate agents, bartenders, tailors, or storekeepers. To others, the policeman may be someone despised! Neighborhood conditioning is strong in such situations. In the case of Nancy and Mike, police were accepted, and Mike was a policeman's son. Nancy evidently did not realize the full connotations of "being drunk," but she accepted size as a symbol of power. Fortunately, no one to whom drunkenness was a social disgrace heard her. Small children growing up in an area where drunkenness is common frequently have been seen by the author to go and look at a prone figure on the sidewalk and then to announce, "I don't know him," in matter of fact terms. When they do know him, shame is not usually present until six or seven. The neighborhood and family reactions can influence reaction earlier but attitudes influenced from the outside come later.

In the above situations, it is to be noted, that an alert teacher diverted some observations into broader channels. Early confusions can lead to later conflicts. Understanding and sometimes explanation and interpretation at the proper moment are helpful.

INDIVIDUAL-SOCIAL CONSTRUCTS

New patterns, which are the children's own constructs, begin to emerge, especially in the fourth year. Generally by age four, dramatic play is small group play. These groups often have a nucleus of two, three, or four children and about the same number of other peripheral additions, who come and go. Dramatic play of the same group may be repetitive of basic patterns of baby care, cooking, and eating, but be embellished with additional factors such as trips, shopping, visits, etc. The most favored of the latter may be repeated daily for several days in one particular way. New patterns which permit additional participants may come from the children or teacher. The role of Aunt Molly permitted Betty to join but did not challenge Mary's leadership. The child who burst into a group, similar to the one described above, announcing, "I'm the shoe shiner. Give me your shoes." was stared at until one child said, "No." When the request was repeated, another child said, "You can't. We are wearing sneakers." Laughter did not deter the shoe shiner and he said, "O.K. You can run soft. Can I play? I'll be soft, too." The children continued to use the term "run soft" and "being soft" during the remainder of the year whenever sneakers were worn.

The quick transition from shoe shine to "running soft" was primarily association. However, the child did solve his problem and "construct" a means to join the play. Such "constructs" are means of solving individual or group difficulties. They indicate some initiative and may be taken over by the group as "running soft" was. The child who announced, "You can't come in without 'the word' was asked by a little girl, "What's the word?" "Midnight" was the answer. "O.K., midnight," she said and was admitted to the dramatic play then in progress. The little group accepted this use of their "word" and continued to require "midnight" for acceptance into their group play. This was a social "construct" made by the group for control. The word "midnight" continued to act as a control to play of this group. It also became significant as the word accepted by this group and acted as an "in group" control. It would be stated at any time, and when so used, be solemnly repeated. It seemed to indicate not only an original means of control but a kind of security. Eventually, the whole class was included as it was chanted, but not members of other classes. It served as a social construct meaning "this class only."

Dramatic play at age three is still primarily egocentric. A second child may well enter the activity of the first as a self-sufficient entity. The activity of the two may be initiated in a "processional" or "parallel" way and then develop interaction through exchange or distribution of materials. The relation may continue to manifest itself in considerable "processional" running about, or "parallel" action with moments of interaction. Thus it is a loose social "construct" and does indicate a relationship.

By age four, leadership tends to be evident and interaction more intricate. Roles tend to be permanent for the duration of the play underway, and although the situational context may shift, the dominant child tends to remain the leader. Domination can at times be extreme enough to require teacher intervention and guidance. Leaders at four may begin to build their following through such "constructs" as bribery. For instance, "If you come, I'll bring you a candy," or threats such as "If you don't, I won't invite you to my party." Teacher intervention can shift these "constructs" into more acceptable ones.

By age five, leadership and followership may be interchanged in the course of what is played. A new idea, stated loudly as, "Let's ride to the country" may mean a new leader. He drives the vehicle and collects all of the children on the ladder gym. Three minutes before, house play had been led by another child. Although they may argue, some small groupings may be composed of several leaders.

An age level mixture can be helpful. (Courtesy Ethical Culture Schools, New York City and Celeste Muschel.)

Age level mixture needs careful supervision. Otherwise, all too often, the older children place the younger in passive roles. "You're the baby" means you are the live doll and better than a stuffed one. You move, BUT I can still control you. Older children can be helpful and younger ones can learn from them. Too often though, it is a new form of the pecking order system. The youngest as well as the oldest needs some sense of control over what he is doing. When children create or help to create their own individual and social "constructs," they begin to achieve control.

Attention to the "constructs" created by individuals and by groups to govern their own action and to control interaction need to be judged by the teacher. Are the children's own "constructs" or ways to reach their ends socially acceptable and means to realize wholesome individual strengths? Guidance into changed actions is necessary when "constructs" are unacceptable from a broad perspective.

One important consideration for the teacher is: What, if any, props need to be introduced during dramatic play? Just when, and how, should this be done?

PROPS FOR DRAMATIC PLAY

Most basic equipment for dramatic play is already built into the indoor or outdoor facilities. Standard furnishings are likely to include:

> jungle gym or similar equipment;
> large and small blocks, sawhorses, boards, etc.;
> large and small transportation toys (some large enough to be ridden on or sat in, such as a rocking boat, wagons, tricycles, etc.);
> sandbox, and spoons, pails, sieves, etc.;
> housekeeping equipment usually in a corner or in a separate area;
> other equipment designed for sustained large and small muscle development through play.*

Equipment for preschool activities should be *durable* because it will often be dropped. It will be used by individuals whose coordination is just developing. The truck, for instance, must have wheels that are fastened firmly, not just with a staple through the axle! Things must be *large enough* to be used without frustration. The snaps or buttons or zippers on the doll's coat must be big enough for a child to manage and to manipulate. The floor blocks and outdoor blocks must be large. Equipment should be *smooth*—no splinters—and *safe*. Tambourines, for example, are fun, but they often have sharp edged jingles, and sandbox shovels can be so sharp on the edge that they give a cruel cut to an unsuspecting finger. Ropes should not be freely available before age five, if then. Large crayons—four- and five-year-olds may grasp small ones so hard that they bend—and blunt scissors should be provided. Paints, of course, should be nontoxic and

---

*See list of Equipment Companies in Appendix 2.

everything fireproof. Climbing apparatus should have mats under it. *Simple* materials without too much detail are best for three- and four-year-olds while five-year-olds can have more parts on the dump truck and more pieces in their wooden puzzles. Materials need to have the "do-with" quality; in other words, Jay is to use them, not merely sit and watch a mechanism move around. Wind-up toys are really of very little use! Things which go in mouths, such as bubble pipes, should be collected right after use for *sanitary* reasons. After a little experience, the teacher will be able to judge readily and will be among those who turn down shoddy equipment and materials.

The teacher's supplements tend to be in terms of enlarging the possibilities of what already exists when the dramatic play of the children indicates the need. Thus, for example, while not leaving ropes out as regular equipment, lengths of rope are brought out as props when the firemen ride their tricycles to a "fire" under the jungle gym. While ropes do require supervision, they do serve well as hoses, also.

Extra doll pots, pans, and washing equipment as well as a reserve telephone or two add—when brought out at the right time—to what is being played out and may be helpful in incorporating more children. They may lend added dimension to the play already underway and perhaps raise it to a more advanced level of maturity. A completely new item, such as bubble bath for the baby, a double boiler, or a new "old" hat are such items. Two small suitcases added to the housekeeping corner can cause the taking of trips to be added quite spontaneously to the dramatic play already going on.

Children do not need elaborate, intricate equipment. Simple equipment encourages them to do more, to use their imaginations, and frequently to supplement together. New basic equipment such as a mop, or broom, or a wagon can be brought out when something new will add a new turn to activity or be there as a surprise some morning. Opening a large package is fun. It also stimulates interest, speculation, and problem solving about delivery, stores, and transportation.

Most preschool teachers learn early that various items which are stored in the closet can be brought out when needed and that having them "on the spot" is advantageous to the children's dramatic play. As the teacher grows more experienced, the props in the closet tend to grow in number and in variety.

THE ENVIRONMENT

Beyond the classroom and separate though connected to home relations exists the community. As the three-, four-, and five-year-old matures, this environment becomes more important. At age three, steam shovels and transportation vehicles are watched as the child slowly distinguishes the operator or driver from the object. By age four, he "drives" the steam shovel and "flies" the plane. His identification with such environmental occupations is often more self-expansive than affirmative of social or group needs.

The garbage truck and the sanitation men handle things fascinating to a four-year-old. Parental attitudes, however, toward dirt, odor, and what is "not nice" may impinge upon direct social learning. The teacher's positive attitude and affirmation of the job and who does it can have a positive influence on the four- and five-year-old's attitude. The five-year-old who moved the kindergarten furniture in his express wagon "van" identified with the mover and understood something of the job. Imitation, projection, and interaction all helped Joe to understand what moving meant. In certain social strata, types of parent employment can be so understood and appreciated.

The social environment of the larger world is peripheral to the small child's activities. However, it does impinge—often in verbal recall and reiteration. Verbally, there is the statement, but social understanding is rare. However, the *emotional* impact is often felt strongly, and colors everything else. Some interpretation by the teacher can help. Even more important is acceptance through calm acknowledgment by the teacher. U.N. collections, for instance may mean little, but bringing toys to a nearby children's center to help furnish it is understood. This helps the four- and five-year-old to make the transition to understanding that children he cannot see because they are very far away will have things brought for them by people who know them. Although such factors may be rather unrelated to the child's immediate experiences, the teacher decides what, if anything, to do about them! For instance, the child who had seen home movies of Oriental children and their environment sat on the floor and said, "I'm going to eat here. I'm Japanese." The teacher explained, "Some people who live far away across the ocean eat from low tables. They sit on the floor when they eat." The children were too young for a detailed explanation, but this fact could be understood. Thus the child's immediate environment is clearest, the community environment is becoming understood more fully, and that of the larger world outside of the immediate community has some clear areas as well as much that awaits future exploration.

A FINAL WORD

Much of the dramatic play of children comes as a reflection of home and the immediate environment and the changes and developments introduced as extensions of these. However, items from this wider environment may impinge at times. This is usually an interjection from outside and not instigated by the child. Nina, at age four, put on all the "clothes" that she could because "I am going to the North Pole." She knew little about it except that it was cold. Three three-and-a-half-year-olds tucked in the dolls, donned doll sheets for wraps, and announced, "We're going to the Club." This was repeated at various intervals, but when asked what they would do at the Club, there was no answer! ". . . no answer! TV has made cowboys and space men more real in one sense— they can be observed. However, such vicarious experience is not firsthand. Children imitate it, but the kind of understanding they get is not the stimulation of firsthand experience.

People met in the outer environment may present positive experiences. Pow-dermaker's example of the white children's prejudice against black people—before any had been met—is still an excellent illustration of what "pictures" can be painted.[6] Strange appearances, such as the wearing of a turban by a visiting Indian, can be treated in a positive way by the teacher. If the teacher is interested and accepting, the children also will tend to be.

The role of the people with whom the child inter-acts is of great importance. (Courtesy Ethical Culture Schools, New York City and Celeste Muschel.)

In considering social interactions, it has been evident that the role of the peo-ple with whom the child interacts and the guidance and sympathetic interven-tion received when necessary are of great importance. How important the con-text, or environment, is has been implied. Teachers, though, need to spell these implications out into full considerations. Is the classroom environment arranged to be conducive to dramatic as well as quiet play? Are there materials and equipment which encourage children to participate actively? Is the program arranged with time blocks long enough to permit scope for play? Above all, does the teacher keep so aware of what is taking place that he/she knows when to add new items so that the activities continue to expand in richness in an environ-ment open enough to permit the free flowing use of what is offered. In the preschool, the world beyond the fairly immediate community is rather vague. The impingements from "out there" may reach in to the child, however, and must be met as they do so.

In his various activities, both individual and social. Jon finds out many things. Much of what he acquires in this way is a functional part of his further experiences. Parents are frequently aware of precociousness in language but rarely in their child's use of mathematical concepts. A brief look at how beginning mathematical concepts are acquired and of how they function deserves consideration next.

Notes

1. Mildred B. Parten, "Social Play Among Pre-School Children" in *Child's Play*, ed. R.E. Herron and Brian Sutton-Smith (New York: John Wiley and Sons, Inc., 1971), pp. 83-95.

2. Kenneth B. Clark, *Prejudice and Your Child* (Boston: Beacon Press, 1964), p. 48.

3. Harry Levin and Elinor Wardwell, "The Research Uses of Doll Play" in *Child's Play*, ed. R.E. Herron and Brian Sutton-Smith (New York: John Wiley and Sons, Inc., 1971) p. 173.

4. Mary Ellen Goodman, *Race Awareness in Young Children* (New York: Collier, 1970), p. 252.

5. It appears to coincide, too, with Piaget's period of preconceptual thought. As Honstead says, he "makes judgments in terms of how things *look* to him." See Carole Honstead, "The Developmental Theory of Jean Piaget" *Early Childhood Education Rediscovered*, ed. Joe Frost (New York: Holt, Rinehart and Winston, 1968), p. 138.

6. Hortense Powdermaker, *Probing Our Prejudices* (New York: Harper and Brothers, 1944).

CHAPTER 9

Mathematical Beginnings

"Of course you know that Tom is so advanced that he should not waste a year in this group. Why he knows his letters, he can write his name, and he can read *The Little Red Hen.* I have not been able to see the principal yet, but we are insisting that he be placed in the first grade."

During the course of many years as teacher of the four-year-old group of preschool classes, the writer invariably had one, two, or three parents per year, who thought that their children should be skipped ahead because they knew the alphabet or could read a few words. Actually the "reading" in most cases was memorization, but in a few cases it was genuine reading. However, never once did a parent request speedup because of mathematical understandings or rote performance with numbers. But, children do evidence individual differences in mathematical understandings as with anything else.

Young children use simple mathematical concepts frequently. Dave says, "*Four* children are wearing red shirts"; Diane says, "My doll is *bigger than* yours"; Donna asks for *more* juice; Tim brags, "I have *hundreds* of pennies. I have *ten* cents"; Jane states, "My house is *26.* It has a *2* and a *6.*" Mrs. Jones says, "Goodbye, Peter, I have to go to the *third* floor," and Peter answers, "We get our juice from the *top* floor. Its over where you are going." Ian carefully chooses a second unit block and sets it up near the first one. He understands that both are the same height when erect, although perhaps he is not able to put it into words. Children use mathematics. Some use more and some less! Large dominoes, when available, will be used and the dots matched by some and not by others. Some bases for later mathematical concepts are being experienced daily.

163

The teacher who is aware of the possibilities utilizes such experiences and expressions when and as they arise so that they will be meaningful. While mathematics, as such, is not taught formally, the teacher does further such experiences as the above when they arise and helps children to clarify their expressions about numbers and related concepts. Nixon and Nixon state it well when they say, "The kindergarten teacher needs to emphasize meaning. She will do so in many ways. In part, she simply takes advantage of the mathematical implications of everything that is done. The list can be endless. There are mathematical concepts in work with blocks, in art, at lunch, in supplies for the store, in groups of children working together."[1] If the teacher is alert, she will seize the situations when they arise in relation to what the children are doing.

Underlying concepts can be developed through incidental and unexpected events and situations. The teacher needs to be able to judge what to seize upon and develop in terms of the meaning it has for some, or all, of the children.

Care must be taken to explain this to parents. Actually, the development of simple mathematical concepts differs not at all in basic theory from that underlying reading, science, and/or social studies. During the course of the experience of preschool children, there are numerous occasions during which math in simple form is used or can be used.

As Widmer says "Experience in manipulating objects in a variety of ways is important for young children's developing mathematical concepts."[2] While it is hard to conceive of a preschool situation in which children do not manipulate objects in a variety of ways, it is easy to overlook the importance of using terms with mathematical implications. As Patty and Sam use cube blocks, Patty says, "Gimme more. Teacher, Sam has more." If Sam has most of the cube blocks, the teacher might need to intervene, "Sam, you have almost all of the cube blocks. You have more than Patty. Can you give her some of your blocks." At age four, this utilizes terms more mathematical than, "Sam, can you share with Patty?" At age five, the teacher may say, "Patty, do you know how many blocks Sam gave you?" (if not more than ten).

Division into half is a common experience, but the term needs to be used during the experience. "Never mind, Sue. Here is half of my cookie." "Here is your other mitten. You had one mitten before. You had half of your pair of mittens."

It does seem possible that many children develop an understanding of math concepts without verbalization. They put on mittens and note that one is missing or that one for each hand is what is expected. However, although they may understand functionally, they do not state the situation in mathematical terms.

Most children who hear *Millions of Cats*[3] tend to repeat, "Hundreds and thousands and millions and billions and trillions", even though they may not repeat each number and may mix the order. Having heard the story and seen the illustrations, they know that these terms stand for many cats. Other children's books use numbers and children gain some understanding of them depending somewhat upon what is done by the teacher.

Simple obstacles may be overcome, associations made, clarifications achieved, and/or learning experiences made more understandable by stopping to clarify the developing mathematical concept.

Three-year-olds, for instance, often use the term "upstairs" as they climb to a higher floor. They talk about a "big" dog and demand "more" juice. By age four, such concepts are part of the understanding of most of the group. However, utilizing the term upstairs may not be clear enough to be related to anything else. The child who says that the plane is "down" in the air needs to relate the two experiences of "up." Thus the concept develops. Numerous experiences which place the developing concept in a variety of situations need to be lived through and understood. Looking up at the ceiling, watching the elevator go up, and noting the pigeon's flight up to the high ledge add to the understanding of "up."

The number of quantitative concepts which three- and four-year-olds use and which are well understood are likely to include the following: up and down; more (sometimes less or few); little and big (small and large); a half; a pound (sometimes ton); a quart (sometimes pint or gallon); spoonful; foot (sometimes inch and yard); mile as a distance; long and short.

Temporal concepts are usually less accurate, but such terms as "a little while," "five minutes," yesterday, tomorrow, and sometimes last week and last year are frequently understood by the time the child is four-and-a-half. Temporal sequence may take longer to establish with some children. By four-and-a-half and five, twelve o'clock, three-thirty (or the time of departure), and nine (or some important morning time such as that of arrival at school) may be understood and utilized as well as being noted on the clock.

Simple groupings—a pair; two; the heavy and the light weight balls or blocks; the matching of colors (like) or the same—and separating those that are different (unlike) are often done quite spontaneously. "I want the red clothes for the doll" or "I have all of the blue cubes," for instance. Five-year-olds often can match large dominoes. Simple lotto is useful for prereading and premath experiences because it utilizes the likes and differents in the symbols and sometimes more and less. Symbol recognition is usually easier after basic shapes are familiar. "These two squares are red." "My box is square." These objects are large and can be manipulated easily by small hands.

Counting is frequently by rote and quite mechanical, if learned at home. However, the child who carefully counts the napkins for the table, who counts four children and four cookies—one for each—has utilized one-to-one correspondence. Some develop the concept that four children and four napkins are both four. In more advanced terms, we might say that they have found that equivalent sets have the same number even though it is not stated in these terms.

On rare occasions, a mature four-and-a-half-year-old has been known to say, "We need four napkins." In response to "Why?," he answered "Because

*Symbol recognition usually is easier after basic
shapes are familiar. (Courtesy Department of Health,
Education and Welfare and Dick Swartz.)*

four people are going to sit here." Later, he answered the same way about five
napkins and five people.

Four-year-olds in one group had baby rabbits one spring. They marked off
the age by marking a line through each day in the week as it occurred. The calendar had days and a few red boxes for the day the rabbits were born, the day
their eyes opened, the day they first ate lettuce, etc. Most of the children could
count the spaces from the day of birth and state that "they are fifteen days old,"
etc. As they counted, they said "one day old, two days old, etc." They also
learned what one week was on the large calendar and that days were part of a
week.

Measurement may be done quite spontaneously by using feet or a unit block.
A foot ruler or yardstick can be introduced, if Pat announces that she "needs a
rug four of her feet long" to lead into her block house. The child making a road
for cars may say, "It's big. It's *bigger* than Tony's." If he is asked, "How *long* is

it," the answer may be, "twelve blocks" (unit blocks). A ruler can be introduced with the suggestion, "Let's try this. It may be easier." After he has laid it down three times, this is called to Alan's attention, "You made it three feet long, didn't you, Alan." Later, this may be shown to the other children, "Alan made a road. Alan, how long was it?" "Yes, Alan measured his road with a ruler. Can you show us?"

Mature four-year-olds can vote for the book that they wish to hear. The first time this is done, it is wisest to choose a favorite and one which only a few children seem to like. Each child is given a cube block. "Today we'll vote for the book that *more* of you want to hear." As the teacher holds out one of the books in each hand, each child is asked to lay his block on the book that he most wants to hear. After each has done this, the teacher asks, "Which book do more of you, children, want to hear?" After some have pointed to it, the teacher says, "Let's see." She takes each block and lines it up on the book on which it has been placed, "Here is Jon's vote, here is Mary's," etc. Then the same is done with the less popular choice. The difference is quite obvious. More children voted for this book. Fewer children (or less) voted for this book. She lines up the blocks near enough, so that three for one book and ten for the other are obvious and clear to the children. "*More* children wanted to hear this book today, so I'll read it (pointing)." Pointing, "And fewer children voted for this. I'll read it later. This," pointing, "had only one, two, three children vote for it, and it had fewer or less votes than this one. This one (pointing) had *more* votes. It had ten votes." "Now," moving the blocks into two groups, "there are *more* blocks on this book and *fewer* (or less) on that." The teacher should decide whether to use fewer or less depending on what she hears most from the children. With some classes, it is best to go through the above on several occasions without counting the blocks. Later, books are chosen which may have more nearly equal votes. Looking at the two groups, lining them up, and, for some children, counting them fuctions as the means to the "voted for" choice.

Large durable scales can be introduced in the five-year-old group. Finding which is the heavier baby guinea big or the lighter doll or car is useful experience. Weighing on a kitchen or baby scales is also a functional experience.

Quart and pint containers from milk or orange juice should be available for use by the children. These are called by name and children find out for themselves, usually, that two pints fill one quart container.

Children often learn to recognize a number rather readily due to its experiential association. "I live at twenty six. It has a two and a six." "My floor is nine." "My father has some numbers on his license." "Our school is at sixty-fourth street." "The numbers are on the sign." "There is a three and another three on the steps." Functional use usually precedes sequential understanding.

Five cents for a meter means more than one cent if the child has experienced use of the former and not the latter. Thus the functional experience determines the learning. After the children recognize a nickel, the teacher may utilize a penny or dime in an experience. However, the concept that five pennies equal one nickel should be delayed in most cases.

It is interesting to note Westcott and Smith's reference to tri-point progression. They stress the concrete which is three-dimensional; the semi-concrete which is two dimensional; and abstract symbols.[4] Although directed to the elementary grades, a high percentage of preschool children, in the writer's experience, have had considerable experience with the first, such as in counting children and blocks; some experience with the second, such as counting the number of puppies in a picture; a little experience with the abstract symbols, such as recognizing number six and perhaps making it with a crayon if Tim lives on floor number six. The point should be emphasized here though that although the preschooler has experiences with tri-point progression, it is not sequential. He may utilize progression functionally in various situations, but rarely in an overall sense. In other words, he has experienced various islands of meaning which will help him to navigate further on the vast ocean of mathematics.

Westcott and Smith state that the four basic math processes used by elementary school children involve the two actions of "putting together" and "taking apart."[5] In considering this, the preschool teacher concludes that the former is more in evidence than the latter. However, many teachers, with their group, decide which children are "away from" the group and state that Jon's pair of boots is now only one boot because one is still in his cubby and "away from" the other.

Todd and Heffernan discuss their version of the "take away game" which most teachers have used in one form or another.[6] The version used by this writer is as follows: the teacher places a small table in front of her when the children are seated in a group; three, four, or five children, depending on the maturity level, are sent to get a small article such as a crayon, a small car, a cube block, a doll cup, etc.; these are placed in a row on the table; the teacher lifts each in turn and says, "this is a cube block," etc. and places it back where it had been; one child covers his eyes; another takes away one object and holds it behind his back, the first child opens his eyes and tells what has been taken away. Care must be taken to return each object to the same place. It is also wise to say, "What did Polly *take away?*" Although Todd and Heffernan suggest using three closely related objects with three-year-olds,[7] the writer has found that starting with familiar but different objects makes for an easier beginning. Similar objects can be used later. The number of objects should be three at the start, but may be increased to six, seven, or eight by age four-and-a-half. One object can be added, also. It is usually wisest for the teacher to govern the placing and replacing of the objects because it is important that each be seen or not seen in its place.

Another game, used by the writer occasionally, is one in which the teacher directs one child, "Go and get one small thing and put it on the table" (in front of the teacher). Then, "Peter, did Sarah get one object?" The numbers can be increased to two, three, and sometimes four or five objects at age five. After a group of objects has been collected, the teacher says, "Addy, take away two things and put them away." Thus there is simple adding and subtracting.

Thus the child, who has distinguished *my* self from my mother and who has understood that *I* am Shelly, begins through daily experiences to distinguish groupings, quantities, spatial and temporal concepts and to use some number concepts as he recognizes a few symbols. "Four candles and one to grow on are on my cake. When I am five, I'll have five candles and one to grow on." So it goes! Mathematics concepts are developing constantly. The teacher must utilize the experiences of every day in which the child is engaged for further mathematical clarification and concept development.

Foundational to all that has been said in relation to children and what they are when they enter the preschool is the parent. We turn now to a consideration of parents in the next chapter.

Notes

1. Ruth Nixon and Clifford Nixon, *Introduction to Early Childhood Education* (New York: Random House, Inc., 1971), p. 164.

2. Emmy Louise Widmer, *The Critical Years: Early Childhood Education at the Crossroads* (Scranton: International Textbook Company, 1970), p. 120.

3. Wanda Gag, *Millions of Cats* (New York: Coward-McCann Incorporated, 1938).

4. Alvin Westcott and James Smith, *Creative Teaching of Mathematics in the Elementary School* (Boston: Allyn and Bacon, Inc., 1967), pp. 18-19.

5. Ibid, p. 34.

6. Vivian Todd and Helen Heffernan, *The Years Before School* (New York: The Macmillan Co., 1971), pp. 380-81.

7. Ibid., p. 380.

CHAPTER 10

Parents as a Part of the Program

DEVELOPING POSITIVE RELATIONSHIPS WITH PARENTS AND THE COMMUNITY

Rafaelo's eyes opened wider and his grip on his mother's hand tightened as mother and four-year-old drew closer to the big green door of the center. In response to the teacher's welcome two minutes later, Rafaelo responded, "Rafaelo fine."

Within five minutes, Rafaelo's sweater had been removed and hung up on a hook under the picture of a yellow cow by Rafaelo with the teacher's insistent encouragement, his mother had departed, and Rafaelo had shifted the grip of his right hand from the left hand of his mother to that of the head teacher. The latter had led him to the block corner where large building blocks and all sorts of other manipulative materials were housed. There was an assortment of cars, "wedgie" people, and animals made of wood and plastic. Rafaelo reached out with his left hand and took a "wedgie" horse. Following his teacher, who had slowly released her hand from his, Rafaelo went back across the room and sat on a chair near the book table. Holding the horse tightly, he watched the other children for several minutes. He got up slowly, then, went back across the room to the block shelves, and removed six blocks. As he stood them up around the horse, he said, "Horse-house."

Alexandra Jane trotted happily beside her father chatting gaily. Her talk was interspersed with such comments as, "Daddy watch Sandra Yay yump, Daddy watch Sandra Yay paint, Daddy drink with Sandra Yay." The two saw the school nurse, walked down the long hall, and reached the three-year group's room. Here Alexandra Jane quickly greeted the teacher with "Hello, Sandra Yay here." After pointing out yesterday's finger painting to her father, she hugged him and said, "Bye, Daddy." Within three minutes, Alexandra Jane was engrossed in dressing a large doll in the housekeeping corner along side of Mollie, who was performing a similar task.

In each of the above situations, a parent had entered the room, the child had been greeted by a teacher, and the first activity of the child's day had begun.

For each teacher, there were similar general expectations as well as specific goals for each child in terms of the context of parent-teacher relationships. One desired to further the development of Rafaelo, on the one hand, and of Alexandra Jane, on the other.

The general expectations held by both teachers and kept operational with parents follow. Each general expectation is qualified by a brief explication of the kind of specific subgoals and considerations applicable to the particular situation. After a little experience, any teacher can add her specific examples to the list.

1. *To establish rapport with each parent* in order to build a cooperative relationship to work with, understand, and foster the maximum development of each child.

Although the school that is able to tell the parents that their cooperation is essential to maintaining a place in the group for their child is rare, almost every preschool teacher seeks to establish rapport with each parent. Otherwise, a reservoir of knowledge about each child is missing. General means, such as parent conferences, meetings, and assessments, will be discussed later. However, for these to be successful, the necessary positive rapport with the parent is established more gradually. Each little encounter is important. While the teacher is filling in her picture of each child in terms of background and home, the parent also is registering his or her impressions of the teacher.

The means to positive rapport vary from meeting the affluent parent like Alexandra Jane's in a local restaurant to greeting the "inner city" father of Rafaelo in his little grocery. Each meeting, no matter how brief, should reflect the teacher's attempt to be in the role of an understanding and helpful friend who shares the parents' concern for their child. This does not mean letting a parent enter unannounced to monopolize the teacher's full time when she is needed in the middle of the work-play time. It does mean that the teacher should try to find a way to meet the parent well over half way, that she should utilize every possible opportunity, and that she should constantly seek to develop the relationship.

"Oh, Mrs. Green, I am so glad to see you. We are attaching this bell to Jimmy and Joe's garage so that they will know when customers come. Won't you sit down? Jimmy, just where do you think the bell should be?"

After Jimmy and Joe had been assisted and Mary's smock found, Miss Berns returned to Mrs. Green and said, "How are you? I see that Linda wants to show you our rabbit. Will you stay for our snack time?" Thus Miss Berns was friendly, although she was occupied; she informed the parent of what was happening; she tried to put Mrs. Green at ease by giving her a hint of what her Linda wanted; at the same time, she let Mrs. Green know that she was welcome to stay for the snack which would come later. From the above, Mrs. Green began to develop an understanding of Miss Berns as a professional person with certain obligations.

Some parents, like Alexandra Jane's, who bring a son or daughter may need a little urging to see what is important to the child. "Mr. Fink, have you a minute? Sandra Jane would like you to see what she painted."*

In localities where the father has not visited the room, this will get father into the room and, hopefully, make him feel more at home. Once inside the room, he will see the other children and gain some information about what is taking place. Fathers sometimes think that visiting is for mothers. Teachers can, and should, exert every effort to make fathers feel at home.

Fathers' Day is fun! (Courtesy Ethical Culture Schools, New York City and Celeste Muschel.)

A cup of instant coffee or a chance to sit down for a few minutes is welcomed late in the day by the tired working parent. With a little encouragement, this

---

*Mr. Fink may need the stages of painting explained.

may be an opening wedge for numerous short, informal exchanges. "How about a cup of coffee, Mrs. Santos? Just sit down there, the water will be hot in a minute." Mrs. Santos has been on her feet most of the day and the chair and cup of coffee are genuinely appreciated.

Being aware of the needs and interests of her children are part of the teacher's stock in trade. Trying to decipher the best approach to establishing a friendly relationship to a group of parents whose backgrounds, work, speech, and attitudes differ widely is a requisite to a well-functioning preschool group.

2. *To endeavor to keep manner, approach, and the growing relationship with each parent on a positive, interactive basis.* Some parents try, consciously or unconsciously, to put the teacher on the defensive. "Oh, Mrs. Small, Toddler Town has a better block supply. Why don't you have yours painted in bright colors?" "Oh, Mrs. Jenkins, this book says that girls are more adept at making initial social relationships than boys. Don't you think that every parent should read it?" "Well, I am tired and he is tired, too. Why can't he sleep all afternoon? My friend says that they do at Small Villa." And so it goes!

A defensive reply by the teacher may simply encourage the insecure parent to continue. A smile of acknowledgment, backed by a phrase or two to let the parent know that a point of view does underlie what is done, can be followed by a change of subject. This should be chosen to put the parent at ease and may suffice to meet the challenge. The teacher also may indicate that materials and the program will be discussed at an early meeting.

The parent who enters the room with a critical and comparative eye may soon become the teacher' greatest ally if answered in a calm matter-of-fact tone. If the parent knows a little about equipment or programs and finds that the teacher knows more and can justify the blocks or rest hour, the parent is more likely to respect her judgment. After all, when a parent sees an item in one place and not in another, a quantitative judgment may be all that can be given.

"Mrs. Jones, I know that you need to leave. Could you wait for Jill to finish the book that she is looking at?" begins to indicate to Jill's mother that the teacher respects her as well as Jill. Some parents need to understand the need a child has to finish what she has begun.

3. *To understand and to meet the needs of the individual child* as well as possible at the same time that each child is seen *in relation to the social and cultural context* of his family, neighborhood, community, and general background.

If Mary Jane insists upon kissing her teacher every morning, while Si merely says "Hi" shyly, the teacher needs to accept each child's expression. Parental concern for amenities can be discussed and explained at another time. Sometimes a remark—out of Si's hearing—to his mother such as, "Si speaks more spontaneously now" indicates understanding and appreciation of Si. His mother is quick to pick up Si's teacher's positive attitude.

The strict parent, who insists that his four-year-old say, "Good morning" and shake hands is probably overly strict in other ways. Frequently, these can best be discussed and need for a more relaxed approach be met at a general meeting.

To seek a change in something by making an issue over one small aspect of behavior may do more to harm than to help the situation. The Puerto Rican child, who looks away, should not be forced to "look at me." His cultural background encourages the former not the latter. When he has not done what is expected, he feels guilty and looks away. Insistence upon having him "look at you" only makes him feel more ashamed. The child who has been taught to challenge everything with his fists first needs to be led slowly but surely to learn that there are other approaches. This should be explained to his parents in terms of what "we do here." Jon needs to learn to *say* what he does not like rather than to hit. "Let's ask him to tell us what is bothering him." To build up a "My Mommy says . . ." versus a "My teacher says . . ." attitude does little to foster a unified approach toward the child and, of course, merely fragments the child's approach to himself and to what he does.

Cultural differences—yes! A pluralistic approach at the start, especially, encourages open interaction. At the same time, the few necessary regulations must be stressed. "We do not talk during a fire drill" means more when explained and practiced *and* when it is one of a few regulations. A few rules are necessary and these need to be introduced in ways to make them clear to those of the many cultural backgrounds found in some groups.

4. *To maintain a growing understanding of each child within the perspective of general patterns of physical, mental, social, and emotional growth and development.*

Elias's need to take his time to climb the jungle gym during the early weeks of the fall may need to be explained to his mother. She sees that other children climb it readily. Having not had opportunities for climbing, Elias may not speed to the top for several weeks. A discussion with his parents about the need for physical activities which utilize large muscles should enlighten Elias's parents at the same time that it proves once again to his teacher that all children are individuals.

Debbie's desire to tap dance for everyone during rhythms should be accepted at the same time that she is led to rhythmic expression of other kinds *and* given approbation for other activities. Her parents can be helped to understand that Debbie is part of a group and that free rhythmic expression has values, too. Debbie does not need to be a star performer to gain acceptance. While her parents' pride must be accepted, their desire to put their child in the spotlight can be diminished with an understanding approach as well as an introduction to the benefits of free, creative rhythmic development.

Many parents come to the preschool with a one-sided or two-sided view of its advantages. Usually this is in terms of social development or added advantages in first grade. Elias's parents probably had never considered development in the full sense of the four major aspects. The well-educated teacher has an educational job to do here—full development of all aspects for maximum child development.*

---

*Physical, mental, social, and emotional growth and development. See chapter 1.

5. *To know where parental and professional obligations are similar as well as dissimilar.* While every teacher tries to help each child make an easy transition from home to school, he/she does not become another parent. Being a parent surrogate is necessary at times, but no parent should enter the room to find the teacher hugging and kissing several children and referring to them as "My own children" and that "Susie is so cute that I could eat her up!"

Affection and supplementary love where needed are coupled with a growing perspective of the child as a whole individual with needs, interests, and definite wants which require skilled and professional handling. Each child has the right to the teacher's professional judgment. He needs to be seen in terms of himself and in the large group context. Perspective is what the teacher can contribute!

Sentimentality is neither genuine respect and affection nor is it an indication of a professional approach to a serious matter—namely the profession of educating children. The teacher is a professional and this should be clear. Being a professional means, among other things, possessing judgment, a sense of responsibility, and the obligation to bring the best* of an ever-enlarging background of theory and practice in education to the preschool scene regardless of where it is housed!

6. *To be sympathetic with the parent* and to seek to encourage the child's potentialities at the same time that parental problems, point of view, and aspirations are understood and kept in focus.

"Good afternoon, Mrs. Shapiro. I was sorry to hear that the twins have been so sick" does far more for Mr. Allen's relationship with Mrs. Shapiro than greeting her with, "We do need to discuss Sam's social relationships. He hit Tommy over the head twice today." If the teacher can see that Tommy isn't hurt and give Sam the support he needs, due to his mother's preoccupation with the ailing twins and subsequent lack of attention to him, the situation can be carried temporarily by Mr. Allen. On the other hand, when the change in health is long-term or even permanent, Mr. Allen should see Sam's mother in order to discuss the relation of Sam and his behavior to the problem situation as soon as possible.

In the first, the home context is temporarily and understandably disturbed. In the second, new patterns need to be established as early and as soon as possible. Most parents are deeply appreciative of such concern on the teacher's part. If the parent seems resentful of the teacher's concern, a much slower approach needs to be taken.

In the case of the parent who speaks little English the teacher needs to spend plenty of time to assure and reassure her/him that she wants to be friendly and helpful and that she is not being critical. The teacher must guard against letting the parent think that she is assuming responsibility for everything or that she is critical and trying to gain the child's love and turn him against his parent. At the school, the teacher can take over Sam and his problem until things are straightened out, BUT this is not a long-term taking over of the parents' role!

---

*Best as tried out and judged by the teacher.

7. *To realize that the apt suggestion made at an apt time will accomplish more* than an impersonal directive or an authoritarian dictum.

"Does Jimmy ever have children over for lunch on Saturday?" for one parent, and "Teddy's mother would be glad to bring Jimmy home on Fridays, if you would be willing to have her do so," for another, are both geared to furthering Jimmy's social development.

The directive, "Jimmy must play with other children as much as possible. If you would invite Teddy to come over, it would help Jimmy" is not guaranteed to foster an interactive relationship. It implies criticism, it commands that some act be performed. It implies, too, that Teddy is somewhat superior.

A quiet, uninterrupted conference is usually the best means to approach a discussion of problems of this sort. This allows a gradual approach to the problem as the teacher assesses Jimmy's parents' acceptance of themselves as parents, of problems, and of Jimmy each step of the way. Being requested to invite another child versus being able to see the need through discussion and perhaps suggesting herself/himself that another child visit are two radically different approaches. The second keeps the parent in a position of authority in the home and makes the parent feel good because he/she has helped with a possible solution to a problem and been assured by the teacher that it is worth trying.

8. *To note when and where greater, and perhaps external, authority may be necessary.*

The child who arrives dirty, who has bruises, or who is excessively apprehensive may be indicating the need for external authority. Terry who arrived a half hour late wearing two kinds of sox, a very dirty shirt, and grease on his face announced, "I brought myself on the bus." Mr. Shores helped Terry wash his face, asked him whether his mother was at home, and a few questions about the public bus. Through this means, he was trying to ascertain whether the four-year-old really had come alone. Terry's teacher went to the principal that afternoon.

Mrs. Anderssen, who found bruises on Selma's arms and neck and who got a glum, "I jest bumped" from Selma, took her to the center nurse and asked the director of the center to meet her there. While children do get dirty, do fabricate, and do bump themselves, there are numerous cases of child neglect and abuse. Inasmuch as the child is powerless to do anything, the teacher must gain whatever cooperation is necessary from the center or school attended by the child, from legal and/or professional authorities, from medical authorities, and often, as added support, from a clergyman, doctor, or social worker who may know the family. Just what is the situation? Who is at fault? Who needs help? What intervention may be necessary to assure Terry and Selma a decent, safe childhood? These questions may be asked by Mr. Shores and Mrs. Anderssen, but the answers must be made by authorities external to the school and center.

9. *To realize that being in school may rouse old feelings of hostility* which the parent may not fully comprehend and thus that agreement, affirmation, and understanding may be the best means of meeting this.

"Anthony's a good kid. Why I getta as' go to his teacha?" The neighborhood coordinator had a job to do. Perhaps the teacher had tried to reach Anthony's mother! Perhaps her means of contacting her had roused old feelings of hostility. In the past, the school as a rigid bastion of discipline and authority held an awesome role for many children. Now these children are parents. Many educational developments may be completely unknown. "Anthony not bad." No, but his mother had to be urged to go to school to meet his teacher. She must be welcomed heartily and her attitude, which may be very hostile, met head on. "I have been trying to meet all of the mothers. Anthony is a fine child. Does he help you at home? He likes to set the table and to help pass the milk here." This should give Anthony's mother some reassurance. It should be followed by some indication of a need for her contribution. "Was Anthony ever scared by a big dog? Oh, won't you tell me about it? Perhaps we can help him get over it," or "There will be a little get-to-gether for parents on Tuesday at five. My assistant will stay with the children. We'll have coffee. I was wondering whether you would be able to help me pour it?"

Old fears are not overcome in an instant, but a friendly smile, a positive approach, and a cooperative attitude are helpful. A discussion of the parents' own early school days can be helpful. This aids the teacher often, in finding a few obvious differences. The teacher can comment sympathetically and then indicate that some things are different now. Once the parent finds out that Anthony is not "bad", that she is welcome, and that the teacher is friendly, Anthony's mother is less hostile and her reeducation about modern education begins. Furthermore, she can be very reassuring to other parents.

10. *To realize that one can learn constantly from this kind of experience* as well as from any other.

The vast difference between "knowing," which indicates competence and understanding, and being a "know-it-all," which is calculated to try to put the teacher on a level superior to that of the parent, should be obvious. The teacher can, and should, be learning constantly. No matter how long and intense the past experience, the teacher is constantly refining old conclusions, meeting new problems, and continuously experiencing and undergoing the results of all of these daily situations. This is part of the teaching profession. Parents, too, improve their own self-images when they learn that they are contributing to this ongoing learning. Mutual learning in an interactive relationship constantly sharpens the alertness of each participant to new understandings.

The teacher who responded to Mrs. Klein's, "I learned so much that I didn't know" with "I found out some things, too," is on the way to a positive relationship and ever-widening experience.

OTHER CONSIDERATIONS

There are various other considerations of which the teacher should be aware. Some of these, stated as questions, are discussed briefly.

How can the teacher get parents to come to school?

In certain localities, a note, a phone call, or word of mouth is enough. Upper and middle class parents, whose children attend a preschool as part of a whole school experience, often expect to come to school for various functions. Such parents may request a conference or ask about the first meeting. However, it must be remembered that since many affluent parents hold busy positions, too, problems about meeting times as well as means of initial contact may be just as difficult to manage as with the nonaffluent working parents. In preschool groups housed in projects, there may be need to utilize the services of the community coordinator if the child attending is the oldest in the family. When there is a language problem, this is necessary. A social worker or the community worker may need to be present as an interpreter during conferences or meetings. Once the purpose of conferences and meetings becomes clear, the parent tends to co-operate providing there is no embarrassment. (This, of course, points up the reason for teachers to speak some of the language of the minority dominant in the district in which they teach.) Provision needs to be made for younger children as well as for the child concerned. If the meeting is after hours, care must be taken at the beginning of the planning to assure the teacher that most parents are free at the proposed time.

Food helps! Ask parents to come for a cup of coffee and more are likely to come. Initial anxiety tends to disappear as people share coffee (or similar drink). Most parents want to hear about their own child. "Come and see what Billy does all day" is an inducement. Each parent is a valuable source of information about his or her own children and no teacher should be deprived of this resource.

To expect a three-year-old to travel home with someone else, other than his parent, and to deliver a note is a bit unrealistic unless it is pinned to his clothing. On too many occasions it never reaches home anyway—or the parent may not be able to read it.

Direct word-of-mouth followed by a mailed note is best except for non—English-speaking parents. The latter need a person-to-person approach. If there is an assistant, this person may call on parents or otherwise try to contact them.

At age five, and sometimes before, the child, himself, can sometimes assist in getting parents to attend a meeting. If the child helps to arrange the room for a meeting, he will want his parents to come. In some instances, if there is a staff to assist, the children can greet their parents and remain until all have arrived, then the assistant or other adult can take them to another room or to the playground. Occasionally, children may remain long enough to pass the cookies that they have frosted for their parents. However, this should not be at the very first meeting.

What should one say and do when parents are there?

Many of the suggestions made in the preceding section are applicable here. Generally, the following are useful guidelines: (a) greet the parent as though genuinely glad to see him or her; (b) use simple language, but do *not* talk down to the parent whose English is poor; (c) be positive; (d) try to give each something of importance about his or her child that is specific; (e) be encouraging; (f) be appreciative of evidences of cooperation; (g) stress that this is for the parent's child and that we are all cooperating for his benefit. If coffee or other refreshments are planned, it helps to have them ready when the parents begin to arrive. If this is your first conference or meeting with these parents, keep your plans clear and make the event short. Leave plenty of time for questions and to get suggestions for the future.

How should one conduct a conference?

Role playing the initial conference before it takes place can be most helpful if one has the opportunity. The new teacher needs to remember that the parent should be put at ease, that she or he (the teacher) is a source of information sought by a high percentage of parents, but that these parents may become very apprehensive if the teacher is too critical. In turn the parent is of great benefit to the teacher in furthering understanding of the child. The parent is not there to be embarrassed nor to be talked down to because this is a time for cooperation and interactive sharing. Even though parent education may be in order, it should be carried out in so far as is possible, in a way that is mutually supportive.

Many teachers have a kind of outline in their heads of the information sought in a conference.* Writing down the things a parent says while he/she is there at the conference is not a good idea except for such things as ages of siblings or dates of contagious diseases if there have been changes from earlier records. At such times, the teacher should plainly state what is being written down and why. Most parents appreciate the teacher's concern.

The teacher needs to remember to "gear" language to the parent's understanding. Telling the parent, who speaks little English that "sibling rivalry can be emotionally destructive" is potentially useless. How many teachers are guilty of using some such phrases? Thus the teacher needs to know how to translate information into language understood by the parent. The use of certain words differs in different localities, and awareness of this is helpful.

Say something positive about each child. Try to end a conference during which problems have been discussed on a positive note of encouragement. Make suggestions, if you can, about affirmative actions that the parent can perform and assure the parent that you will have another conference soon. Assure each parent(s) that you will confer at his/her (their) request and that frequent conferences are sometimes necessary when special problems arise.

How should one conduct a meeting?

To help assure success, initial meetings should start on time, not be longer than an hour or an hour and a half, and end at the time stated. The parents are greeted warmly, given some information that they want, and incorporated into —but not allowed to dominate—the meeting. Announcements made should be clear, and necessary plans and/or elections be followed succinctly. When possible, children's work—that of *every* child—should be in evidence. The meet-

---

*See Appendix 6.

ing should be planned for plenty of interaction. The time and manner is to be determined by the subject matter under consideration.

If parents are slow to participate, those most anxious to verbalize should be given a chance and as others appear to show an interest, the question might be asked rather casually, "Mrs. Simon, do you agree with what Mrs. Morris said?" A nod "yes" from Mrs. Simon has opened the door for her to participate. Reference made later to her agreement or disagreement keeps her in focus. Care must be exercised constantly that one, two, or three parents do not dominate. If others are slow to particpate, an example may be given by the teacher. This broadens discussion and may bring in a necessary second point of view.

Meetings should be lively—a joke or two may help. Weber's suggestion to show slide recordings of children's work to aid discussion should be noted.[1] The writer has found that children's actual work, when displayed and discussed, adds a great deal of meaning to what is said. Slides meet the problem of permitting children to take their work home, however.

What should be considered at meetings?

What the child does all day is interesting to parents. Thus a brief rundown of a typical day is helpful. Parents can try out the materials and equipment and those of mature four- and five-year-olds can be guided through a typical day in abbreviated form. The chance to try clay or dough, to put together a puzzle, or to connect a bell to make it ring may be new experiences for some parents. Explanations and/or discussion of certain common developmental problems such as how to broaden a child's interests and activities and the relation of these to first grade reading activities, what to do about TV, how to get Jon to be less subservient to his brother are useful and worthwhile starters. A call for anonymous written suggestions for future meetings can be helpful. The parent who really wants to know why children rest, why they are encouraged to taste each food, or why building blocks are considered important may hesitate because he or she thinks that everyone knows. The subject does depend upon the community, parental concerns, and teacher assessment of needs. To quote Weber again, she states in her discussion of the Plowden Report that English Infant Schools were provided as a response to parents' as well as to children's needs and that the close and warm parent-teacher relationship has a base from which to expand its educational role with parents and community.[2] There are numerous examples of this in the United States. For instance, some independent school parents seek to work for the community as well as the school in making surveys, in service to neighborhood agencies, and in public relations, while inner city centers may disseminate information of an educational nature about items ranging from drug abuse to inexpensive books for preschool children. Cooperative nurseries often expand their services through benefits put on by parents and by distributing information about child care, education, or legislation. There are new subjects possible all of the time.

What other roles can parents perform?

The parent who is free to help occasionally usually likes to do so. The parent who does assist needs to clarify his role with his own child with the teacher. Oversolicitous parents, parents who are outspoken about children in their presence, and apprehensive parents benefit from a few suggestions. This caution on the part of the teacher is essential if the group experience with the teacher is to be of maximum benefit to the child as well as to his parent(s).

Parent officers, or room parents, can help the teacher plan meetings, and notify other parents about meetings, events of common interest, or situations such as a seriously ill child, which should be known to all. Parent officers can often bridge a gap between the teacher and a reticent parent. They can spend a morning and/or have lunch with the group in order to become more knowing about the children, teacher, and the program.

Parent assistance on short field trips needs to be planned carefully. Otherwise the teacher sometimes may have to guide the parents into concern for the children and to end their own chatting along the way. Giving each parent a definite group or place in which to function is helpful. If parents drive, care must be taken to be sure that they have the insurance necessary to protect the children.

How can reluctant or busy fathers be included?

Fathers should participate in conferences when possible. Some fathers are able to come in alone for conferences and should be encouraged to do so when they cannot accompany their wives. Their insights about their children as well as their wives' relationship to them is important. At such times, they may be able to remain and visit for awhile. One school initiated a yearly Father's Day successfully many years ago. On this day, usually one of the February holidays, the mother is asked to keep the child at home, if the father, a male relative, or friend is unable to come. Otherwise it is too hard on the child. A grandfather, uncle, brother, or friend is just as welcome in the case of the young child of divorced parents. Mothers are told that they may visit any day but this. It is interesting to note how much fun it can be for the children, if a father can be invited for lunch, and also, how enlightening it may be for the father.

In cooperative nurseries, fathers can often provide needed equipment, repair equipment, and paint. Needless to say, their understanding is greater, if they can visit and see how the equipment is used. Fathers, who can participate occasionally, add a great deal to a preschool situation.

Parent specialties can be incorporated into the day's program providing that they are not too overstimulating. The teacher should plan beforehand with such a parent and then the naturalist, the violinist, the sketch artist, or the lolly pop maker can be utilized to the fullest extent for the children's advantage. Many a mother and father can provide fine learning experiences, if encouraged to do so.

What can children and parents share?

Although three-, four-, and five-year-olds may be included advantageously, occasionally, in part of a conference of parent with teacher, it is generally best for the two adults to confer without them at this age level. Children do sometimes clarify a situation by explaining what they like to do, why they perform certain activities, and what they wish they could do.[3] Their unfulfilled wants may range from "building an ocean" as Dick's did, to "riding that chain bike 'cause I never did." The latter should alert the teacher either to what may be an unfair use of equipment or to a hesitancy on the part of Dick to try something new. At the same time the teacher realizes that "never" in a child's conception may not yet be equivalent to that concept held by the adult! Even in such cases, parent and teacher should have some time to confer alone. It is essential though that the child not gain the impression that parent and teacher are critical of him behind his back. Laughter on their part when he knows that they are conferring, may be misinterpretted as ridicule by the little boy or girl.

In cooperative nurseries or preschool groups, the presence of a parent becomes an acceptable part of the adult context. Many schools prefer to have the parent in a group other than the one in which the child is placed. This tends to be to the advantage of the child and his activities. When, however, parents are regular assistants, children usually grow accustomed to it. Parent and teacher plan for the assisting which is usually to the mutual advantage of both. A parent sees her child from a broader perspective, the teacher gains assistance, and the child benefits from a shared experience—usually after the first or second time. (See Auerbach and Roche;[4] Todd[5] for helpful discussions of the role of the parent and/or aide.)

At pre-holiday times and on a child's birthday, one or both parents usually expect to come, if they are able to do so. At pre-holiday times at the three-year-old level, a song sung together, cookies shared, and the giving of a simple gift made by the child is often enough. A total of fifteen minutes for these activities is plenty. At age four, most can sing several songs, perhaps using simple rhythm band instruments for one, hear a story, and then have cookies and candy. If the group is a stable one, twenty to thirty minutes may be so spent. If children have made simple gifts, these may be given. Five-year-olds can, and often do, request and benefit from a longer time. They add more rhythmic activities and perhaps cookies that they have iced. A simple planned event in which children follow the usual procedure tends to be most successful. A song that children and parents can sing together is fun. Children do tend to become overstimulated easily by the presence of their parents, if the situation is not a co-op with parents present every day. Chairs placed in the room, sitting in a new place to sing, and any other act performed differently than usual can be upsetting to some children. The child's birthday also can be overstimulating. A simple cake, cupcake, or cookie at lunch time or before going home in the afternoon is enough. Once the bars are down and other things are permitted, competition is likely to arise either from child or parent. A short, happy, simple time is more satisfying, and if all goes well, children can add to it by showing their parents around the room after the simple planned events.

If the parent is visiting, the child may use the occasion to call attention to himself. He can frequently be set at ease by showing his parent materials or activities that he likes. After he grows more accustomed to the presence of his parent(s), what he does, in relation to what is available and to others present can be very informative to his mother and/or father. Some children become so emotionally overstimulated, that it is best for the parents to dovetail their day with another parent and thus not to remain too long until the child becomes more accustomed to their presence.

What problems may arise with separated/divorced parents?

In the situation which includes divorced parents, the teacher as well as the child and one or both parents will be spared the possibility of considerable grief if the teacher knows what specifically are the rights of each parent. Custodial rights differ. It is not unknown at all for one parent to use the school situation as an opportunity to get the child away from the other. Who calls for the child, who can and cannot take him must be clear. There are various cases of one parent suddenly appearing and whisking away the child counter to legal agreement. The parent not living in the home may not have the right to take the child to another state. If the teacher has signed permission to take the child anywhere, she should know about such arrangements or she may find herself in great difficulty.

The teacher, also needs to try to ascertain the attitude of each parent toward the other. It is not the teacher's responsibility to take sides, but it is the teacher's obligation to try to assist the child, who goes back and forth, to make as smooth a transition as is possible.

Needless to say, all groups utilize some sort of signed permission slips for trips. There should be a place on them for the noting of special considerations. As was said earlier, records also must be clear concerning who is to pick up the child after school. It takes only one misunderstanding on the teacher's part to cause serious consequences for all concerned. The children of famous people attend preschool groups, too, and have the right to very careful attention to these matters at going home time. Abductions have occurred after school. While these admonitions may not affect too many teachers, they must be respected where they do apply.

How may older children be included?

Older children can frequently assist in groups of preschool children. In one school situation sixth, fifth, and later fourth graders were excellent assistants at lunch, during quiet activities between lunch and rest, and on the playground.

They assist best when given some instruction about "why" and "how" certain things are done. Otherwise, they may overassist and be an obstacle to development. When they are given a brief introduction to the preschool situation and to what the teacher is trying to accomplish, many become excellent helpers. In the school situation, referred to above, a short course of six weeks duration was used to induct upper graders. For three-quarters of an hour each week, they looked at materials and equipment and heard simple "whys" and "wherefores." This was followed by a time for questions.

What other adults may function in important roles?

The teacher often has other adults present to help, to explain, or to do things with the children. Again, they need instruction in how to help the children help themselves. If the situation seems predominately feminine, inviting the male science or art teacher or the librarian to eat lunch with the children is helpful. Fortunately, the supply of male educators in the preschool field is increasing. Workers about the building can explain what they are doing. One teacher had a bus driver drop in occasionally because he could speak to the Russian child and help to explain things in his own language. Another brought in the policeman from the corner often enough for him to become a friend to each member of the four-year-old group, most of whom lived in a large inner-city project.

While each three-, four-, and five-year-old needs a close relationship to his own teacher who really knows him, each should be expanding his relationships enough to include other adults. What better way than with his group and his teacher!

Toward the end of the year, the next teacher should be visited enough to be considered a friend. This aids in a smooth transition during the following fall.

After some experience, answers to some of the above problems come rather easily. However, teachers are likely to transfer, communities to change, and teachers find that no two professional years are alike. The few succinct suggestions made should be helpful. However, each teacher will be able to add findings from similar experiences as he/she has them.

THE SURROUNDING COMMUNITY

The teacher and his/her children are a part of the larger community, while at the same time they form their own smaller social unit. If the teacher comes from outside of the immediate area, it is necessary that he/she become conversant enough with the context of the school community to help the children who live in it to constantly greater advantage. Then the teacher's plans and daily living with the children will form an extension to their home living. If school is an extension of home living, it will clarify, simplify, and be an addition to their lives. At the same time it may provide the richest and most satisfying hours that the child lives. The teacher who understands the Cuban, Puerto

Rican, or Polish milieu, for instance, meets Florita, Jose, or Stella in terms of their backgrounds—which will be utilized—and then guides the children into further activities from where they are. For example, five-year-old Carmen was convinced that babies were found under cabbage leaves. Seeing no cabbage leaves on the mainland, she asked where Mrs. Fernandez had found her baby!

The teacher should know which community agencies are located within the school area and whether these have help and/or materials available to her. Which religious groups serve the area? What parks and other facilities are available? Most important, who are the people who man these agencies and facilities? The four-year-olds in one school with their teacher set up the materials in a play room for a preschool group in a local neighborhood house. They brought good, usable materials and toys which they no longer used. "This is for the children 'cause they might like to see the horse move. I used it when I was little!" If their teacher had not become acquainted with the neighborhood house, with several of its workers, and with its needs, this experience would not have been possible.

A complex industrial area may be overpowering to small children. The noise and activity veritably seem to swallow them up. A noisy highway or elevated train can be observed and discussed by three-year-olds. At age four, a short ride, or at least a trip to a station of the El, as well as discussion about where it is going, give further understanding to the child. By age five, a highway or elevated train begins to be understood more fully in its context. "My father's car goes there. We went to see Bo. We went there." "I went under the turnstile, but my mother put a token in the box." "We sat on the train. We saw the water." Gradual extension of simple clear experiences increases the child's clarification of where he lives, of what surrounds him, and of relationships which are a part of his daily living. People in the community are interwoven into his experiences, and some of these people should become individuals whom he can call by name.

A row of bars down the avenue troubled the teacher. To the children, who darted in unannounced, two of these were the sources of pretzels and a hearty welcome from the proprietors. Miss Johnson eventually came to appreciate these two proprietors and their interest in the children.

A potato chip bakery was a place to visit, to enjoy the smell, and to watch the trucks while "we stand out of the way." "Jenny's father works there. He makes potato chips."

While the policeman may be a negative figure to some children, it was rather easy to encourage a constantly developing friendship between Officer Jones and the four-year-olds of the Singer Street Center. Officer Jones was invited to visit frequently and came to know each child by name as each child learned how he could help him.

The teacher who is at home in the neighborhood finds parents employed there. These parents as well as other adults help her to interpret a busy environment for the greater understanding of her class.

While rural children are less beset by large, frightening machines, dark door-ways, and confusing sights and sounds, they may need guided understanding of their experiences with noisy sawmills, express truck depots, milk plants, and heavy powerful farm machinery. Planes flying ominously low in order to fight a forest fire on a nearby mountain should be understood as helpers. "The pilot in the plane is trying to help us." The need for these planes, at this time, should be explained in a matter of fact way in order not to frighten the children.

The more a child understands through his daily interactive experiences, the less he feels overwhelmed. Eventually, he will take some part in controlling these surroundings. The people are all a part of this milieu in which he is inter-acting. Many of these people have some part in the direction or control of ac-tivities which affect the child and his community. He begins to relate people to these environmental phenomena. Each child is a small part of the larger com-munity, but a large contributing part to the small school community. He is just beginning to find his way in the former, but in the latter, he is developing the relationships which eventually will earn him his place in the former.

THE CHILD AND HIS FAMILY

The inner city child may see less of his parents than the so-called middle class child. The children of parents who are financially well-off are often just as de-void of direct daily parent solicitude than those known to be financially poor.

Patsy is given over to the care of a strict nurse, who is intent on seeing her particular peers in the park. Patsy will see those children of those nurses with whom her nurse is friendly. Her parents believe that she is being well cared for—they need to be sure just what is happening when she is out with her paid guardian!

Sol arrives in prekindergarten. He is a tall, handsome, friendly child, but his teacher soon finds that he is unable to climb stairs in four-year-old fashion, to run, or to ride a tricycle fast. Patient encouragement with various materials, in-cluding a ladder, soon help him. But, why? To keep a long investigation short, Sol's governess had kept him seated on a bench or in a sandbox for the two pre-ceding years!

Those able to afford nurses or governesses or the like do not always fare so poorly. However, attention does need to be given to what happens during a child's daily routine.

Tony, who lived in a large inner-city project, was left alone occasionally. Once he fell off the table during the time he was left alone because he was climb-ing up to reach the light after dark. On another occasion, he was left with an elderly neighbor. He ran out of her apartment and was found in the basement with two older boys, who were abusing him.

Stevie ran away from his elderly grandparents. He was found sometime later by the police miles from home. He had run down the subway stairs just as a train was coming in! He dashed under the turnstile, and onto the train. The police found him half a mile from the end of the line throwing pebbles into a small lake.

None of these children had proper care. Their parents or guardian grandparents needed information about other possibilities. Many of Patsy and Sol's peers attended private nursery schools. Their parents believed that their children would benefit more from individual attention which they were not really receiving. Some parent education would be useful.

Tony's mother had not been long on the mainland from Puerto Rico. Stevie's parents had deserted him: the father left before he was born; his mother left when he was six months old. His grandparents spoke only Croatian. This mother and these grandparents needed information about day care centers.

It has been said that deprivation deficits increase. Patsy and Sol had good opportunities to overcome their deficits and did so rather rapidly. However, Tony and Stevie should have similar opportunities!

While Patsy and Sol heard English, were well fed, and were spoken to often, Tony and Stevie heard Spanish and Croatian, were not properly fed, and were rarely spoken to as individuals.

These are but four synoptic situations out of many. The preschool teacher who knows about such situations must try to reach such children. Agencies are doing a tremendous job, but they are not always able to reach everyone. Other parents in the neighborhood who speak the same language are the best means through which to reach the parents and guardians of these children.

Familiarity with a neighborhood comes as one lives in it, shops in it, uses its streets and public conveyances. Strangers or minority group members can be reached. Despite welfare agencies and Spanish language coordinators, there are unreached individuals. These, too, deserve a chance as they are found and their young children brought to day care centers.

RECENT ARRIVALS

As said earlier, conversational ability in the dominant minority language of the area is helpful to the teacher of young children. Through being able to converse, simple facts can be clarified and questions answered: Does Jose have a warm coat for wear this winter? Has Kathy seen a doctor to find out why she coughs? Does Joanna eat any supper? Is your older child coming to the after-school center? Do you know about summer day camp? These and dozens of other questions can be asked, answered, and explained. The names and addresses of service agencies can be given to the parent(s) of the young child.

Orientation to the country, to the neighborhood, and to its daily customs are necessary for the new parent and child. Expectations and reality may differ widely. Comparatively simple things like the weather and its changes, the need for supplementary vitamin pills, and the availablity of service agencies are all items of information vital to those in need of them.

CULTURAL AND RACIAL DIFFERENCES

Mary Ellen Goodman notes "a grim, hard fact, to be added to the growing collection of grim, hard facts about race relations in America." She points to what some of us know all too well that race prejudice "flourishes among us . . ., and even into early childhood . . . It is all too clear that Negro children not yet five can sense that they are marked . . . ."

She adds that "each child grows his own set of thoughts and feelings about race, and he achieves them out of the materials at hand." She holds that "each individual *generates* his own attitudes, out of the personal, social, and cultural materials which happen to be his."[6]

The writer has seen the positive and negative generated. It is the responsibility of every teacher to be aware of the "materials" with which she and her children work. "Generation" can be the construction of a positive view toward self and others and the reception of an equal view in interactive relationships. The teacher's attitude toward parents is one such material!

Cultural differences are too little recognized. The middle class white teacher with a long American heritage may insist to Carmelita, "Look at me." In Carmelita's culture doing something wrong causes shame, and one looks away. Teachers must steep themselves, insofar as it is possible to do so, in the cultural milieu of the children they will teach. Hess and Croft wisely say that "The desire or the decision to intervene in the life of a young child or his family and the attempt to change his style of life, cultural pattern or socioeconomic level is a critical one."[7]

They do say that the teacher can help give the child more alternatives than he would otherwise have. Families do need help in finding that there are more possibilities available than they may have realized. However, the writer has found that sometimes expectations are too utopian. The teacher needs to try to understand the community, the needs and aspirations of the community, and then to try to guide individuals into understanding feasible options. To quote Hess and Croft again, "Perhaps the most difficult task she (the teacher) has is to give the child a versatility and competence to be successful in both his own world and in others he may encounter and wish to enter."[8] The parents, who understand this task of the teacher can be the best facilitating agents the teacher has!

Notes

1. Lillian Weber, *The English Infant School and Informal Education* (Englewood Cliffs, N.J.: Prentice-Hall, 1971), p. 102.

2. Ibid., pp. 32-33.

3. Heffernan and Todd remind us, wisely, that the teacher helps parents to look at any problem they may have from the viewpoint of the child. See Vivian Todd and Helen Heffernan, *The Years Before School* (New York: The MacMillan Co., 1971), p. 563.

4. Aline Auerbach and Sandra Roche, *Creating a Preschool Center* (New York: John Wiley and Sons, 1971), Chapter 2.

5. Vivian Todd, *The Aide in Early Childhood Education* (New York: The Macmillan Co., 1973), Chapter I.

6. Mary Ellen Goodman, *Race Awareness in Young Children* (London: Collier Books, 1970 edition), pp. 245-46.

7. Robert D. Hess and Doreen Croft, *Teachers of Young Children* (New York: Houghton Mifflin Co., 1972), pp. 131-32.

8. Ibid.

CHAPTER 11

Problems

Some days seem filled with problems. Young children can become negative easily. At times this seems very sudden! Their hostility is frequently aroused because they understand what they refuse to do, in their own way, but cannot explain easily—if at all—to someone else. Self-protection, physically and emotionally, is maintained by refusal. Blunt refusal can be aggravating. It may precede an unnecessary emotional storm if the teacher continues to urge the child.

Reasons, when uncovered, are sometimes humorous! Sometimes, they indicate a deep-seated emotional problem for the expert. Frequently, the reason for refusal, for minsinterpretation, or for unusual behavior has a clear justification when understood from the child's point of view.

Numerous problems have been presented in context in the preceding pages. Here are a few more! They are given here in order to help us realize that teachers often do not comprehend a situation immediately. A little more understanding can be helpful.

"I WON'T SIT ON THE FLOOR."

Marilyn arrived in a thin, highly starched pink dress complete with a large pink sash tied in a big bow. After the mid-morning rest, Mrs. Jonas asked the prekindergarten children to sit on the floor in front of the piano. This was their usual "collection spot." "Come, children, David has a new record to play for us."

"No, I won't," said Marilyn.

"Come on, Marilyn," said Penny, her best friend.

"No," said Marilyn.

"Marilyn," said David, "we can't start until you are ready."

"I won't," screamed Marilyn, and hitting the air in the general direction of the group, she added, "and no one can make me."

"Come, Marilyn," said Mrs. Jonas.

"I won't," said Marilyn, and she burst into tears.

What did Mrs. Jonas do?

Insisting would produce a temper tantrum. Not insisting would be unfair to David, who expected to play his record for everyone. Mrs. Jonas considered the possible cause.

> Marilyn was beautifully dressed, and so she said, "Marilyn, why don't you want to sit on the floor?"
> Marilyn sniffed and said, "Mommy told me not to get dirty." (Mrs. Jonas had suspected this.)
> Mrs. Jonas said, "All right, Marilyn, sit on a chair, today. We want you to hear David's record."

Mrs. Jonas had spoken to all of the parents, and had sent home *Requests to Parents.* In both cases, it was requested that girls be dressed in slacks or dark skirts that would not soil easily. Mrs. Jonas knew that she would need to ask Mrs. Martin, Marilyn's mother, again and that she would need to be quite insistent about it. Inasmuch as she did not want Marilyn to feel the conflict between her mother and her teacher, she asked Marilyn to sit on a chair. (Previously, the class had decided that, "if we sit on the floor, we can get up to 'dance' more quickly.")

It is easy to conflict with a parent's admonition and not be aware of it! This situation was not Marilyn's fault and so Mrs. Jonas had tried to settle it as quickly as possible. She would, however, speak to Mrs. Martin so that Marilyn would be neither in conflict nor stand out as different in one of the simple routines which had been agreed upon by the prekindergarten. Mrs. Jonas was aware, too, of not wanting to promote an impasse which would develop in Marilyn a situation of trying to "pit" one adult against the other. This, too, can happen and produce a miserable situation.

"I DON'T WANT TO PAINT."

Jonathan had not painted at all at the easel during the first four weeks of kindergarten. He had been given a free choice of activities but had never chosen to paint. On two occasions when he had stood near the easel watching another child painting, Miss Sanderson had asked casually, "Jonathan, would you like a turn to paint next after Jay (or whoever was painting) finishes?"

"No," said Jonathan, as he walked quickly from the easel. His response had been the same on both occasions.

Painting seemed to fascinate Jonathan, yet he never asked to paint and refused when the suggestion was made. On one occasion, he was heard to ask another child, "Paul, why do you do that?"

One day, Miss Sanderson decided that Jonathan should be "pushed" a bit in order to find out the basis for his seeming interest and yet definite refusal to paint. She was sure that there was some special problem here but was not certain what it was. He had finished several crayon pictures of the "design" type. These had been made with great care. The following dialogue took place.

> Miss Sanderson: "Jonathan, everyone else has painted. Let's give you a turn today."
>
> Jonathan: "I don't want to paint."
>
> Miss Sanderson: "Jonathan, you don't *have* to paint, but perhaps, you would *like* to try the new brushes, today."
>
> Jonathan: "I have brushes like that at home."
>
> Miss Sanderson: "Your place for hanging your paintings is over there." (She pointed to an empty place near the door.)
>
> Jonathan: "I know it."
>
> Miss Sanderson: "Jonathan, today, suppose you make one quick picture to put up in your space."
>
> Jonathan: "No, I don't want to paint."
>
> Miss Sanderson: "Do you paint at home?"
>
> Jonathan: "Yep, some of the time."
>
> Miss Sanderson: "Jonathan, before we clear up, paint one picture—today. Your smock is in your cubby."
>
> Jonathan: "No, I won't paint here." (He pointed to Joanna, who was wearing a smock and busily painting.) "I'm not like Joanna. I don't want to wear a dress!"

"IT'S A HOSPITAL!"

Marcus's mother rushed in during the week preceding the opening of school. She was practically weeping as she said, "Oh, Miss Jensen, Marcus won't come into the building."

Miss Jensen invited Marcus's mother to be seated and then said, "But, Marcus came to visit last May, didn't he?"

"Oh, yes," said his mother. "He wanted to come back the next day."

"Didn't you bring him over in June, too?"

"Yes, we saw you when you were putting away the equipment," answered Marcus's mother. "Suddenly, after we came back from the shore, Marcus refused to come up the steps. Oh, dear, we tried so hard. We wanted him to adjust easily."

"Refused to come up the steps?" asked Miss Jensen.

"Yes," said his mother. "We walked by three times in August. When I suggested that we walk up the steps in order to look through the front door of his school, he refused. The last time, he stamped his foot and said that he would *never* go in."

"Did he look in?" asked Miss Jensen.

"No, he refused to go up above the first step. When I took his arm to urge him, he screamed at me."

"What did he say?"

"He said, 'no,' I *won't* go in there ever!"

Miss Jensen thought a minute and then said, "Let's think this through together."

"Fine."

"Now, he came in May, returned in June, and was at the shore in July?"

"That's right, we went as soon as his tonsils were out and the doctor said that it was O.K."

"Ah ha," said Miss Jensen. "What hospital was it?"

"Menorah."

"Isn't that a dark red brick building?"

"Yes."

"Where is Marcus now?"

"At home."

"Bring him over, and I'll meet you on the sidewalk, in front, in fifteen minutes."

Fifteen minutes later, Marcus and his mother met Miss Jensen on the sidewalk near the front of the school.

Marcus greeted Miss Jensen with "Hi."

"Marcus," said Miss Jensen, "do you know what that is?" (pointing to the school).

"Yes," said Marcus, "the hospital."

"ONE, TWO, GO 'WAY WITH YOU."

Terry arrived in nursery school with an angry look on his face. After responding to his teacher's greeting with a glum, "Hi," he removed his sweater and hung it up. Turning, he began to walk across the floor, and then he stopped abruptly. Suddenly, he ran to the housekeeping corner, grabbed a rubber doll by the leg, and threw it on the floor. He jumped on the doll, shouting, "One, two, go 'way with you." After about three minutes, he stopped, picked up the doll, threw it into the bed, and went to the block corner where he began to build. Terry repeated this action during the two remaining days of the week.

On Friday, Mrs. Anders, his mother, and Mrs. Carlton, his teacher, had a conference. Mrs. Anders had requested it even before Mrs. Carlton had a chance to do so.

Mrs. Anders said that Terry was being very destructive at home and that she could not understand it. Responding to Mrs. Carlton's questions about the Anders's only other child, Mrs. Anders said that when Kathie was born, Terry had adjusted well. He had helped her with Kathie's powder, her bath towel, and later with the bottle.

"How old is Kathie, now?" asked Mrs. Carlton.

"She's just two weeks less than a year," answered her mother.

"Does she walk yet?" asked Mrs. Carlton.

Mrs. Anders replied that Kathie was walking with help.

"You can't imagine how patient my husband is with her," she added. "Why he comes home from a long day's work and helps Kathie walk all about while I get supper."

"Where is Terry then?" asked Mrs. Carlton.

"Lately, he's been in his room before we eat. He gets ready for his bath before supper, now," she added.

"Is this something new?" asked Mrs. Carlton.

"Yes, it was his idea to do this before we eat," said his mother.

"There is a possibility that he resents his father's sudden added attention to Kathie," said Mrs. Carlton. "This happens often. The initial adjustment is fine, but then when the baby begins to walk, everyone's attention is suddenly focussed on her again. It's too hard on Terry. He is trying to do something to gain praise, too, by getting himself ready early for his bath."

After further discussion, Mrs. Anders decided to try to have Terry and his father share some activity immediately after he arrived home. After about fifteen minutes, Mr. Anders would go into the living room and Terry into his room. Then, while Terry got ready for his bath, Mr. Anders could help Kathie.

At the end of the next week, Mrs. Anders reported that the plan had worked well. "You know," she said, "we tried so hard, but we just didn't see this from Terry's point of view. We read up on sibling rivalry and then didn't recognize it when we had it. Now, Terry is less destructive. Last night he said to my husband, 'You're *my* Daddy, too.' "

"DON'T ALISON 'AH'?"

Alison ran to her teacher, held up her arms, and literally climbed up Mrs. Bohm. The three-year-old wrapped both arms tightly around Mrs. Bohm's neck and did not move.

The school nurse had just appeared in the door for her morning visit. The children ran to her from the playground. Mrs. Bohm, with Alison still clinging to her neck, walked to the group about the nurse.

"Why Alison, dat?" asked Nick.

Mrs. Bohm said quickly, "We'll stay over here. Who can say 'ah' loud enough for us to hear?"

"Me, me, me," came the response.

"Don't Alison 'ah'?" asked Nick.

"She will, later," said Mrs. Bohm.

Mrs. Bohm realized that Alison was terrified of nurses due to an unfortunate experience in a doctor's office. She had held Alison each day, but today she came much closer and requested to hear the children.

The next day Mrs. Bohm put on a little white starched cap and said, "Today, I'm going to play nurse." Everyone lined up quickly except Alison.

"Nurse?" she questioned softly.

"Yes," said Mrs. Bohm, while she looked into the children's throats. Alison stood watching her from a little distance, sucking her thumb as she did so.

When the children went inside, Mrs. Bohm took off her cap and said, "If anyone wants to play nurse, there are caps in the dresser drawer."

Several children immediately put them on and began to play nurse. Alison watched but said nothing.

The next morning when she arrived, Alison looked at Mrs. Bohm and said, "No hat."

"No," said Mrs. Bohm, "I'm not a nurse today." Reaching into her pocket, she pulled out a little starched cap and said, "Alison is the nurse."

Before Alison could say anything, she laid the cap on top of her head and bent in front of the child saying, "Ah."

"Mrs. Bohm is 'ahing'," shouted Dave.

"Look," said Sue, "like us."

"Look into my mouth, Alison," said Mrs. Bohm.

Alison looked toward her, and then reaching up, took off the cap and looked at it. She smoothed it and laid it carefully on the window sill.

Two days later, after the same behavior was repeated during the intervening day, Alison looked into Mrs. Bohm's mouth and Dave's mouth as they said "ah."

Mrs. Bohm could sympathize with Alison. She believed, however, that if Alison could be induced to identify herself with the source of her fear, she might be able to accept it. The next day when Alison arrived, she went up to Mrs. Bohm and said, "Please, cap." When it was given to her, Alison took it, looked at it, and then putting it on, she said, "Nurse." Alison walked about, patting the cap every few steps, and saying "Nurse, nurse."

This time when the school nurse appeared at the door, Alison walked over hesitantly but straight to her and permitted the nurse to look into her mouth. She then shut her mouth abruptly and walked away. A few minutes later, she removed the cap, smoothed it carefully, and holding it out toward Mrs. Bohm, said, "I'm finished." Alison then went over to the swings and began to swing.

Mrs. Bohm knew that Alison had had a traumatic experience, but also that Alison needed to act in some positive way in order to overcome it. By eventually accepting the nurse role, which represented power, Alison identified with it and overcame her fear. She repeated the same behavior of wearing the cap and saying "Nurse, nurse" for the remainder of the week. On Monday, she came to school in a new nurse outfit which she had been given at home. Although her mother had endeavored to have her wear it earlier, Alison refused even to put it on. Now, that she had been led to face her fear and to play it out with Mrs. Bohm, whom she trusted, and in a secure and supportive situation, Alison was ready to accept the role at home, in school, or anywhere else. A month later, when she had to return to the doctor's office, she wore it and was met by the doctor rather than his nurse. The latter came in after the doctor had examined Alison. Although she was looked at suspiciously by Alison, the child said in a loud voice, "I'm a nurse now."

"I'M A BIG MAN."

Kate arrived in kindergarten with a belligerent look one morning during the second month of school. When she was asked whether anything was the matter, she replied, "I won't wear a dress. I'm a big man." Hiking up her jeans, she added, "I'm a boss."

Later, Kate's mother appeared and told Mrs. Johns that Kate had some lovely dresses but that she refused to wear any of them. She had recently refused to attend an all girls birthday party unless she could wear jeans. She usually refused to wear a slacks outfit, too, although earlier she had been willing to do so on one or two occasions.

Mrs. Johns knew that Kate preferred to play with boys, whom she called "Fellas," but that Doreen was often included. Doreen usually wore slacks and was a physically active child. Kate responded well to the suggestions that Mrs. Johns made to her, but Mrs. Johns was aware that the girl student teacher had had many difficulties with her. She recalled, also, that Kate had not left a visiting male intern. She had followed him, sat on his knee, played ball with him on the playground, and had asked him when he would return.

Later, during the morning when Kate had arrived looking so belligerent, Mrs. Johns heard her say to the student teacher, "No, you're not the boss of *me*." Going over to them, she said, "Kate, Miss Austin is a 'boss' here and I am a 'boss' here."

"No," said Kate, "she is not the boss of me."

"Kate, why isn't she the boss of you?"

" 'Cause she's a girl. Girls and ladies are not bosses."

"Am I a boss, Kate?" asked Mrs. Johns.

"Sure," said Kate, "but, I like you. You are a *nice* lady. Ladies are *not* bosses—just you."

"Mrs. Rose is the boss of the school," said Mrs. Johns. Mrs. Johns knew that Kate had spoken to Mrs. Rose when the latter, who was the school's principal, had visited one morning. Kate had asked what her name was after Mrs. Rose had gone.

"No, she's not. She's a lady. Ladies are *not* bosses," said Kate.

A quick phone call was made to Mrs. Rose, and Mrs. Johns left the class with the student teacher and took Kate up to visit Mrs. Rose in her office.

When they arrived, Mrs. Johns said, "Mrs. Rose, this is Kate. Kate, this is Mrs. Rose. She is the boss of our whole school. See her telephones. She uses her telephones to be sure that we are all right, and she uses her telephones to tell people what to do."

As Kate looked, Mrs. Rose said, "Yes, Kate, I'm the boss of the school. I am a lady and *I* am a boss."

Kate was very quiet. As they went back to the kindergarten room, Kate said, "I'm going to be a boss like Mrs. Rose."

Kate's mother and Mrs. Johns had a number of conferences. During them, Mrs. Johns tried to help Kate's mother to strengthen her role with her daughter. Mrs. Johns had watched Kate carefully. She saw that she identified with the boys and Doreen. She had heard Kate state repeatedly that she was a man and a boss many times.

Kate was having trouble adjusting to her mother's second marriage. She had accepted her new father readily and called him Daddy Joe. Her own father had died two years before.

Sensing real disturbance here due to Kate's rejection of any semblance to a feminine role—in any observable way—and her obvious identification with males and power, Mrs. Johns suggested further help. Kate's mother agreed. This was a case which was too complicated for a layman. Mrs. Johns sensed feelings of withdrawal and frustration in Kate's mother and knew, too, that the home situation demanded help which only a professional could render. Mrs. Johns believed, rightly, that her job was to provide security for Kate, a ready ear for her parents, and not to be too demanding of Kate for the present time.

"I GOTTA NEW DADDY."

Nat bounced into prekindergarten one morning. "I gotta new Daddy," he said.

"That's fine," said Mr. Verrano.

"Yep," said Nat. "He came out of Mom's bedroom this morning and hugged me. He'll be there when I get home, too."

"Great," said his teacher.

Mr. Verrano hoped that this man would stay. Nat had one father and last name and his two sisters a second. His big brother went by another last name and had been fathered by a man who had left Nat's mother several years before the sisters had been born.

Mr. Verrano did not believe that he could change Nat's mother's mode of life. The children were well fed and clothed, but he knew, too, that a succession of men or "Daddys," as Nat called them, made for little security. As he thought it over, he reminded himself that all he could do at this juncture, was to be a strong support for Nat.

He had visited Nat's home once after setting a time agreeable to Nat's mother. Nat's mother appeared to have an independent establishment, but Mr. Verrano wondered about the number of doors opening on to the hall which ran the length of the long, large apartment. The children's rooms were at the back. Nat was insecure, but always hopeful or so it seemed to Mr. Verrano. Nat's mother had greeted Mr. Verrano warmly when he had called at the old and somewhat rundown apartment building. He noticed though, that he had been carefully scrutinized by the barber in his shop on the first floor. When he rang the bell and started up the stairs, he was sure that at least two doors had closed quietly as he approached landings before reaching the sixth floor where Nat lived.

In the discussion, Nat's mother referred to the fact that she was usually busy at night. She said that someone slept back near the children in case they woke up or needed anything, in response to Mr. Verrano's question about care of the children at night. She offered Mr. Verrano a drink and gave him cake and coffee. Mr. Verrano found himself appreciating her general courtesy and warmth.

Nat's mother was proud of her son and pleased to hear about his progress. She obviously loved her children and was supporting them as best she could in terms of her own standards. Mr. Verrano had wondered about Nat's future then— and he still did. If the new Daddy stayed—it would be helpful!

"WHY DID THE FISH DIE?"

"But, why did the fish die?" persisted Bobby.

"He's sleeping," said Gina.

"No," said Bobby, "he deaded. Why?"

[This question of the young four-year-old represents typical inquiry for the age level.]

"He is dead," said Mrs. Jacobs. "Why he died, I don't know. But, everything and everybody dies at some time."

"My Grandpa died," said Bernice.

"Yes," said Mrs. Jacobs. Carefully lifting the goldfish out of the water and putting it on a towel, she let all of the children see it. "Sometimes we do not know why fish, or animals, or people die," she said. "We remember how they were when they were alive."

"My Grandpa let me sit on his lap," said Bernice.

"That is a happy thing to remember about him, isn't it?" said Mrs. Jacobs.

"He's not asleep?" said Gina, with a question in her voice.

"No," said Mrs. Jacobs, "if he were asleep, he would wake up. The fish cannot wake up any more," she added.

Thus the four-year-olds found out that the fish had died, that he would not swim again, and that he was not asleep.

Mrs. Jacobs tried to meet each question as it came. She had found the fish dead upon her arrival and decided to let the children experience finding it. She thought it a wise introduction to a common problem. She tried to avoid any religious connotations in what was said because she knew that this was the parents' responsibility.

Teachers and parents used to remove children from situations involving death or remove the dead animal quickly from the child's view. Death is a common enough experience, and today people tend to agree that children should participate in it. The dead fish in the classroom was a simple introduction since children do not tend to be very emotional about a fish. They could see that it looked the same, but that it neither breathed nor moved.

Parents often ask what to do when a family member dies. If the child is an average child and healthy, he should share in the family's grief as well as its joys. The child who is removed from the scene asks where the dead person is, why his parents are not with him, and feels "pushed away" from something important. Furthermore, this "something" is emotion-laden. The writer had occasion to spend time with a child who had been removed from home at the death of a brother. Sarah had many questions and wanted answers. Her parents later regretted what they had done. Granting that a child usually meets upset best when carrying through his usual routine, he should share his family's deepest feelings. When sent away, he may feel rejected. When he returns and finds someone missing, he feels more upset. Will he be next? Was he, in any way, the cause?

When someone close dies, out of the home, and a four- or five-year-old is told, he may seemingly accept the statement and then ask whether it isn't time to leave for school. One such youngster appeared in kindergarten the morning after her father had died. "Since she wanted to come, and thought she belonged here, we sent her," the mother explained later. The child later attended the services.

When such an event has happened, four- and five-year-olds frequently want to discuss it in their own time. One child walked to the center of the hall and after standing there a moment said—almost to herself—"Now, I'll never hear Daddy come up the steps again." She seemed to be meeting the situation herself and trying to deal with it. Her aunt heard her and said softly, "No, Shirley, we won't." In a minute she added, "But, we can remember how he sounded and how he smiled, can't we?"

At such times, adults in the environment need to be reassuring to a child. Some children wonder, if everyone who is sick, for instance, will die and disappear suddenly. If he sleeps, will he move and awaken again? Stating more emphatically, "We'll see you in the morning" or "Tomorrow morning, we'll—" helps to focus the child's feelings and thinking on the next day in a positive way. Grief is an observable emotion, but so is the assurance of people and shared anticipation. The individual child's reaction is the key to what to say and do. Avoiding the whole issue is not the answer at age four and five or for mature three-year-olds.

Support for this view is found in a number of places. For example, Kastenbaum says that when children ask questions about death, their parents often think that there is no answer that would not appear threatening. However, children may fantasize death. Most of us have seen "gun play" in which a child is "shot" and arises two seconds later. Kastenbaum says that, up to age five, children do not fully grasp the fact of finality and usually relate death to sleep.[1] His suggestion to help a child by sharing it with him is sound and in accord with the views expressed above.

Ethical concerns support what the teacher does, the ends sought, and how problems are settled. Such concerns underlie the teacher's treatment of the children and determine the role played in the community. Living and interacting in an environment of nature, people, and things whether face-to-face or at a distance necessitates a point of view or a philosophy. Philosophy is a unified view which includes insights, beliefs, and convictions of an ethical nature. Why do we perform one action and not another? What governs our choices? How do we judge self and other? Can we ascertain any changes and progress in relationships? If so, toward what ends? How and why are our ends and those of others to be realized? Is realization attainable for everyone? Should it be? Answers to these questions may become ethical convictions and set standards for living. They usually develop slowly as we have experiences and weigh and consider them in the context of our total living. Children can begin to develop ethical concerns as they attend preschool groups. In the next chapter, this will be considered briefly.

Notes

1. Robert Kastenbaum, "The Kingdom Where Nobody Dies" *Saturday Review* (December 23, 1972): 33-38.

CHAPTER 12

Toward an Ethics

Ethics can become the central imperative for living and learning. If so accepted, it governs attitudes and behavior, penetrates thinking as a dynamic, and officiates as a standard, or standards, for judgment. Ethical goals serve as foci for ethical means, and, they control—or can control—an entire experience or situation. Ethical means and goals stem from beliefs and convictions. Belief may be defined as confidence in some thing, person, or idea and conviction as a strong persuasion about some thing, person, or idea. It needs to involve motion or action to be a genuine conviction, otherwise it may be an unattached dream or wish fulfillment. Although this difference seems more quantitative than qualitative, the conviction is more basic where as the belief is more dependent upon the conviction and seems more capable of change. A conviction is more general and a belief more specific.

A person's ethical beliefs and convictions are formulated from beliefs and projections. They make him what he, as a person, is: able to carry out, in some part, what he believes or an inactive dreamer; responsible or irresponsible; outgoing or withdrawn; able to share or completely self-centered; able to choose in broad cultural terms without loss of self or unable to consider a perspective broader than his immediate concerns; a participant in furthering the means and ends of common humanity or a rugged individualist out only for his own comforts here and now. Ethical goals can be expansive for an individual concerned with maximum realization for self, for other, and for the manifestation of groups in cultural and worldwide terms.

Relationships are definable in major categories: individual to individual; individual to small face-to-face group; small face-to-face group to individual; individual to large group or culture; this large group to individual; individual to unseen group (international, for instance); international or unseen group to individual. The individual may be a member of more than one group at a time. He may be a Polish-American, a Roman Catholic, a Democrat, and a member of several professional organizations. He interacts with all of these groups and gradually develops as a major or minor representative. His group memberships may bring conflicts or harmony, but each calls for some expression from him. As he responds in these interactive relationships, he may do so from a tradition which is habitual or from convictions which he has formed for himself. In the latter case, there has been both firsthand and projective experiences, reflective thinking, and weighed judgment.

Participating in the building and implementing of ethical concerns is a lifelong task. However, a beginning can be made in the preschool. It will be noted that an interactive situation has been implied. X acts and responds because *inter*action implies a two-way experience—a doing and an undergoing. X acts and something external responds to X. X, in turn, responds when acted upon by something external. The "something" may be persons, living things, or objects in the natural-social environment. For instance, Billy, as the leader, makes suggestions to which his followers respond. There must, however, be times for Billy to respond to the statements, actions, and ideas of the others. This interaction also takes place with things. Billy hammers a nail. If it goes into the wood and fastens two pieces of wood together, Billy responds by using his airplane. If his hammering is less skillful, his response may be a hurt thumb. Thus, in either case, Billy reacts. Billy also gives something to his initial act. What he gives, or puts into it, is the result of his development thus far. Some of this is his natural biological growth including inherited proclivities, and some of this is the result of the social and cultural conditioning which has been applied to him. Thus what he does is the combination of internal development projected outward and external action from without to which he has (or has not) responded inwardly. The combination is Billy. In the two examples which follow, Louise more fully exemplifies the latter and Bobby the former. Both Louise and Bobby have had much experiential learning of both types of the beginnings of ethical action.

The young child gradually adds to his internal development through new relationships and strengthens or weakens his own developing self-concept. He is the social reflector of his home, his school, his neighborhood, and cultural background. If he has been encouraged to respond, to interact, and welcomed as a part of these units, he may already participate.

Early participation is likely to be largely conditioned and habitual. However, if encouraged to choose, he may initiate his own particular responses and means of relating. Certain obligations are exerted on him as a young participator. He can acquiesce, he an acquiesce with understanding, or he can refuse. Early social mores are likely to insist on acquiescence. However, understanding can make the individual response conscious and later social as he becomes able to choose and to decide whether or not to participate. Thus he will be commencing to develop his individual means of becoming a participator in these manifestations of group social behavior.

An illustration should clarify this. Acceptable means and clear ends which become the individual's own eventually and develop as his personal ethics, may begin as a simple social dictum or conditioning from without. However, in this case the outer dictum was not an authoritarian dictum. The attempt was made to treat Louise as a feeling, learning child throughout.

At age three, Louise hangs up her hat. It is her individual responsibility and a social dictum accompanied by social pressure. She hangs her hat on the hook provided by the nursery school and gains self-satisfaction; her Ego expands through the doing of it, and she becomes aware that it is *her* hook. She gains social acceptance in the social context because she is helping to keep *our* room clean.

At age four, Louise hangs up her hat. She identifies with prekindergarten society and carries through the act. Louise may identify with the social pressure and say, "Jane, hang up your hat." She achieves satisfaction; as an individual, she accepts and carries out the dictum as she interprets it; as a participator in the social context she accepts its regulation and thus identifies with that little society. Furthermore, she incorporates her identity with that of Jane and seeks to bring her under the dictum of their social context.

At age five, Louise hangs up her hat. In kindergarten, *we* hang up *our* hats. This is complete identification with group "custom" which is used to regulate the kindergarten society. As a person, Louise may say, "I got to hang up my hat." In terms of another, she may say, "Hang up your hat, Peter." As a group member, she may say, "We hang up our hats."

An act which is ethical at this age is regulatory of Louise's behavior and for Louise's benefit; regulatory of the group's behavior and for the group's benefit. The means of performing the act are clear to Louise and acceptable. The ends— to clean up our room—are achieved because it is clear. It is a functional act which develops from individual behavior to group behavior because Louise consciously identified the behavior with herself and as part of group behavior in accord with the dictum from the context of this group. The behavior was initiated and carried out as a result of conditioning and it was internalized by Louise's acceptance of it.

The two-year-old falls down and then screams, "Bad floor hitted Bobby." As he distinguishes Bobby from what is around Bobby and as he begins to develop his own controls, he tends at age three to shout, "Bobby fall down." Bobby is responsible for his own ability or inability to stay upright. At age four, he is very sensitive to the possibility of slipping on some ice. "I will walk slow. I don't want to fall down." Bobby has begun to control his own choice—to walk slowly and to take his own responsibility to not want to fall down.

At age four, or so, Bobby may say to Joe and Emma, "Walk slow. Ice is there." He is choosing to be concerned about Joe and Emma and is projecting his concern outward to the two children with whom he has been playing.

At four-and-a-half when he has achieved group identification, Bobby may try to guard the group. Bobby paces up and down before a shattered window, "Stay away. Glass is there. Glass cuts." Esther comes too close and Bobby pushes her back with, "Esther go back. Glass is there. It broke. Go back, Esther. You will bleed." His concern is now projected to the group with which he is identified as he seeks to control a recalcitrant member.

Through his experiences, Bobby has taken some responsibility for himself, then for Joe and Emma, and then for the whole group. As his socio-emotional development has matured, his identity with these others has been expressed. With his responsibility came simple controls. Bobby controlled his behavior and sought to control that of Joe, Emma, and the group for their benefit. His concern showed the beginning of ability to project beyond himself. Had he not developed socially and emotionally, would he be able to project and identify? Isn't this the beginning of ethical behavior? In his own way, Billy was controlling his own, Joe's, Emma's, and the group's behavior in order to benefit those involved. He deemed it necessary to be responsible for them.

Bobby's goals were safety from falling on the ice and from being cut. He did not want to "hurt" and thus controlled himself and adhered to his goal. Furthermore, he was able to project his concern to his two friends and then to the entire group. He was convinced of the importance of not being cut—enough to push Esther back when she did not immediately respond to his verbal warning.

In a small way, Bobby was trying to control a situation which assured realization or achievement of the ends of himself and of others, too. The "good" for him and for them was furthered by his simple action which may be termed an ethical action.

Several items should be noted: Bobby developed his behavior through his own experiences; Bobby was not given any authoritarian admonitions at this time; Bobby was not told to tell the others; Bobby's concerns seemed to be self-sustained and socially acceptable. How did Bobby reach this level of development?

As a toddler, Bobby had been given a few firm "No's." When he first reached toward a candle, he was told, "No." At first his hand was moved, and then he was controlled verbally. During the same period, he was taught "hot." His finger touched a "hot" bath after his mother's hand had. Her word "hot" was imitated. His mother continued to develop the concept through experiences with soup, cocoa, a water pipe. Then, after first giving physical protection from the candle, Bobby seemed able to understand the concept "hot" applied to various objects, and he needed only the verbal admonition. Of course, his mother's firm voice, also, was associated with it. Bobby learned "cold" in relation to ice cubes, ice cream, water, and milk. The word was accompanied by direct experience—initiated by him as often as possible.

At two-and-a-half, Bobby looked at a puddle and said questioningly, "Cold?" His mother said, "Let's find out." She bent over and cautiously put one finger into the puddle. She smiled at Bobby and said, "Bobby do it." After he had, Bobby said, "Cold, not hot, cold."

Thus we see that prior to nursery school, Bobby was told "no" firmly only when it was necessary for his physical safety as a toddler. He was encouraged to find out, given the appropriate terms, and as soon as possible led to draw his own conclusions. Actually, this was a longer and more involved process than our brief illustration indicates. However, his parents' attitude of letting him find out when he could, of sharing with him, rather than dominating, and of taking time for him to have experiences and to develop his own concepts was important to the entire situation. Bobby's parents' controls over him were restricting when physical safety was involved, were kept to a minimum, and were clear and simple. Bobby's experiences were broad, varied, and as unhurried as possible. The controls were Bobby's to the greatest possible extent, although neither parent let him dominate a group situation nor refuse to act upon the few regulations established.

At the same time, Bobby began to see and to play with children of varied backgrounds. Activity at ages two, three, and four is what interests children. As Bobby progressed through the various stages of social development, his attitude toward others was kept open and positive. In the kindergarten Bobby knew and occasionally remarked in matter-of-fact tones about skin, hair, and eye coloring. He appeared to have no emotional tension, anxiety, or to put special emphasis on the color when he did. He went through the usual stages of social development. When he hit, he was told firmly, that "We do not hit," but he was not made to say that he was sorry when, obviously, he was not. When his sister was two and Bobby four, his mother would say, "We have to help, Bonnie," if she fell, for instance. Words were never put into Bobby's mouth but his rights as to his possessions and Bonnie's were respected. At age four, Bobby spent two weeks alone with his aunt. One day, at the beginning of the second week, she passed him some cherries. Bobby was told that he might have four. He carefully counted out the four cherries and put them in his hand. An hour later, he was found still holding two tightly clenched cherries in one hand. "Why, Bobby," said his Aunt, "I thought that you liked cherries." "Yes," said Bobby. "These I am keeping for Bonnie."

Bobby's social interactions tended to be positive, although he could and would defend himself, if necessary. He showed a tendency to lead, but he could follow another's suggestion, especially if it was a new or different one. Bobby was on the road to ethical behavior. At first it was little more than an aura around his ego concerns. The well-being of all was a responsibility he began to assume as a class member.

His background had given Bobby: numerous experiences through which his activity led him to undergo the consequences of his actions; various opportunities to interact with a variety of children and others in differing situations; opportunities to not only explore alone but also to find out with those, who said, "Let's . . ."; ego-strengthening experiences balanced, as he developed, with a broadening social context which functioned as an interactive field; chances to share and again to undergo the results with increasing awareness and some comparative understanding; by age four, chances to discuss stories, actions, observations, and experiences; an attitude of openness, awareness, and simple problem solving so that through his own efforts he could continue activities to try to achieve what he was trying to do. By age five, he was slowly inducted into experiences which gave some insight into others through activities with which he could identify and draw some conclusions. Seeing a neighborhood play center, for example, brought associations and comparisons with his own classroom. "What would children like to have there?" became a simple problem which he helped to answer. This was, in a sense, thinking with things, as he asked, "Where is the tricycle, crayons, etc.?" Every such room should have such things that he associated with it, so that his own contribution was not based on social altruism but rather—I have cars. If this is a playroom, cars should be here. By putting cars into the situation and being told that Danny, Laura, etc. would use them and then, later being told about their use of the things he had brought completes his simple expectation of what the term playroom means. (Unfortunately, he was not able to see the playroom in use.) His conviction about what *ought* to be there was strong. Granting that this was rather limited, the "ought" functioned as an end sought and this was a factor in his actions to bring it into being. The "ought" was primarily an item or person in the situation, hitherto associated with them. Thus a playroom ought to have a car, Grandma ought to be in her house, etc. By age five, he began to discuss these with broadening associations. If Grandma was not in her house, where might she be? Sight unseen, Bobby projected his imagination into situations where Grandma might be. His parents discussed such matters with him but encouraged him to try to decide such matters. When possible, his suggestions were verified. Gradually, in relation to himself, Bobby had begun to protest physical and emotional hurts to himself. "Bud hit me"—"I did not hit him. I told him, but he hit me."

In another situation, Edward hit Don. Don took the truck which Edward was using. Don was "bad" according to Edward because he, Edward, got it, was using it, and had a right to it. Edward's individual right was negated. Edward's hit was an effective means to his end—Edward got the truck. Through verbal means, Edward told Don: the telling was effective and Don gave the truck back to Edward. To Edward and Don, the physical means—the hit—was still functional, but the verbal means is a higher form and is psychologically and socially acceptable. The end was peace between Edward, who had the truck, and Don, who understood why the truck was for Edward at that time, *and* that he, too, would have a turn. Don was beginning to identify his feelings with those of Edward. He said, to his teacher, "We want that red truck. Edward is driving it. *I'm going* to drive it."

Ethics has functional imperatives. They function on this level to achieve behavior and to affirm (a) the realization of the self; (b) the realization of the other; (c) the realization of the group. In the preceding illustration, Don was at the beginning of stage b. Behavior adds its quality to a situation. It can add and be a plus, or detract and be a minus, or make no difference and be a neutral. If it is plus to self and other, it is social. It can be a plus to more than two, to two, and to one. In the latter case, it would be most likely to be individual, depending upon the situation.

Convictions are the sum total of pluses which regulate the individual and group. Ethical convictions are imperatives which foster maximum realization and which sanction behavior or means to realization or ends.

A conviction should be strong enough to propel its possessor beyond himself and possible objectors into a state of the socially positive. However, the individual does not lose sight of the means as being judged ethically.

For instance, in the case cited earlier of Louise, she developed the conviction —minor though it may seem—that: (a) "I hang up my hat"; (b) "Peter hangs up his hat"; (c) "We hang up our hats." It becomes an ethical act when a, b, and c are all understood. Blind acquiesence, or strict obedience, or acceptance due to threats do not cause Louise to perform an ethical act. In the latter cases, it is not her act because the motive, the act itself, and the consequences are not acceptable in terms of the realization of either herself or her social group.

An ethical act is composed of motive—Louise chooses and wants to hang up her hat; free performance of the act—hanging up the hat; undergoing the positive consequences—feeling "good" or having a sense of achievement herself and as time goes on in relation to the social context which, in this case, is her class. She acts and undergoes the consequences. She feels "good" about herself or has a positive Ego image of herself, and her participation in a group-accepted role gives her positive social identity.

Although life and ethics will not continue to be as simple as this, Louise has begun to function in terms of self-social dictums which she understands and which add to realization.

Alan began to discuss stories that he had heard. For instance, there was no authoritarian edict about *The Little Red Hen*.[1] But, Alan said, "She did it—so she ate it." A simple cause and effect situation. *My Dog is Lost*[2] was discussed without any moral note being interjected. Alan said, "He got him (the dog) back. They helped him. They looked." No one said that one must help others, but Alan was beginning to understand that cooperation brought results. Although it is usually presented to older children, Alan's teacher showed him *Two is a Team*.[3] Alan said of this, after he had studied the pictures, "They were friends. They did it with each other."

When Alan heard *The Snowy Day*[4] and had studied the pictures, he said, "He took care of *himself* outside." This seemed important to the four-year-old. Later, Alan said, "I took care of my coat and hat *myself*." He was realizing something about himself as an independent. The situation in *My Dog is Lost* and *Two is a Team* is mentioned above. Alan was able to identify with both situations. In each case, he appeared to realize that another person was essential to one's realization. About this time, "I can do it myself" and "Tim and me did it" were used frequently. Although interaction with another country through books was postponed for later, Alan was introduced to those whom he could not see. The unseen are central in *While Susie Sleeps*[5] and some are given roles in *The Park Book*.[6] One night Alan said, as he went to bed, "I go to bed, but men and ladies are in the park and in the street." When *The Little Engine That*

"We're going to see Mrs. Brant"—Relating to people in the environment brings reciprocal satisfaction. (Courtesy Brooklyn-Parma Coop Preschool, Cleveland, Ohio and Lois Overbeck.)

Could[1] was read, Alan said, "Two pushed it. Up it went. Two did it. They were friends." Cooperation was becoming clearer to Alan!

In this age of ever-growing technology, Alan's teacher and parents encouraged him to relate to himself and to achieve positive self-identification; to relate to those people and animals, too, in his environment and thus to gain some reciprocal satisfaction. Interaction with things was also reciprocal up to a point. Using clay and eventually forming the clay ball into "a man" was partly a reciprocal act. Alan developed feelings of achievement, but he had to work for them as he handled the moist clay. The "man" was an object of comment and thus led to social interaction.

Pets are often a stepping stone to self-other relationships. Alan's guinea pig squealed when he was hungry. Alan took this seriously and after he had fed him one day he said, "Now you're happy. *I* made you happy with your dinner. I like you." Alan gained a feeling of control as he shared satisfaction with his pet. Alan's sense of realization was broadening. Concern for another would soon stretch into a greater concern for others.

His desire to have his birthday party at school gave some evidence of this development. He said, "They will all eat *my* cake. We can all sing 'Happy Birthday'."

Gerald's parents could afford to sponsor a child in Brazil. This was explained to Gerald, and Isa's picture was placed on the sideboard. Gerald asked, "She can't see me. Is she my friend?" The unknown Isa began to achieve more reality when a letter arrived telling more about Isa, her mother, her sister, her brother, and the boat that her father used for fishing. One night when Gerald was in bed, he said, "Isa is sleeping, too." Gerald's relationships were broadening.

If the room should be clean—and Alan wanted to dance—the need for no blocks on the floor was apparent! Alan wanted to paint when he arrived one morning and thus the brushes needed to be clean. These became little "oughts" in relation to his needs. Alan was learning that what he wanted and needed was gained through means over which he and his friends had some control. The time element lengthened to include not only the full act (the motive—I want to paint; the act—I am painting; the consequence—I painted a picture) but also what Alan needed to do it. He said, "I need the paper on the easel, the paint. I choose red, green, yellow, blue, and black, and clean brushes." An admonition to "wash the brushes for tomorrow" would cause him to wash them without any real conviction, at age four. However, slowly getting him to project himself into he, Alan, painting, and what he needed to do this did develop his conviction about it. The next step came when Alan said, after he had painted a picture, "I'm washing the brush. Marla is painting. Marla needs it."

In the cases of Louise and Bobby, the child was in a social milieu and accepted its functioning. However, each decided on the affirmative behavior, by choice.

As time went on, each assumed the role of cooperator, and then last decided upon his own action and carried it through. Motive, act, and consequence gradually assume, or should assume, a balance. Bobby desires to do something. This desire or motive is nothing without the expected accompanying act. Once Bobby is acting, he undergoes the consequence. Thus his act is neither without a motive or, unless he is too habituated, without a recognition by Bobby of what he is doing. The actual action is like a headless horseman unless it develops from its own motive. To disregard the result or consequence is to put others at a disadvantage because, although constant action may seem fine, one must undergo the consequences and look back over it with the conviction that he has carried the act through completely. Judgment develops as each undergoes the consequence stage. "I spilled the juice because I ran," for instance. All action makes for a constancy of movement at these ages. This is different from the complete act in that it can become an almost frenetic doing for doing's sake! Children's activities are so continuous, however, that the little achievements or consequences are sometimes missed. They often turn into means for the next act. However, they should be noted.

With this general attitude, as developed so far, both Louise and Bobby have the beginnings of ethical behavior. As they develop so, too, should this behavior. Motives will soon become more complicated, the actions more varied, and the results almost impossible to predict as to extent and variation.

Neither child was "talked at," but each was dealt with in terms of his level of action and capacity for understanding.

We have said that interaction is important. Interaction with the things and people in one's environment. The inner city child has one type of environment and the rural child another. As the latter matures, he should experience the former and vice versa. However, at a preschool age, the child can experience a little of nature even if he does not have full rural experience. Granting that he won't have the number of interactions of a country child, he can still have living plants and animals in his environment. They broaden his giving and taking in terms of natural surroundings and help to determine the breadth and understanding of what he does. Many a shy child, for instance, has related to a guinea pig as he cuddled it and felt a bit more secure. It has encouraged interaction with other children in some cases. All children need to experience what it means to see plants and animals grow, reproduce, and pass away. To learn how to relate to these and to recognize them as part of one's environment is an important dimension of life.

Ecological concerns, in a major sense, come later. However, interactions with natural life, where possible, with living things, and with simple pollution control and wildlife preservation can begin in the preschool. Simple controls of his own are learned from some of these experiences as the child reaches out to interact with other life around him. Recollected activities and the learning which results from undergoing experiences with plants and animals extends the child's environment, furthers his feeling relationships, and adds a new dimension to his life.

As his purposes develop and his scope of activity widens, he comes to realize that interactions, experiences, and resulting relationships benefit from what he has done, and that in turn, he also gains immeasurably. What he is and what he is becoming become more clear. (The child's behavior speaks!) In maintaining one's self, in concern for others, and in looking ahead to the world we should like to have, we need nature, too. It should speak to the child as he learns to speak to it!

Other factors enter into the situation as Louise, Bobby, and the other children, mature. They see how their parents are treated. Much of their parents' attitude is reflected in them, not because of clear acts necessarily nor because of interactions with their parents, but because they have adjusted to their parents' feeling responses. If Mr. Jones constantly sounds hostile in statements that he makes about his neighbors, or if Mrs. Stevens constantly withdraws or acquiesces in her relations with her neighbors, Bobby, Louise, and Alan tend to react, as conditioned or unconsciously learned behavior, in the same way. They replicate the family member's action behavior or patterns.

The teacher of the three-, four-, and five-year-old has to recognize this. Attitudes of teachers toward parents has already been discussed. However, there are certain imperatives for the teacher in an early childhood and/or preschool center. As these function, the child sees his parent in a positive regard in this little social center anyway. Some of the ethical imperatives for the teacher to keep in mind may be listed as follows:

1. Parents of the children in attendance at a preschool center need to be involved;
2. Involvement of all implies constant interaction;
3. The individuality of each child and each parent must be kept foremost;
4. The term social-self-realization* is apt because it keeps realization foremost and divides the stress between the self or individual, and the social or group;
5. A core of general human ends and means must be spelled out in terms of specific individual and group objectives to achievement which will serve to unify the group and to serve as a focus for the actions of the group.

Many a parent group has talked endlessly, but carefully thought-out ends and then agreement about the means to their achievement are necessary for positive

---

*Borrowed from the philosophical Reconstructionist, Theodore Brameld, and used in other writings of the author.

action to take place. With adults, motive, act, and consequence may cover a longer time span. However, they can be ethical, too. Achievement of the action and its consequence stem from their motive. Once the consequence or conclusion of the particular act has taken place, the entire act may be judged. Did it further the realization of each individual, and of the group, and was it a plus to realization without minus characteristics?

Although there is nothing finished about the beginnings of ethical behavior in the preschool, there are things that a teacher can do to encourage feeling and the problem solving or reflective thinking process as well as evaluation of actions. The teacher can foster an ethical highlighting of daily experiential situations which arise. The teacher

1. Can be alert to where children are in their development and foster pride of background, especially in urban Puerto Rican, Black, Mexican-American, Indian, and other minority group children by appreciating what the child's cultural, religious, national, and racial background has to offer for the sake of the child's individual realization and to accustom others to it through their interaction;

2. Can be aware of the functional level of one child with the other, with the social context, and inklings he has of the larger unseen culture which may need interpretation so that he will feel a growing relationship and not be overwhelmed by the unknown as he experiences relationships with it;

3. Can help each child to consider what *is* as fully as he is ready for it, lead him gradually to comprehend what *was,* and then encourage each to begin to look toward what *can* be in terms of what he will be able to do alone and with others.

The teacher neither dictates to the child nor talks too much about what he has not actually experienced. However, in some instances each child will project beyond the immediate and this should be considered in a way which makes it understandable and thus somewhat within the control of the child and discussed.

A series of events shared between four-year-olds and eight-year-olds worked out to the mutual advantage of both groups. Each group planned for its part in the interactive experience with the other and was able to regulate its own behavior and, when necessary, that of the other group. For example, when the eight-year-olds wanted to climb the ladder gym after a pleasant lunch in the younger children's room, the four-year-olds forbade it, saying, "It will make your stomach sick." Instead, it was planned when this much desired activity could take place. Control over one's self and over a shared situation was achieved as the two teachers watched and endeavored to make of these experiences a shared enrichment in which neither dominated the other. Domination, they knew could happen easily in a completely open interchange between various age groups. Sometimes, too, older children, near the younger age, will tend to regress to the younger level. Thus, for instance in a trial situation with five-year-olds, it was found that they tended to regress to the more immature behavior of the four-year-olds. Other ages were tried, but four-year-olds and eight-year-olds seemed in this series of instances to work out to real mutual advantage of both.[8]

The teacher takes the group for what it is and each child with his strengths and weaknesses. The teacher does not impart the values and attitudes of her social strata unthinkingly but tries to accomodate each child with the gifts and with the expression of his potentialities into the class community which is being created. When possible, each class is accomodated into the larger school community which is functioning for the realization of all. The positive attitudes in the situation are fostered for the realization of each child and for that of the whole group as shared experiences increase. Highlighting the positive, when it functions, judged in terms of realization of self, of other, and eventually of the larger cultural environment, is the task of the preschool teacher. This is ongoing. It is daily. The teacher can see some of the future implications while Jim and Joan experience preschool life as fully as possible. This is the beginning of an ethics![9]

Notes

1. *The Little Red Hen* (Racine, Wis.: Western Publishing Company, 1953).

2. Ezra Jack Keats, *My Dog Is Lost* (New York: Thomas Crowell Company, 1960).

3. Lorraine Beim and Jerrold Beim, *Two Is a Team* (New York: Harcourt Co., 1945).

4. Ezra Jack Keats, *The Snowy Day* (New York: The Viking Press, 1962).

5. Nina Schneider, *While Susie Sleeps* (New York: William R. Scott, Inc., 1948).

6. Charlotte Zolotow, *The Park Book* (New York: Harper and Brothers, 1944).

7. Watty Piper, *The Little Engine That Could* (New York: The Platt and Munk Co., 1930).

8. Grace K. Pratt, "Vertical Interaction in the Pre-School," *Peabody Journal of Education* (November 1953).

9. See also Grace K. Pratt-Butler, "Ethical Imperatives for Head Start," *The Educational Forum* (January 1972): 215-16.

APPENDIX 1

Selected References for Preschool Education

Anderson, Robert, and Shane, Harold. *As The Twig is Bent.* Readings in Early Childhood Education. New York: Houghton Mifflin and Co., 1971.

Auerbach, Aline, and Roche, Sandra. *Creating a Preschool Center: Parent Development in Our Integrated Neighborhood Project.* New York: John Wiley and Sons, 1971.

Auleta, Michael, *Foundations of Early Childhood Education: Readings.* New York: Random House, 1968.

Chisholm, Johnnie B. *What Makes a Good Head Start?* Wolfe City, Texas: Hennington Publishing Co., 1968.

Christianson, Helen; Rogers, Mary; and Ludlum, Blanche. *The Nursery School.* Boston: Houghton Mifflin and Co., 1961.

Croft, Doreen, and Hess, Robert. *An Activities Handbook for Teachers of Young Children.* Boston: Houghton Mifflin and Co., 1972.

———. *Teachers of Young Children.* Boston: Houghton Mifflin and Co., 1972.

Evans, Ellis D. *Contemporary Influences in Early Childhood Education.* New York: Holt Rinehart and Winston, 1971.

Foster, Josephine, and Headley, Neith. *Education in the Kindergarten.* New York: American Book Co., latest edition.

Frost, Joe, ed. *Early Childhood Education Rediscovered: Readings.* New York: Holt, Rinehart and Winston, 1968.

Hammond, Sarah Lou; Dales, Ruth; Skipper, Dora; and Witherspoon, Ralph; *Good Schools for Young Children.* New York: The Macmillan Co., 1963.

Headley, Neith, *The Kindergarten: Its Place in the Successful Program of Education.* New York: The Center for Applied Research in Education, 1965.

Heffernan, Helen. *Guiding the Young Child.* Boston: D.C. Heath and Co., 1951.

Heffernan, Helen, and Todd, Vivian. *The Kindergarten Teacher.* Boston: D.C. Heath and Co., 1960.

Herron, R.E., and Sutton-Smith, Brian. *Child's Play.* New York: John Wiley and Sons, 1971.

Hurd, Helen. *Teaching in the Kindergarten.* Minneapolis: The Burgess Publishing Co., 1965.

Isaacs, Susan. *The Nursery Years.* New York: The Vanguard Press, 1929, 1936.

Lambert, Hazel. *Teaching the Kindergarten Child.* New York: Harcourt Brace and Co., 1958.

Landreth, Catherine. *Early Childhood Behavior and Learning.* New York: Alfred A. Knopf, 1967.

_____. *Education of the Young Child.* New York: John Wiley and Sons, Inc., 1942.

_____. *Preschool Learning and Teaching.* New York: Harper and Row, 1972.

Leonard, Edith; Van Deman, Dorothy; and Miles, Lillian. *Foundations of Learning in Childhood Education.* Columbus: Charles E. Merrill Books, 1963.

Miller, Neabel. *A Practical Guide for Kindergarten Teachers.* West Nyack, N.Y.; Parker Publishing Co., 1970.

Moore, Sallie Beth, and Richards, Phyllis. *Teaching in the Nursery School.* New York: Harper and Brothers, 1959.

Nixon, Ruth H., and Nixon, Clifford L. *Introduction to Early Childhood Education.* New York: Random House, Inc., 1970.

Parker, Ronald. *The Pre-School in Action.* Boston: Allyn and Bacon, 1972.

Pitcher, Evelyn, and Ames, Louise. *The Guidance Nursery School.* New York: Harper and Row, 1964.

Pratt-Butler, Grace K. "Ethical Imperatives for Head Start," in *The Educational Forum* (January 1972): 215-16.

Read, Katherine. *The Nursery School.* Philadelphia: W.B. Saunders Co., 1964.

Rudolph, Marguerita, and Cohen, Dorothy. *Kindergarten: A Year of Learning.* New York: Appleton, Century and Crofts, 1964.

Ryan, Bernard, Jr. *Your Child and the First Year of School.* New York: World Publishing Co., 1969.

Silberman, Charles E. *The Open Classroom Reader.* New York: Vintage Books, 1973.

Sinclair, Caroline B. *Movement of the Young Child.* Columbus: Charles E. Merrill Publishing Co., 1973.

Todd, Vivian. *The Aide in Early Childhood Education.* New York: The Macmillan Co., 1973.

Todd, Vivian, and Heffernan, Helen. *The Years Before School: Guiding Preschool Children.* New York: The Macmillan Co., 1971.

Weber, Evelyn. *The Kindergarten.* New York: Teachers College Press, 1969.

Widmer, Emmy Louise. *The Critical Years: Early Childhood Education at the Cross-roads.* Scranton: International Textbook Co., 1970.

Yamamoto, Kaoru. *The Child and His Image: Self-concept in the Early Years.* Boston: Houghton Mifflin Co., 1972.

APPENDIX 2

Sources

FILMS

It is wise to write and request film catalogues and then to study them before deciding upon what to order. Many excellent films are available for use at parent meetings, for educating assistants, student teachers, etc.

Atlantis Productions, Inc.
Thousand Oaks, California 91360

Community Playthings
Rifton, New York 12471 (Slides on loan)

Contemporary Films
McGraw-Hill Films
Princeton Road
Hightstown, New Jersey 08520

Coronet Films (Instructional)
488 Madison Avenue
New York, New York 10010

Education Development Center, Inc.
55 Chapel Street
Newton, Massachusetts 02160

Encyclopedia Britannica Films
1150 Wilmette Avenue
Wilmette, Illinois 60091

Eye Gate House Inc.
146-01 Archer Avenue
Jamaica, New York 11435

Film Associates of California
11559 Santa Monica Boulevard
Los Angeles, California 90025

International Film Bureau Inc.
Chicago, Illinois 60607

James, Phoebe
Box 286
Verdiego City, California 91046

Long Film Service
El Cerrito, California 94530

McGraw-Hill Text Films
330 West 42 Street
New York, New York 10036

National Film Board of Canada
Suite 819
1540 Broadway
New York, New York 10036

Polymorph Films, Inc.
331 Newbury Street
Boston, Massachusetts 02115

Science Research Associates, Inc.
259 East Erie Street
Chicago, Illinois 60611

UNIVERSITIES

University of California at Berkeley
Media Center-Extension Department
Berkeley, California 94704

University of Indiana
Audio-Visual Center
Bloomington, Indiana 47401

New York University Film Library
Washington Square
New York, New York 10003

Columbia University
Bureau of Publications
1234 Amsterdam Avenue
New York, New York 10025

Pennsylvania State University
University Park, Pennsylvania 16802

Southern Illinois University
Department of Audio-Visual Aids
Edwardsville, Illinois 62025

Vassar College
Poughkeepsie, New York 12601

Wayne State University
Audio-Visual Center
Detroit, Michigan 48221

Weston Woods Studios
Weston, Connecticut 06880

RECORDS

Angel-Capitol Records Inc.
1290 Avenue of the Americas
New York, New York 10036

Bowmar Records, Inc.
10515 Burbank Boulevard
North Hollywood, California 91601

Child Craft Education Corporation
964 Third Avenue
New York, New York 10022

Creative Playthings Inc.
P.O. Box 1100
Princeton, New Jersey 08540

Folkways Scholastic Records
906 Sylvan Avenue Dept. B3
Englewood Cliffs, New Jersey 07632

Metro-Goldwyn-Mayer Records
1540 Broadway
New York, New York 10036

RCA Records
Camden, New Jersey 08101

Rhythm Record Company
9208 Nichols Road
Oklahoma City, Oklahoma 73120

Sound Book Press Society, Inc.
Scarsdale, New York 10583

Young People's Records (Children's Record Guild)
100 Sixth Avenue
New York, New York 10013

EDUCATIONAL EQUIPMENT

Childcraft Equipment Company, Inc.
115 East 23 Street
New York, New York 10010

Community Playthings
Rifton, New York 12471

Creative Playthings
P.O. Box 1100
Princeton, New Jersey 08540
and
1 East 53 Street
New York, New York 10022

Fisher Price Toys
East Aurora, New York 14052

Judy Company
310 North 2 Street
Minneapolis, Minnesota 55401

Milton Bradley Company
Springfield, Massachusetts 01101

APPENDIX 3

Selected Materials

CHANTS, RHYMES, VERSE, AND POETRY

This is a representative listing. A careful choice should be made in terms of group, maturity, and situational context. Sometimes the first verse of a long poem is apt.

Aldis, Dorothy. *All Together*. New York: G.P. Putnam's Sons, 1925.

———. *Hello, Day*. New York: G.P. Putnam's Sons, 1959.

———. *Quick as a Wink*. New York: G.P. Putnam's Sons, 1960.

Arbuthnot, May H. Compiler. *Time For Poetry*. Chicago: Scott-Foresman and Company, 1952.

Arnstein, Flora.* *Adventure Into Poetry*. Stanford: Stanford University Press, 1949.

———.* *Poetry in the Elementary School*. New York: Appleton, Century and Crofts, 1962.

Association for Childhood Education. *Told Under the Silver Umbrella*. New York: The Macmillan Company, 1935.

Baruch, Dorothy. *I Would Like to be a Pony and Other Wishes*. New York: Harper and Row, 1959.

Brooks, Gwendolyn.** *Bronzeville Boys and Girls*. New York: Harper and Row, 1956.

Brown, Helen, and Helt, Harry J., ed. *Let's Read Together Poems*. Evanston: Row, Peterson, and Co., 1954.

Ciardi, John. *I Met a Man*. New York: Houghton Mifflin, 1961.

---

*Discussion of uses of poetry with the appropriate poems.

**Mostly for older children, but parts may be used.

Coatsworth, Elizabeth. *Poems* (mostly for older children) New York: The Macmillan Company, 1958.

Conkling, Hilda, *Rhymes and Verses: Collected Poems for Children.* New York: Holt, 1947.

De La Mare, Walter. *Peacock Pie.* New York: Holt, 1929.

_____. *Rhymes and Verses: Collected Poems for Young People.* New York: Holt, Rinehart, and Winston, 1947.

DeRegniers, Beatrice Schenk. *Something Special.* New York: Harcourt, Brace and World, 1958.

Doane, Pelagie, ed. *A Small Child's Book of Verse.* New York: Oxford University Press, 1948.

Farjeon, Eleanor. *Eleanor Farjeon's Poems for Children.* Philadelphia: J.B. Lippincott Company, 1951.

Ferris, Helen, ed. *Favorite Poems Old and New.* New York: Doubleday and Company, Inc., 1957.

Field, Rachel.* *Poems.* New York: The Macmillan Company, 1951.

_____.* *Pointed People.* New York: The Macmillan Company, 1933.

_____.* *Taxis and Toadstools.* New York: Doubleday and Company, 1926.

Fisher, Aileen. *Going Barefoot.* New York: Thomas Y. Crowell, 1960.

_____. *In the Woods, In the Meadow, In the Sky.* New York: Charles Scribner's Sons, 1965.

Frank, Josette. *Poems to Read to the Very Young.* New York: Random House, 1961.

Gay, Zhenya. *Jingle Jangle.* New York: The Viking Press, 1953.

Geismer, Barbara, and Geismer, Sutter. *Very Young Verses.* Boston: Houghton Mifflin, 1945.

Giovanni, Nikki.* *Spin a Soft Black Song.* New York: Hill and Wang Inc., 1971.

Kuskin, Karla. *In the Middle of the Trees.* New York: Harper and Row, 1958.

Lear, Edward. *The Complete Nonsense Book.* New York: Dodd, Mead and Company, 1946.

Lenski, Lois. *Now It's Fall.* New York: Oxford University Press, 1948.

Lewis, Richard, compiler. *In a Spring Garden.* New York: The Dial Press, 1965.

Lindsay, Vachel. *Johnny Appleseed and Other Poems.* New York: The Macmillan Company, 1928.

Livingston, Myra Cohn. *Wide Awake and Other Poems.* New York: Harcourt, Brace and World, 1959.

Love, Katherine, ed. *A Pocket Full of Rhymes.* New York: Thomas Y. Crowell, 1946.

Merriam, Eve. *Catch a Little Rhyme.* New York: Atheneum, 1966.

*Mostly for older children, but parts may be used.

Milne, A.A.* *Now We Are Six.* New York: E.P. Dutton and Company, 1924.

———* *When We Were Very Young.* New York: E.P. Dutton, 1924.

O'Neill, Mary.** *Hailstones and Halibut Bones.* New York: Doubleday and Company, 1961.

Petersham, Maude, and Petersham, Miska. *The Rooster Crows.* (Abridged *Book of American Rhymes and Jingles.*) New York: Collier, 1971.

Richards, Laura E. *Tirra Lirra.* Boston: Little Brown and Company, 1955 edition.

Rossetti, Christina.* *Sing Song.* New York: The Macmillan Company, 1924.

Starbird, Kaye. *Speaking of Cows.* Philadelphia: L.B. Lippincott, 1960.

Stevenson, Robertson L. *A Child's Garden of Verses.* New York: Oxford University Press, 1947.

Thomson, Jean. *Poems to Grow On.* Boston: Beacon University, 1957.

Tippett, James. *I Go A-Traveling.* New York: Harper and Brothers, 1929.

——— *I Live in a City.* New York: Harper and Brothers, 1927.

——— *I Spend the Summer.* New York: Harper and Row, 1930.

Tudor, Tasha. *First Poems of Childhood.* New York: Platt and Munk, 1967.

MOTHER GOOSE COLLECTIONS

As stated in chapter 5, *if* Mother Goose rhymes are used, a careful selection should be made of appropriate rhymes.

Anglund, Joan Walsh. *In a Pumpkin Shell.* New York: Harcourt, Brace, and World, 1960.

Benet, William. *Mother Goose.* New York: Heritage Press, 1943.

Briggs, Raymond. *Ring-O'Roses.* New York: Coward-McCann, 1962.

Brooke, L. Leslie. *The Nursery Rhyme Book.* London: Frederick Warne and Company, 1947.

Buffum, Katherine. *Mother Goose.* Boston: Houghton Mifflin Company, 1927.

Caldecott, Randolph. *Randolph Caldecott's First Collection of Pictures and Songs.* London: Frederick Warne and Company, no date.

De Angeli, Marguerite. *A Pocket Full of Posies: The Merry Mother Goose.* Garden City: Doubleday and Company, 1961.

Françoise, *The Gay Mother Goose.* New York: Scribner and Sons, 1938.

Fujihawa, Gyo. *Mother Goose.* New York: Grosset and Dunlap, 1973.

Galdone, Paul. *Old Mother Hubbard and Her Dog.* New York: Wittlesey House, 1960.

---

*Select with care for today's child.
**Mostly for older children, but parts may be used.

Greenaway, Kate. *Mother Goose: Or The Old Nursery Rhymes.* London: Frederick Warne and Company, no date.

Latham, Hugh. *Mother Goose in French* (trans.). New York: Thomas Y. Crowell and Company, 1946.

Lenski, Lois. *Jack Horner's Pie.* New York: Harper and Brothers, 1927.

Opper, F. *Mother Goose's Nursery Rhymes.* London: J.M. Dent and Sons, 1960.

Perrault, Charles. *Histories or Tales of Past Times Told by Mother Goose.* London: Fortune Press, nodate.

Rackham, Arthur. *The Old Nursery Rhymes.* London: Heinemann and Company, 1952.

Reed, Philip, *Mother Goose and Nursery Rhymes.* New York: Atheneum, 1963.

Rojankovsky, Feodor. *The Tall Book of Mother Goose.* New York: Harper and Brothers, 1942.

Scott, William R. *This is the Milk that Jack Drank.* New York: William R. Scott, 1944.

Smith, Jessie Wilcox. *The Little Mother Goose.* New York: Harper and Brothers, 1942.

Tenggren, Gustaf. *Mother Goose.* Boston: Little Brown and Company, 1940.

Thomas, Isaiah. *Mother Goose Melodies,* Part I. (Worchester, I. Thomas, 1794) New York: Bowker and Company, 1945.

Thomas, Katherine. *The Real Personages of Mother Goose.* Boston: Lothrop, Lee, and Shepard, 1930.

Tudor, Tasha. *Mother Goose.* New York: Oxford University Press, 1944.

Weisgard, Leonard. *Little Goose.* New York: Harper and Brothers, 1951.

_____ *Mother Goose.* New York: Harper and Brothers, 1951.

Wheeler, William. *Mother Goose Melodies.* Boston: Houghton Mifflin Company, 1869, 1872.

Wildsmith, Brian. *Brian Wildsmith's Mother Goose.* New York: Scholastic Book Services, 1964, 1972.

Wright, Blanche Fisher. *The Real Mother Goose.* Skokie, Ill.: Rand McNally, 1944.

NOTE: *This is a rather long list because it illustrates the variations in title and illustration.*

BOOKS

Adelson, Leone. *All Ready for Winter.* New York: McKay Publishing Company, 1962.

Ardizzone, Edward. *Little Tim and the Brave Sea Captain.* New York: Henry Walck, 1955.

_____ *Tim's Friend Towser.* New York: Henry Walck, 1962.

Bacmeister, Rhoda. *Stories to Begin On.* New York: E.P. Dutton, 1955.

Bancroft, Henrietta, and Van Gelder, Richard. *Animals in Winter*. New York: Thomas Crowell, 1963.

Bemelmans, Ludwig. *Madeline*. New York: The Viking Press, 1939.

———. *Madeline's Rescue*. New York: The Viking Press, 1953.

Beskow, Elsa. *Pelle's New Suit*. New York: Harpers, 1929.

Bond, Jean. *Brown is a Beautiful Color*. New York: Franklin Watts, 1969.

Branley, Franklyn. *Big Tracks, Little Tracks*. New York: Thomas Y. Crowell, 1960.

Brown, Georgiana. *Look and See*. Los Angeles: Melmont Publishers, 1958.

Brown, Margaret Wise, *The City Noisy Book*. New York: Harper and Row, 1939.

———. *The Country Noisy Book*. New York: Harper and Row, 1940.

———. *The Indoor Noisy Book*. New York: William R. Scott, Inc., 1942.

———. *The Noisy Book*. New York: Harper and Row, 1939.

———. *The Sea Shore Noisy Book*. New York: William R. Scott, Inc., 1941.

Buckley, Helen E. *Grandfather and I*. New York: Lothrop, Lee, and Shepard, 1961.

———. *Grandmother and I*. New York: Lothrop, Lee and Shepard, 1961.

———. *Josie and the Snow*. New York: Lothrop, Lee and Shepard, 1964.

Budney, Blossom. *A Kiss is Round*. New York: Lothrop, Lee and Shepard, 1954.

Burton, Virginia, Lee. *Mike Mulligan and His Steam Shovel*. Boston: Houghton Mifflin Co., 1939.

Cleary, Beverly. *The Real Hole*. New York: Morrow Junior Books, 1960.

Conklin, Gladys. *I Caught a Lizard*. New York: Holiday House, 1967.

———. *I Like Caterpillars*. New York: Holiday House, no date.

De Brunhoff, Jean. *The Story of Babar*. New York: Random House, 1960.

Ets, Marie Hall. *Gilberto and the Wind*. New York: The Viking Press, 1965.

———. *Just Like Me*. New York: The Viking Press, 1965.

Flack, Marjorie. *Angus and the Ducks*. New York: Doubleday, 1930.

———. *Ask Mr. Bear*. New York: The Macmillan Company, 1932.

———. *The New Pet*. New York: Doubleday, 1943.

———. *The Story About Ping*. New York: The Viking Press, 1933.

Françoise. *The Things I Like*. New York: Charles Scribner and Sons, 1960.

Freeman, Don, *Mop Top*. New York: The Viking Press, 1955.

Gag, Wanda. *Millions of Cats*. New York: Coward, McCann, 1928.

Garelick, May. *Where Do Butterflies Go When It Rains?* New York: William R. Scott, Inc., 1961.

Goudey, Alice. *The Good Rain*. New York: E.P. Dutton, 1950.

Grifalconi, Ann. *City Rhythms*. New York: Bobbs Merrill, 1965.

Huntington, Harriet. *Let's Go Outdoors*. New York: Doubleday, 1939.

Hutchins, Pat. *Changes, Changes*. New York: The Macmillan Company, 1971.

Jackson, Kathryn, and Jackson, Byron. *The Saggy Baggy Elephant*. New York: The Golden Press-Western Publishing Company, 1952.

Jaynes, Ruth. *My Tricycle and I*. North Hollywood: Bowmar Publications, 1968.

Johnson, Crockett. *Harold and the Purple Crayon*. New York: Harper and Row, 1958.

Joslin, Sesyle. *What Do You Do, Dear?* New York: William R. Scott, Inc., 1961.

_____. *What Do You Say, Dear?* New York: William R. Scott, Inc., 1958.

Kahn, Joan. *See Saw*. New York: Harper and Row, 1964.

Keats, Ezra Jack. *Goggles*. Toronto: The Macmillan Company, 1969.

_____. *Peter's Chair*. New York: Harper and Row, 1967.

_____. *The Snowy Day*. New York: The Viking Press, 1962.

_____. *Whistle For Willie*. New York: The Viking Press, 1964.

Keats, Ezra Jack, and Cherr, Pat. *My Dog Is Lost*. New York: Thomas Y. Crowell, 1960.

Koenig, Marion. *The Beaver*. New York: Grosset and Dunlap. 1969.

_____. *The Bee*. New York: Grosset and Dunlap, 1969.

_____. *The Mouse*. New York: Grosset and Dunlap, 1969.

Krasilovsky, Phyllis. *The Very Little Boy*. New York: Doubleday, 1962.

Krauss, Ruth. *The Carrot Seed*. New York: Harper and Brothers, 1945.

_____. *A Hole Is to Dig*. New York: Harper and Brothers, 1952.

Kunhardt, Dorothy. *Pat the Bunny*. New York: The Golden Press, 1962, 1940.

Kuskin, Karla. *All Sizes of Noises*. New York: Harper and Row, 1962.

_____. *James and the Rain*. New York: Harper and Row, 1957.

Lenski, Lois. *Big Little Davy*. New York: Henry Z. Walck, 1956.

_____. *Cowboy Small*. New York: Henry Z. Walck, 1950.

_____. *Davy's Day*. New York: Henry Z. Walck, 1943.

_____. *Davy Goes Places*. New York: Henry Z. Walck, 1961.

_____. *I Like Winter*. New York: Oxford University Press, 1950.

_____. *The Little Farm*. New York: Oxford University Press, 1942.

_____. *The Little Fire Engine*. New York: Oxford University Press, 1946.

_____. *Now It's Fall*. New York: Henry Z. Walck, 1948.

_____. *Papa Small*. New York: Henry Z. Walck, 1966.

_____. *Policeman Small*. New York: Henry Z. Walck, 1962.

_____. *Spring Is Here*. New York: Oxford University Press, 1945.

————. *Susie Mariar.* * New York: Henry Z. Walck, 1967.

Lionni, Leo. *Inch By Inch.* New York: Obolensky, 1960.

————. *Little Blue and Little Yellow.* New York: Obolensky, 1959.

————. *Swimmy.* New York: Pantheon, 1963.

McCloskey, Robert. *Blueberries for Sal.* New York: The Viking Press, 1948.

————. *Make Way for Ducklings.* New York: The Viking Press, 1941.

————. *Time of Wonder.* New York: The Viking Press, 1957.

MacDonald, Golden. *Red Light, Green Light.* New York: Doubleday, 1944.

McGovern, Ann. *Who Has a Secret?* Boston: Houghton Mifflin, Co., 1964.

Piper, Watty. *The Little Engine That Could.* New York: Platt and Munk, 1954, 1930.

Potter, Beatrix. *The Tale of Peter Rabbit.* New York: Frederick Warne, 1902.

Provensen, A., and Provensen, M. *Who's In the Egg?* New York: The Golden Press, 1970.

Radlauer, Ruth, and Radlauer, Ed. *Father Is Big.* North Hollywood: Bowmar Publishers, 1967.

Rey, Hans Augusto. *Curious George.* Boston: Houghton Mifflin Co., 1941.

————. *Curious George Rides a Bike.* Boston: Houghton Mifflin Co., 1952.

Rockwell, Anne. *Sally's Caterpillar.* New York: Parents' Magazine Press, 1966.

Schlein, Miriam. *Fast Is Not a Lady Bug.* New York: William R. Scott, Inc., 1953.

————. *Heavy Is a Hippopotamus.* New York: William R. Scott, Inc., 1954.

Schneider, Herman. *Let's Look Under the City.* New York: William R. Scott, Inc., 1954.

————. *The Sun Looks Down.* New York: Abelard Schuman, 1954.

Scott, William R. *This Is the Milk That Jack Drank.* New York: William R. Scott, Inc., 1944.

Sendak, Maurice. *The Night Kitchen.* ** New York: Harper and Row Publishers, 1970.

————. *Where the Wild Things Are.* ** New York: Harper and Row, 1963.

Seuss, Dr. (Theodor S. Geisel). *And to Think That I Saw It on Mulberry Street.* New York: Vanguard Press, 1937.

————. *The Cat in the Hat.* New York: Random House, 1947.

————. *McElligot's Pool.* New York: Random House, 1947.

Shapp, Charles, and Shapp, Martha. *Let's Find Out About Fall.* New York: Franklin Watts, 1963.

————. *Let's Find Out About Spring.* New York: Franklin Watts, 1963.

————. *Let's Find Out About Summer.* New York: Franklin Watts, 1963.

Susie Mariar could be listed under verse, too.
**These have raised some controversy.

_____. *Let's Find Out About Winter.* New York: Franklin Watts, 1963.

Shulevitz, Uri. *Rain, Rain, Rivers.* New York: Farrar, Straus, Giroux, 1969.

Sklaar, Grace. *Nothing But Cats* and *All About Dogs.* New York: Young Scott Books, 1947.

Slobodkina, Esphyr. *Caps For Sale.* New York: William R. Scott, Inc., 1947.

Sonneborn, Ruth. *Friday Night Is Papa Night.* New York: The Viking Press, 1970.

Tresselt, Alvin. *Rain Drop Splash.* New York: Lothrop, Lee and Shepard, 1946.

_____. *Wake Up Farm.* New York: Lothrop, Lee and Shepard, 1955.

_____. *White Snow, Bright Snow.* New York: Lothrop, Lee and Shepard, 1956.

Udry, Janice May. *A Tree Is Nice.* New York: Harper and Row, 1956.

Ungerer, Tomi. *Crictor.* New York: Harper and Row, 1958.

Watson, Jane. *Wonders of Nature.* New York: Golden Press, 1966.

Webber, Irma. *Up Above and Down Below.* New York: William R. Scott, 1943.

Yashima, Taro. *Umbrella.* New York: The Viking Press, 1958.

_____. *The Village Tree.* New York: The Viking Press, 1953.

Zaffo, George. *The Big Book of Real Fire Engines.* New York: Grosset and Dunlap, 1949.

_____. *The Giant Book of Things in Space.* Garden City: Doubleday, 1969.

Zolotow, Charlotte. *Flocks of Birds.* New York: Abelard-Schuman, 1965.

_____. *My Friend John.* New York: Harper and Row, 1968.

_____. *The Park Book.* New York: Harper and Brothers, 1944.

_____. *The Storm Book.* New York: Harper and Row, 1952.

MUSIC

Singing, Rhythmic, and Listening Materials

Coleman, Satis and Thorn, Alice. *Another Singing Time.* New York: Reynal and Hitchcock, 1937.

_____. *The New Singing Time.* New York: The John Day Company, 1950.

_____. *Singing Time.* New York: The John Day Company, 1929.

Crowninshield, Ethel. *Sing and Play Book.* Boston: Boston Music Company, 1938.

Dubseky, Dora. *Sing and Dance.* New York: Stephen Daye Press, 1955.

Fisher, ed. *The Animal Songbook.* New York: St. Martin's Press, 1962.

Kapp, Paul. *The Cat Came Fiddling and Other Rhymes.* New York: Harcourt Brace, 1956.

_____. *Cock A Doodle Doo, Cock A Doodle Doo.* New York: Harper and Row, 1966.

Jenkins, Ella; Krane, Sherman; and Lipschutz, Peggy. *The Ella Jenkins Song Book for Children.* New York: Oak Publications, 1966.

Landeck, Beatrice. *Songs to Grow On.* New York: Edward B. Marks Music Corp., William Sloan Associates, Inc., 1950.

Landeck, Beatrice, and Crook, Elizabeth. *Wake Up and Sing.* Edward B. Marks Music Corp., William Morrow and Co., 1969.

McCall, Adeline. *This Is Music for Kindergarten and Nursery School.* Boston: Allyn Bacon, Inc., 1965.

MacCarteney, Laura. *Songs for the Nursery School.* Cincinnati: Willis Music Co., 1937.

Martin, Florence, and Burnett, Elizabeth. *Rime, Rhythm, and Song for the Child of Today.* Chicago: Hall and McCreary Company, 1942.

Watters, Lorrain. *The Magic of Music.* Boston: Ginn and Company, 1970.

APPENDIX 4

Science and Nature

DEVELOPING CONCEPTS ABOUT SCIENCE IN YOUNG CHILDREN*

Grace K. Pratt

How do we encourage young children to develop concepts about science? Gans, Stendler, and Almy say that too many classrooms "neglect the importance of firsthand experiences in developing concepts in children."[1] They add that while five years olds experimenting with a thermometer "would not be able to verbalize their procedure, they were actually using the scientific method." Heffernan and Todd also stress the importance of the scientific methods in developing concepts.[2]

John Dewey believed children were capable of experiences with the scientific method and reflective thinking even though they were not aware they were using it. Dewey's approach may be paraphrased as follows: (a) the child should be engaged actively in a meaningful experience; (b) from such experience, a genuine problem should arise; (c) he should be guided in the collection of data relevant to solving the problem; (d) he should set up a tentative hypothesis or possible solution to the difficulty; (e) the tentative hypothesis is then tested.[3] As a result, it is assumed that the child will be able to continue his experiencing with greater understanding.

The uncomprehending adult frequently asks, "How can a mature theory of developing meaningful concepts be practically exemplified and encouraged from the children's activities, which often seem pointless, uncontrolled, and meaningless?" Let us look

---

*Reprinted with permission from SCIENCE AND CHILDREN 1(December 1963): No. 4. Copyright 1963 by the National Science Teachers Association.
[1] Roma Gans, Celia Stendler, and Millie Almy. *Teaching Young Children.* World Book Company, Yonkers-on-Hudson, N. Y. 1952. p. 241.
[2] Helen Heffernan and Vivian Todd. *The Kindergarten Teacher.* D. C. Heath and Company, Boston, Mass. 1960. p. 175.
[3] John Dewey. *Democracy and Education.* The Macmillan Company, New York City. 1916. p. 192.

more closely in order to find out: (a) how to develop concepts from the natural activities of children; (b) how to determine what the role of the teacher is to be.

Perhaps one example, typical of nursery school, will suffice for the former. The three year olds were playing with newly fallen snow and making the most of this experience, when it became time to go indoors. A number of them responded to the teacher's call carrying balls, or handfulls of snow. "Please let me take it in. I want to play with it inside." The teacher listened to the requests. "Silly," said another child, "it will be water." "No, I want to play with it. Why can't I?" insisted one little boy. At this point the teacher, noting that there was a difference of opinon and that this seemed to arise from a simple genuine problem, produced a pail and said, "Timmy wants to play with the snow indoors. Paul says it will be water. Marie wants to use it for doll food." Thus, she summarized the very simple data supplied by the children. "What shall we do?" asked the teacher. "Put some in a pail, take it to our room, and pretty soon we will see water," said Paul. Although very simple, this was a tentative hypothesis useful to try out one possibility. The teacher smiled and said, "All right, let us find out what will happen. We shall see whether Timmy and Marie can use it, or whether Paul is right." Needless to say, the testing proved quickly and conclusively that snow taken indoors would melt. The word melt was used to designate the concept resulting from the simple experience. Further related activities, such as putting snow in the kitchen refrigerator, on the hot stove, and outside on the window sill were carried out to see whether melting would result. The concept of melting was used freely during snack and lunch time discussion in relation to such other items as ice cream and frozen foods. Thus, we have a simple illustration of the development of a concept about science.

Other experiences from the preschool and early grades, useful in developing concepts, range from how to repair a flashlight that suddenly stops working in the building block garage made by four year olds, to how to adjust a door bell to ring in a first-grade play house, to how the crickets, kept in the kindergarten, chirp, or to finding if a coleus slip will make a new plant for the second grade. The care of a mother rabbit and her babies can be a source of scientific thinking which results in countless concepts about science. The same rabbit and offspring will, of course, be the source of concepts of greater complexity to seven year olds than to four year olds.

The very simplicity of the three year old's snow experience should clarify the role of the teacher. This does not deviate in basic theory whether the teacher is guiding children to understand the basic properties of snow or is encouraging them to find out how a cricket makes his chirping sound. Concepts in science can be developed from the natural activities of children when they are encouraged to pursue their problems through to satisfying conclusions. Their understanding of these conclusions function as concepts which may be verbalized and used for further experiences. This teaching method is quite different from telling children about experience and then asking them to exemplify the concept already given. Although the latter is concise, easy, and faster, it is not nearly as meaningful, developmental, and conducive to real understandings.

The teacher's role may be played in one of three possible kinds of situations: the *incidental*, when a grasshopper is seen on the doorstep; the *unexpected*, when a parent arrives at noon with a baby kitten; and the *planned*, when the teacher and group decide that having chosen to have a pet white mouse rather than a small green turtle, they have to solve problems revolving around suitable living quarters, proper food, and rules about handling. In the first two instances, the teacher's role determines whether much or anything at all is to be developed from the incidental and unexpected situations. The last is usually less of a test of the teacher's initiative. In the incidental and unexpected situations, the teacher needs to consider possible ways to develop worthwhile concepts even though, at the start, she may know little about a Dutch rabbit, a box turtle, or milky quartz.

The teacher's role in developing concepts about science may be summarized by the following traits:

1. Willingness to explore and find out with the group because the importance of science, its method, and its implications in the lives of children are realized;
2. Knowledge of where to acquire further necessary information about simple problems which may arise in science;
3. Knowledge, to which more is constantly added, about plants, animals, and inanimate objects of scientific interest developed through previous experiences and available as functional data for problems which may arise;
4. Conviction that children's experiences, fumblings, and efforts to solve problems within their general capabilities are time-consuming, but far more valuable than the learning of a quick rote answer;
5. Conviction of the importance of trying out (where safe), of failing, of reassessment, and of retrial;
6. Awareness of the breadth of opportunities to utilize new concepts and of the possibilities for constantly extending them;
7. Awareness of how to relate scientific concepts through continuous, meaningful experiences. For example, the concept of how a male cricket chirps and of how a female cricket lays eggs with her ovipositor may be developed into the concept that a male and female cricket perform separate functions.

Above all, the role of the teacher requires the realization that settled, adult acquired knowledge comes as the result of reformulating experienced situations in which there has been enough interest to work through a problem to a satisfying conclusion. The conceptual result is a mere resting place before further experiences and the problems which arise from within them utilize this concept as data in the next development of learning.

To develop science concepts scientifically, it is important to learn how to do it while the child is living through his early childhood years. We must be aware of the many opportunities lying about us which may be developed into concepts about science through which young children may gain greater mastery of themselves and their environment.

A chart showing "Requirements for Various Animals" is located on the next two pages. Reprinted with permission from Pratt, Grace K., "How to Care for Living Things in the Classroom," National Science Teachers Association.

REQUIREMENTS FOR VARIOUS ANIMALS

Food and Water Plants (for fish)	Rabbits	Guinea pigs	Hamsters	Mice	Rats
Daily					
pellets	rabbit pellets:		large dog pellets: one or two		
or					
grain	keep dish half full	corn, wheat, or oats:	1½ tablespoon	canary seeds or oats: 2 teaspoons	3-4 teaspoons
green or leafy vegetables, lettuce, cabbage and celery tops	4-5 leaves	2 leaves	1 leaf	1/8—1/4 leaf	1/4 leaf
or					
grass, plantain, lambs' quarters, clover, alfalfa	2 handfuls	1 handful	1/2 handful	—	—
or					
hay, if water is also given					
carrots	2 medium	1 medium			
Twice a week					
apple (medium)	1/2 apple	1/4 apple	1/8 apple	1/2 core and seeds	1 core
iodized salt (if not contained in pellets)	or salt block	sprinkle over lettuce or greens			
corn, canned or fresh, once or twice a week	1/2 ear	1/4 ear	1 tablespoon 1/3 ear	1/4 tablespoon or end of ear	1/2 tablespoon or end of ear
water	should always be available		necessary only if lettuce or greens are not provided		

236

Goldfish / Guppies

	Goldfish	Guppies
Daily		
dry commercial food	1 small pinch	1 very small pinch; medium size food for adults; fine size food for babies
Twice a week — shrimp—dry—or another kind of dry fish food	4 shrimp pellets, or 1 small pinch	dry shrimp food or other dry food: 1 very small pinch
Two or three times a week — tubifex worms	enough to cover 1/2 area of a dime	enough to cover 1/8 area of a dime
Add enough "conditioned" water to keep tank at required level	allow one gallon per inch of fish	allow 1/4–1/2 gallon per adult fish
	add water of same temperature as that in tank—at least 65°F	add water of same temperature as that in tank—70—80°F
Plants — cabomba, anacharis, etc.	should always be available	

Newts / Frogs

	Newts	Frogs
Daily		
small earthworms or mealworms or tubifex worms or raw chopped beef	1—2 worms	2—3 worms
	enough to cover 1/2 area of a dime	enough to cover 3/4 area of a dime
	enough to cover a dime	enough to cover a dime
water	should always be available at same temperature as that in tank or room temperature	

Water turtles / Land turtles / Small turtles

	Water turtles	Land turtles	Small turtles
Daily			
worms or night crawlers or tubifex or blood worms and/or	1 or 2	1 or 2	1/4 inch of tiny earthworm
raw chopped beef or meat and fish-flavored dog or cat food	1/2 teaspoon	1/2 teaspoon	enough to cover 1/2 area of a dime
fruit and vegetables fresh		1/4 leaf lettuce or 6—10 berries or 1—2 slices peach, apple, tomato, melon or 1 tablespoon corn, peas, beans	
dry ant eggs, insects, or other commercial turtle food			1 small pinch
water	3/4 of container	always available at room temperature; should be ample for swimming and submersion; large enough for shell	half to 3/4 of container

APPENDIX 5

Conservation Groups

Defenders of Wildlife
731 Dupont Circle Building
Washington, D.C. 20036

East African Wildlife Society
P.O. Box 20110
Nairobi, Kenya

The Living Wilderness Society
2144 P Street NW
Washington, D.C. 20037

National Association of Audubon Societies
1130 Fifth Avenue
New York, New York 10028

National Mustang Association
Newcastle, Utah 84756

The National Wildlife Federation
1412 16 Street NW
Washington, D.C. 20036

APPENDIX 6

Parent Conference

Name:
Address:
Birthdate:
Birthplace:
Background
    Cultural Milieu
    Language Spoken
    Birthplace of Parents, Siblings
    Date of Birth of Above (if obtainable)
    Parents' Education
    Parents' Occupation
    Time Living at Present Residence
    Assistance Received
    Others Living in Home (Boarders, Grandparents, State Children, etc.)
    Special Considerations (Recent Moves, Accidents, Deaths etc.)

Physical Development and Health
    General Physical Condition
    Skin and Muscle Tone
    Known Allergies
    Appetite, Food Dislikes, etc.
    Sleep and Rest Patterns
    Toilet Training: Present Status, Problems, Child's Terms for Functions
    Condition of Eyes, Ears, etc.
    Wearing of Braces, Glasses, etc.; Length of Time
    Special Surgery
    Contagious Diseases: Dates:

     Schedule at Home
     Coordination and Development of Large Muscles
     Coordination and Development of Small Muscles
     Intermuscular Development and Coordination

Social Development
     Status of Social Development in Parent's Opinion
     Level of Social Development: Processional Play, Parallel Play, "Fringe" Play,
        Play with One Other, Interactive Play with Small Group—with Large Group,
        etc.
     Leadership and Followership Tendencies
     Preferences for Play (Girls, Boys, Mixed, Tall-Strong, Small-Weak, etc.)
     Interactive Play with Children of Other Backgrounds
     Group Identification
     Relationship to Each Family and Household Member
     Approach to Strangers: Men, Women
     Larger Social-Cultural Environment: Trips, Knowledge of Other People and
        Places

Emotional Development
     General Stability and Security
     Causes of Strong Feeling
     General Attitude
     Sources of, and Manifestations of, Anxiety: Nail Biting, Masturbation, etc.
     Specific Fears: Dogs, Thunder, Loud Noises, etc.
     Crying: Often, Rarely, Causes, etc.
     Hostility and Aggression: Shy, Withdrawn, etc.
     Withdrawn Behavior: Pulls Back—When, etc.
     Family Relationships
     Types of Punishment Used
     Relationships to Others and to Strangers (Emotional)
     Special Problems according to Parents

Mental or Intellectual Development
     Habit Formation: Ways Established, When, What, etc.
     Ability to Follow Requests and Suggestions
     Evidences of Problem-Solving Ability
     Attention Span
     Ability to Connect Cause and Effect
     Special Interests and Abilities
     Breadth of Interests, Skills, Abilities, etc.

Interrelationships
     For Instance: Poor Large Muscular Coordination due to Illness at Age Two

Other
    Parents' General Attitude during Conference
    Parents' Relationships to Each Other and Child
    Impending Trip by one Parent, etc.

APPENDIX 7

Some of Comenius' Prescriptions for Education

In Chapter 17 of *The Great Didactic** Comenius discusses the requisites for easy teaching and learning. In order to make the process of learning and teaching both easy and pleasant, Comenius says that we must follow the steps of nature. Instruction:

1) Must begin early . . .
2) The minds must be made ready for it.
3) It must proceed from the general to the particular, and,
4) From the easier to the more difficult
5) Progress must not be rushed.
6) The minds must not be forced to do anything but that to which they aspire according to their age and motivation.
7) Everything must be related through sense impression . . .
8) Everything must be applied immediately, and,
9) Everything must be taught consistently and according to one and the same method.

---

*Comenius, Jan Amos, *Didactica Magna*, translated by Robert Ulich from Wilhelm Altemoller's edition. Paderborn, Ferdinand Schoniugh, 1905, Chapter 17.
Quoted in Robert Ulich, Editor, *Three Thousand Years of Educational Wisdom.* Cambridge: Harvard University Press, 1954, p. 346.

INDEX